IMAGES
of America

GREENE COUNTY
OHIO

TIME CAPSULE OF 1901

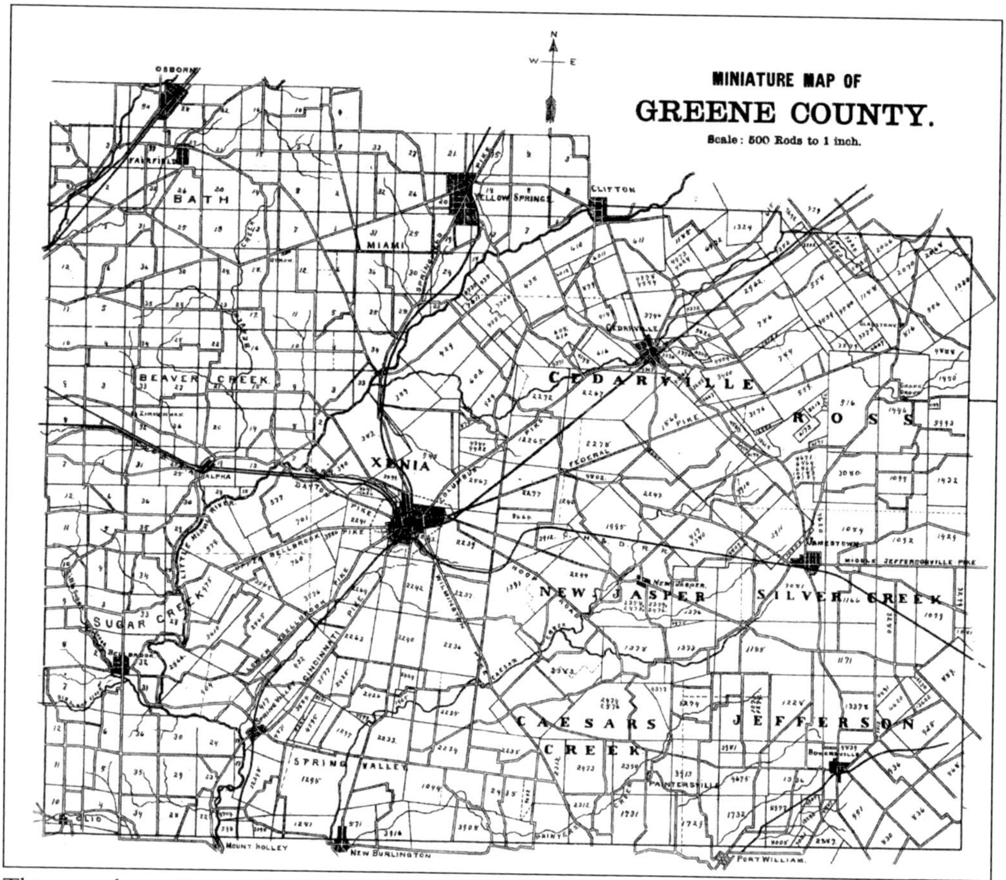

This map shows Greene County in 1896. (Courtesy of Greene County Archives.)

IMAGES
of America

GREENE COUNTY
OHIO
TIME CAPSULE OF 1901

Gillian Hill and Deanna Ulvestad

ARCADIA
PUBLISHING

ISBN 978-0-7385-1959-3

Published by Arcadia Publishing
Charleston, South Carolina

Printed in the United States of America

Library of Congress Catalog Card Number: 2002111594

For all general information contact Arcadia Publishing at:
Telephone 843-853-2070
Fax 843-853-0044
E-mail sales@arcadiapublishing.com
For customer service and orders:
Toll-Free 1-888-313-2665

Visit us on the Internet at www.arcadiapublishing.com

To all past and present citizens of Greene County, Ohio,
especially to the Sophomore Class of Xenia High School in 1901 who asked,
"Now good friends remember our good deeds and us
While we lie sleeping under the dust."

Contents

ACKNOWLEDGMENTS

We would like to thank the following people for their help and support:

All members of the Greene County Bicentennial Committee, chaired by Tim Leiwig, executive director of Greene County Recreation, Parks, and Cultural Events Department; and these members, in particular, for contributing photographs, Joan Baxter of the Greene County Historical Society, Sheila Darrow of Central State University, and Jackie Brown of Wilberforce University Library.

Our employers, the Greene County Board of Commissioners; and the Greene County Public Library, Martha Gardin, Director, and the Library Board of Trustees.

Our staff, Chris Wydman and Barbara Lindsey of the Greene County Records Center and Archives; and Joe Greer, Jennifer Morrow, Susan Chidester, Virginia Mullins, Linda Hasting, and Peggy Leadingham of the Greene County Room, Greene County Public Library.

Others who contributed photographs and/or supporting information, including Sharon Leaming, Russell Shelley, and Aaron Vaughn of the Greene County Sheriff's Department; Janet Steward, Joan Donovan, and Judy Randall of Greene County Microfilm; Sharon Lane and Sharon Allen of Clinton County Records Department; Scott Sanders, of Antiochiana, Antioch College; Jean Mulhern of Wilberforce University Library; Charles Carroll, Ph.D., of St. Brigid's Church; and Bob Empson of the Association of Ex-Pupils, Old Soldiers' and Sailors' Orphans' Home/Ohio Veterans' Children's Home.

INTRODUCTION

In early 2001, the Greene County archivists were asked to help the county commissioners prepare for a small ceremony to commemorate the centennial of the laying of the Greene County Courthouse cornerstone. We remembered having heard that there might be a time capsule buried under the cornerstone, and we thought that if we could find it, it would add some excitement to the occasion. Library research of microfilmed newspapers from the time yielded a description of the box and its contents. With something substantive on which to base a search, digging began. After several fruitless days, as we were contemplating abandoning the project, we finally hit the metal of the sealed copper box. It had been well cemented in and was difficult to extract. The recovery, however, proved to be well worth the effort involved.

The courthouse, in the process of construction in 1901, was the third courthouse to be built specifically for the purpose in Greene County's short history. The county, named for Revolutionary war soldier, Nathaniel Greene, was founded in 1803—the same year that Ohio became a state. It originally ran north to Lake Erie, but its present boundaries had been established by 1819. The Greene County commissioners had been meeting in privately owned properties until the first official county courthouse was ready in 1809. In 1843, an elegant new courthouse in the classical style was built to provide more space. In a little over 30 years, however, this building had also become inadequate for the growing county's needs. An 1875 addition helped temporarily, but by 1883 there were serious safety concerns. The roof fell down and, although it was repaired, calls began for building yet another new courthouse. Votes were taken several times, but the proposal failed to pass. It was not until 1900—when the 1843 building was condemned as unsafe—that a bond issue finally was passed to enable the new courthouse to be built. A building commission was appointed, composed of the three county commissioners, joined by four freehold electors of the county (two Democrats and two Republicans) who served without pay. Remarkably, the courthouse was finished under budget.

Architects Samuel Hannaford and Sons of Cincinnati designed the imposing Romanesque stone courthouse. The Building Commission's records in the Greene County Archives detail the multitude of specifications for the builders, including the latest modern conveniences. In January of 1901, the commission recorded in their minutes that it would be "proper and fitting to commemorate the commencement of the work upon the new courthouse by the laying of a cornerstone with proper ceremonies." They decided to invite Lodge No. 49 of the Free and Accepted Masons to take charge of organizing the occasion. This became a matter of considerable controversy when the Judge of the Probate Court, Joseph Dean, led a doomed protest movement in favor of the Association of Ex-Soldiers, Sailors and Marines. Despite the disputes, the county came together, schools were let out early and businesses were closed to encourage attendance.

A crowd of 5,000 people witnessed the impressive celebrations on the cold and snowy afternoon of March 15, 1901.

In the days leading up to the ceremony, there were notices urgently requesting organizations submit historical sketches and other papers of interest for the proposed time capsule. Business people were invited to advertise their concerns in the extra editions of the commemorative newspapers, copies of which were to be included in the time capsule. Through these advertisements, they were told, they could reach a large number of prospective customers immediately, and be rediscovered in the future.

In 1901, Greene County was a thriving and prosperous area. Although the county was noted for livestock breeding and general farming, there was also much innovation in business and manufacturing. Traditional methods of transportation were being replaced. Nearby, the Wright brothers were experimenting with their flying machines, and the railroads were carrying goods around the country from local factories, such as the cordage company of Hooven and Allison and the Xenia Shoe Manufacturing Company. Automobiles were appearing on the streets of Xenia. Typewriters, telephones, and telegraphs were revolutionizing communications, and electric lights brightened homes and businesses. Perhaps it should therefore not be surprising that on the day the cornerstone was laid an article published in the *Xenia Semi-Weekly Gazette* contained such a lively, imaginative vision of the Xenia of 2001, when the writer thought that the courthouse would likely be torn down and replaced. It painted a fanciful picture of a town full of skyscrapers, with huge, modern factories. Yet the article, which is included in full in this book, presciently described our feelings as we archivists "carefully unfolded" the items in the time capsule. We did indeed handle the "documents with a certain awe," and were intrigued by "the advertisements of queer things that are never needed in this day and age of the world."

We actually opened the time capsule at a public meeting of the county commissioners on February 27, 2001. We gingerly removed the items untouched for 100 years and placed them on a table for viewing. They had been stored well and were in pristine condition. Even the newspapers were fresh looking and not brittle. The material had obviously been handled professionally, using state of the art methods of preservation for the time. The items had come from schools, churches, and organizations across the county, representing most of the townships and municipalities that existed at the time. At the centennial celebration, copies of some of these interesting finds were displayed in a small exhibit in the courthouse.

The 1901 time capsule has given us a fascinating snapshot of the time when it was buried, illustrating how the people then wanted to be remembered. We hope that this book, containing photographs of some of the documents preserved in the time capsule, and supplemental photographs of some of the people and places noted in the documents, will be of interest to the current inhabitants of the county.

One

Background

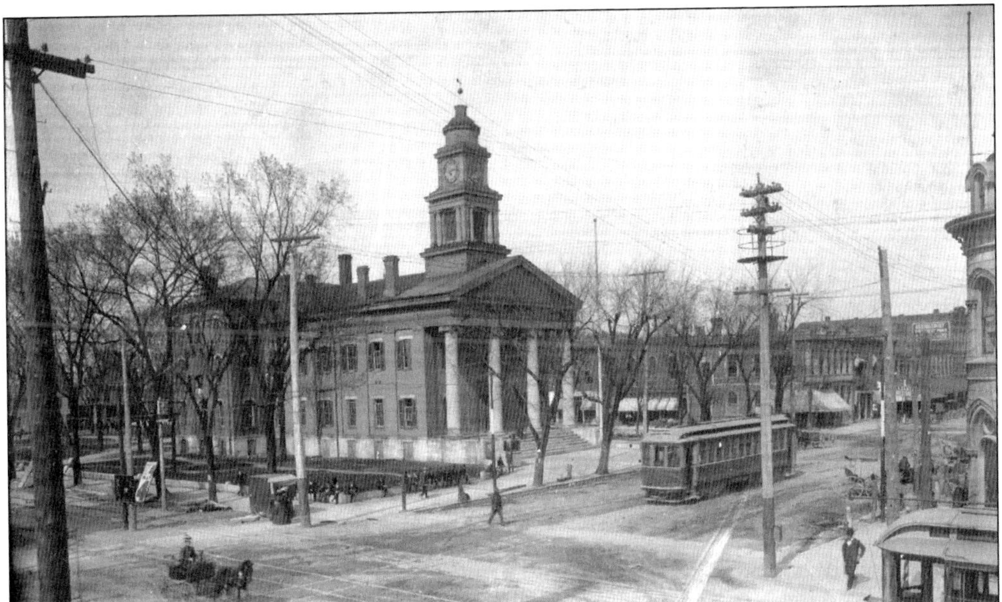

The building first used as a courthouse by Greene County was a privately owned log structure located in Beavercreek Township, west of the city of Xenia. It was used from 1803 until 1804. When Xenia became the county seat, the courts moved to another temporary location across the street from the present site. This location was used from 1804 until 1806. The first courthouse constructed and owned by Greene County was completed in 1809. The classical building shown here was the county's second courthouse, completed in 1843. The addition of 1875 is visible behind the main building. (Courtesy of Greene County Room, Greene County Public Library.)

"AU REVOIR."

Imposing and Fitting Ceremonial on Forsaking the Old Greene County Court House.

On last Thursday afternoon the last session of court was held in the old court house at Xenia, and when the gavel fell the old structure was legally abandoned to the wreckers, and in a few days the once stately and imposing imitation of the old Greek Parthenon will be but a pile of rubbish.

Judge Scroggy assembled the members of the bar, with but few exceptions, and rather imposing ceremonies were had, and many recollections of the old structure were recalled to the minds of the older members of the bar by the somewhat sad occasion. After the last word had been said the bar were all arranged about the old court room by Mr. McGervey, the photographer, and a picture of all those present was taken, which will be prized by them and their families in the after years.

It was suggested by several of those present that Mr. W. A. Paxson, who has been denominated the "Poet Laureate" of the Greene county bar, should compose some ode or tribute to the old court house, and in pursuance thereof Mr Paxson has composed the following:—

ODE TO THE OLD COURT HOUSE.

Venerable pile! Remnant of ages past!
Your builders never dreamed that you would last
So long; they little thought that a future generation
Would be so overcome with veneration,
For the thing constructed years ago
That they would let it stand thus long to show
The ancient styles of structure, pillars and entablature,
Like Carnak's halls or a Parthenon, destined to endure
Through centuries. Your belfry towering high
With ancient clock, proclaiming "Time doth fly;"
Your courtroom that in days long gone
Has echoed with the resonant intone
Of a Corwin, Carey, Blackburn, Clay,
And many more such advocates as they;
Whose bench has highly honored been
By many pure and noble men
Like Ellesberry, Winans, Gilmore, Doan,
Barlow, Williams, Shearer, Sloan;
Munger, Sexton, Shauck and Hawes
Smith and Scroggy learned in laws,
Until at last, with scythe in hand
Old Time took charge and gave command
That thou henceforth no more shall stand.
Could thy old walls but speak! Alas! Alas!
But such things cannot come to pass;
The only things those walls can say
As they condemned stand today.
Is "We like you are common clay,
We now are crumbling in decay
And at no very distant day
This old court house must pass away."

W.A. Paxson, attorney-at-law from Jamestown and a member of the Greene County Bar Association, was called the court's "poet laureate." Here is an extract of a poem he wrote to bid farewell to the old courthouse. (Courtesy of Greene County Archives—Time Capsule Document.)

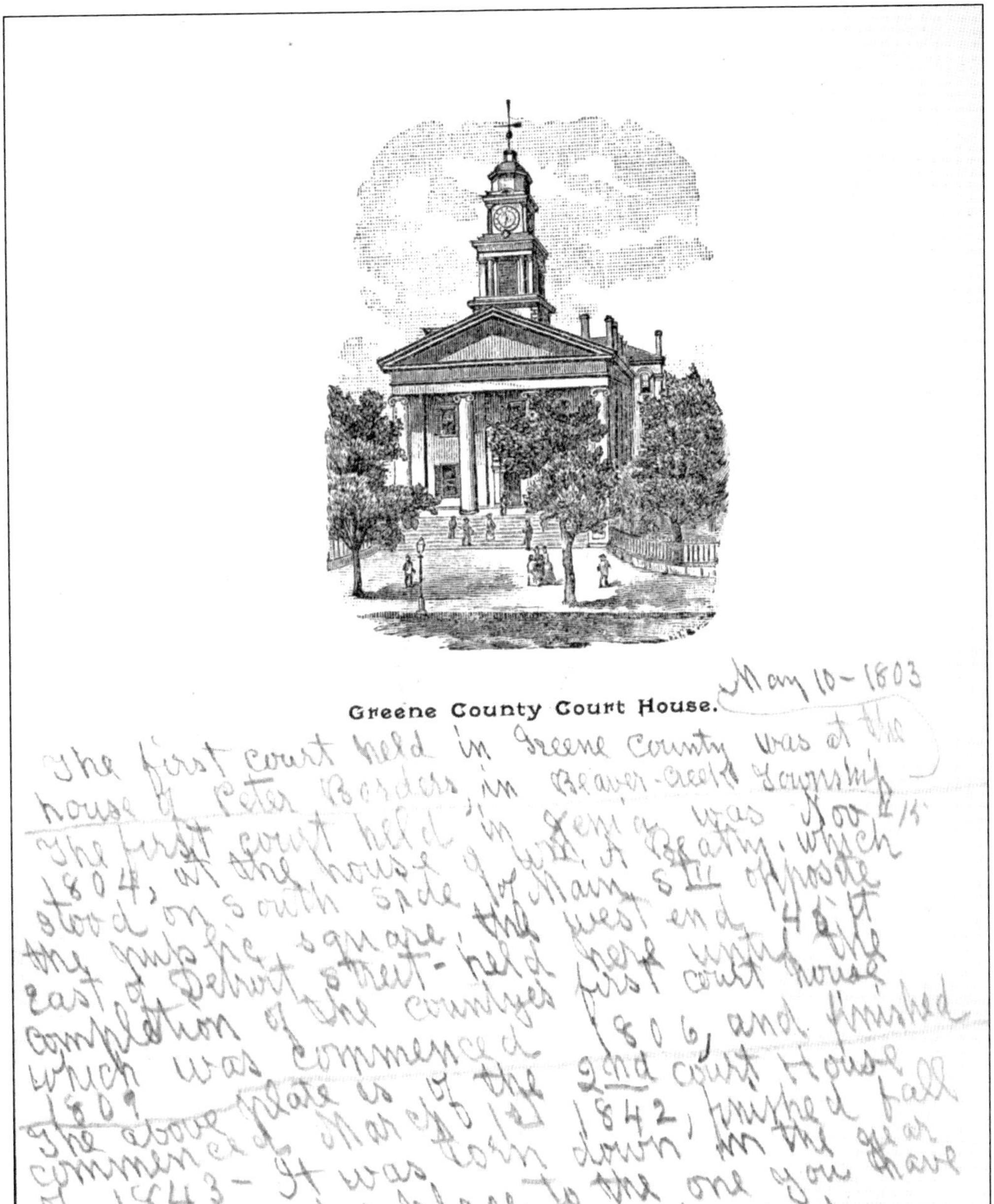
Greene County Court House.

May 10 - 1803

The first court held in Greene County was at the house of Peter Borders, in Beaver-creek Township.

The first court held in Xenia was Nov 15 1804, at the house of Wm. A Beatty, which stood on south side of Main St. opposite the public square, the west end 4th east of Detroit street - held here until the completion of the countyes first court house which was commenced 1806, and finished 1809.

The above plate is of the 2nd court House commenced March 1st 1842, finished fall of 1843 - It was torn down in the year 1900. To give place to the one you have just torn down - !

A copy of a book listing the Civil War soldiers from Greene County, entitled *After Thirty Years*, was enclosed in the time capsule. It included this picture of the 1843 courthouse with a handwritten, brief history of Greene County courthouses. Note that the writer expected that the time capsule would not be found until the new courthouse was demolished. (Courtesy of Greene County Archives—Time Capsule Document.)

Roster of Greene County Bar as they appeared at the final adjournment in the court room of the old Court House.

This photograph was taken by F. E. McGervey (an amateur in photography) Cashier of the Citizens National Bank =

1. C. F. Howard. Pros. Atty.
2. W. A. Paxon.
3. Hugo. Schlesinger.
4 Hon. John. Little
5. D. P. Browder.
6 M. A. Broadstone
7 P. R. Schnebly
8 W. S. Howard.
9 H. S. Armstrong
10 J. A. Cook.
11. F. H. Dean.
12. H. L. Smith. Ex Com. Pleas. Judge.
13 F. N. Shaffer.
14 M. J. Hartley
15. W. F. Trader.
16 E. H. Munger. Ex. Com. Pleas. Judge.
17 T. E. Scroggy. "Judge"
18 W. F. Orr.
19 J. F. Hoverstick. "Clerk"
20. C. C. Shearer Ex Circuit Judge.
21. C. H. Kyle.
22 H. Nesbitt "Bailiff"
23 Charles. Darlington
24 H. Sabin.
25. W. E. Kiser court. Stenographer
26. W. L. Miller
27 J. Thos Harbine
28. F. P. Cunningham
29. J. N. Dean.

March 15th 1901

F. E. McGervey

Here is the back of the photograph of the Greene County Bar Association's last meeting in the old courthouse, listing the members present. (Courtesy of Greene County Archives—Time Capsule Document.)

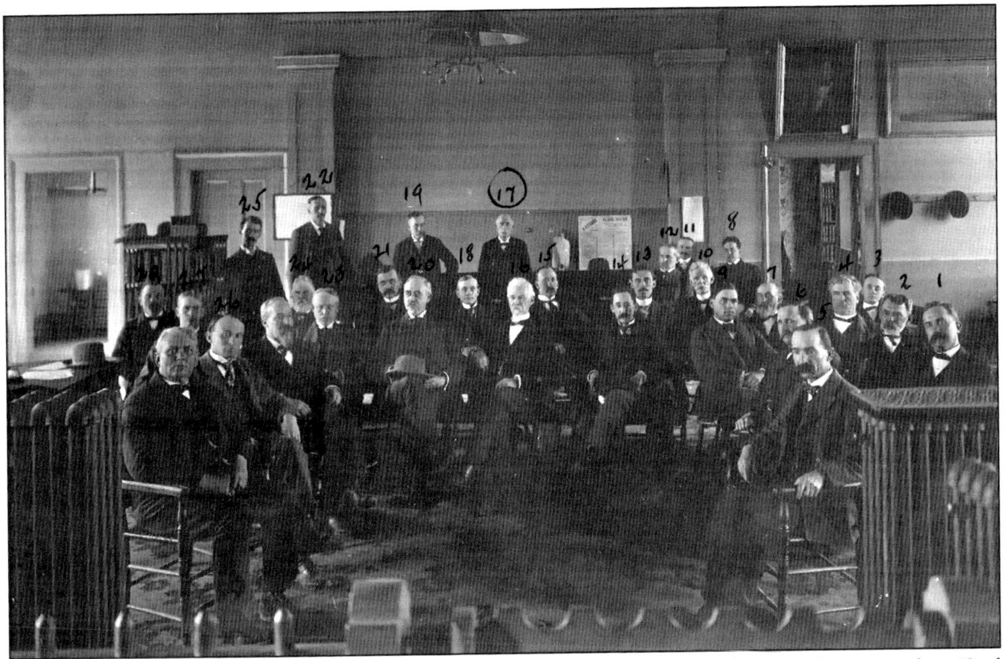

Pictured is the bar association's last meeting in the old courthouse. The members are identified on the back of the photograph. See opposite page. (Courtesy of Greene County Archives—Time Capsule Document.)

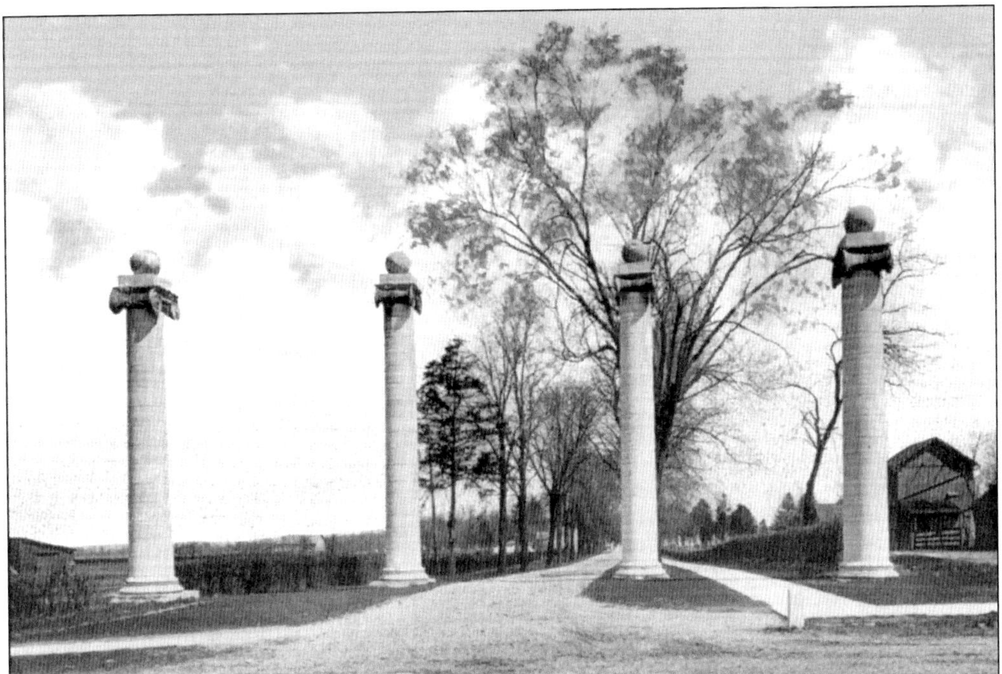

When the 1843 courthouse was pulled down, the four classical columns were transported to the entrance of Xenia's Woodland cemetery, where they still stand today. (Courtesy of Greene County Room, Greene County Public Library.)

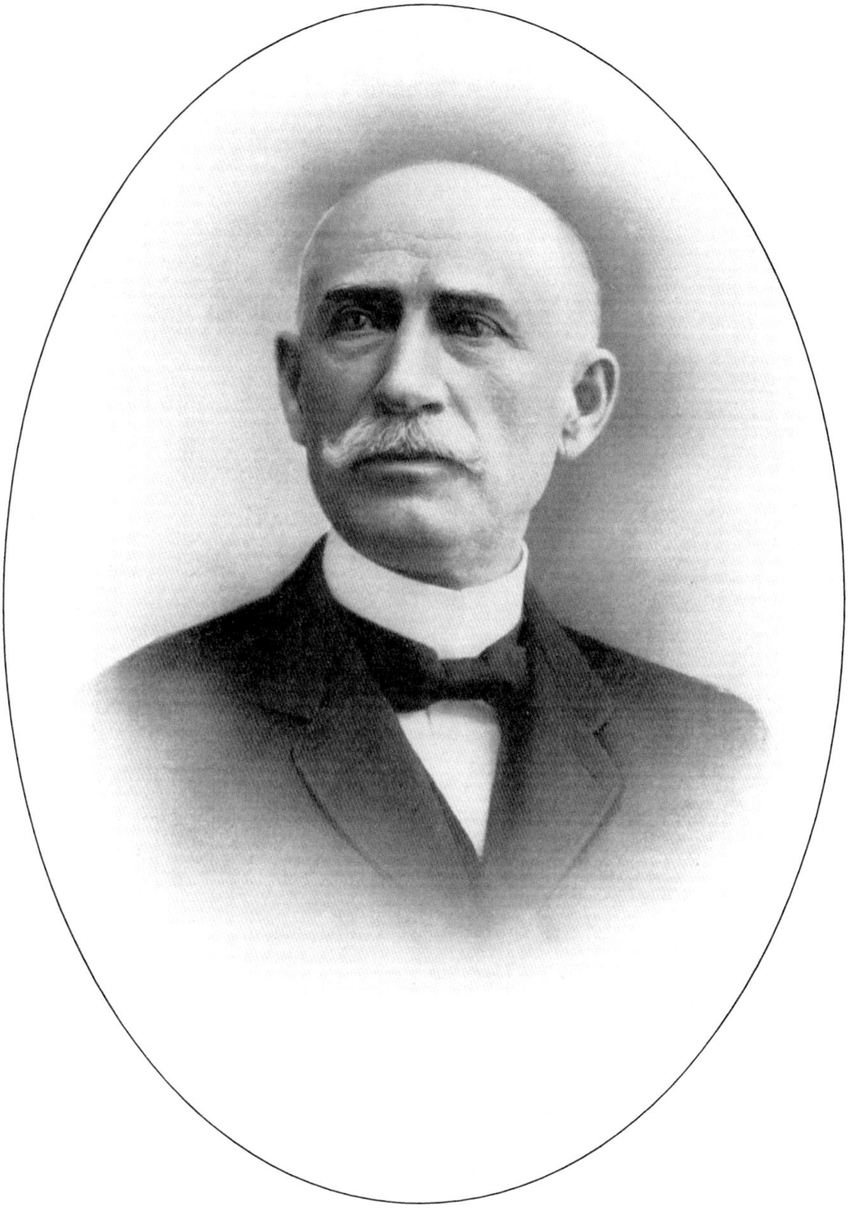

The judge of the Common Pleas Court was Thomas E. Scroggy. Judge Scroggy was a veteran of the Civil War and, as were many men of his generation and standing in society, a member of several fraternal organizations. He belonged to Xenia Lodge, No. 49 of the Free and Accepted Masons (FAM); the Xenia Chapter No. 36 of the Royal Arch Masons; the Benevolent and Protective Order of Elks; the Union Veteran Legion; and was a charter member of the Grand Army of the Republic, Lewis Post, No. 347. (Courtesy of Greene County Room, Greene County Public Library, Robinson's *History of Greene County, Ohio*, 1902.)

The following is a brief summary of the facts disclosed by the minutes of the Court House Building Commission:-

On March 21st, 1900, the Legislature of Ohio passed an Act to provide for the erection of a new Court House in Greene County, Ohio, under the terms of which the County Commissioners, in conjunction with B four free hold electors of the County to be appointed by the Judge of the Court of Common Pleas, were directed to issue bonds to the amount o of $200,000.00 for the purpose of building a new Court House.

The Act further provided that before the Commission should proceed, the question should be submitted to a vote of the people. The question was submitted at the election held April 2nd, 1900, and carried by a vote of 3582 against 908.

Pursuant to the requirement of the said law, Judge Thomas E. Scroggy, on March 21st, 1900, appointed John Little of Xenia, Albert Wickersham of Jamestown, Henry Barber of Cedarville, and Wm. W. Ferguson of Beaver Creek Township as the four members of the Building Commission, who in connection with John Steveson, J. W. Fudge and Lewis Smith, the County Commissioners, constituted the Building Commission.

The first meeting of the Commission was held April 4th, 1900. At the second meeting April 7th, 1900, the Commission decided to tear down the old Court House, and formulated rules therefor. The contract for this work was subsequently let to John McGarey for $

On April 25th, 1900, the Commission met and adopted the following rules for the general guidance of the Architects:-

1- The cost of the main building should not exceed $150,000.00.
2- That it be fire proof, except that the sheeting may be wood, protected below by asbestos plastering.
3- That the roof be tile or slate.
4- That the outside of the outer walls be rocked faced ashler of some standard stone for that purpose, and the rest of the walls of brick.
5- That the halls and corridors above the basement be floored with tile, and wainscoted five feet high withmarble, or some durable and good material in similitude thereof.
6- The outside walls below grade line and all foundations to be of Dayton limestone.
7- That the top of the first floor be as near the grade line as will allow good light and ventilation in the basement.
8- All offices and rooms for accasional use only, including an assembly room, to be in the basement.
9- The offices and rooms of the County Treasurer, Auditor, Commissioners (these to be connected), Recorder and Probate Court to be on the first floor.
10- The Common Pleas Court Room (to be on the north-east corner, with rooms on the west of it), Chambers for Pleas Judge, Chambers for Circuit Judges, Concultation Room, Library, Clerk's office, Sheriff's Office, Prosecuting Att'ys Office, Stenographer's Room, Witness Room, Petit Jury Room, Grand Jury Room, to be on the second floor.
11- There is to be a suitable waiting room, especially for ladies, preferably on the first floor; also a well-lighted and suitable Surveyor's Office, easily accessible, and a Tax Inquisitor's Room.
12- A space for an elevator from basement to garret to be provided.
13- Stairways to be easy and commodious, with marble steps, and glass in risers where useful.
14- The main halls to be well lighted from above as well as from the ends, and all the rooms to have good light; and the windows to be wide, of plate glass, and not stinted in number.

The Commission then and thereafter at various meetings considered the subject of selecting an Architect, and finally agreed upon Messrs. Samuel Hannaford & Sons of Cincinnati, Ohio. The contract with them was signed on the 31st day of July, 1900, they agreeing to do the work, and furnish a Superintendent for the sum of $7000.00. Specifications were prepared and submitted to the Commission at its meeting held August 16, 1900, and at that meeting it was ordered that the letting of the contract for the main building of the Court House be fixed for September 18th, 1900, on which day the bids were opened, and the next meeting, Sept. 19th, all were rejected except that of Hennessey Bros. & Evans Co. of Chicago, and Redmond & Gibson of Logansport, Ind. At this meeting, it was decided by the Commission to go to Bedford and examine the stone in the quarries, which was accordingly done.

The next meeting was held September 22nd, at which meeting the bid of Hennesey Bros. & Evans Co. was accepted, and the contract signed with them on the 4th day of October, 1900, by which contract they were to complete the building, according to plans and specifications, for $140,248.00.

After several meetings, at which unimportant matters were discusss-ed, the Commission met and entered into a contract with the P.C.C & St.L. R.R. for the construction of a swotch into the Court House lot, which switch was subsequently placed in position.

Mr. John Little, one of the Commission, died shortly after this meeting, and the Court appointed his son George Little to fill the vacancy thereby created, and he presented his credentials and became a member of the Commission at the meeting held November 6th, 1900.

Numerous meetings were held by the Commission, at which sundry matters of minor importance relating to the Court House were taken up and discussed, and finally on November 27th, 1900, the bond of Hennessey Bros. & Evans Co was approved and work commenced on the Court House.

On January 2nd, 1901, the Commission met and adopted plans for the construction of a power house to be constructed on the Jail lot, and at this meeting it was resolved that it is the sense of this commission that it will be proper and fitting to commemorate the commencement of the work upon the new Court House by the laying of a corner-stone, with proper ceremonies, and resolved further that the F. & A. M. Lodge, No. 49 be invited to take charge and to perform said ceremonies, at a time to be mutually agreed on, which time was fixed as March 15th, 1901.

At the meeting held January 24th, 1901, it was resolved to issue the first installation of $100,000 4% Gold Bonds, and the same,after being advertised,were sold to N. W. Harris & Co of Chicago, Ill, on February 28th, 1901, for the sum of $109,330 and accrued interest.

Prior thereto, on the 12th day of February, 1901, the contract was let for the building of the Power House to Peter McCurren & Sons of Xenia, Ohio, for the sum of $2747.00.

The last meeting of the Building Commission,prior to the laying of the corner-stone,was held, as were all the other meetings theretofore held since the tearing down of the old court house, in the Commissioners Room, situated on the second floor of the building located on the north-east corner of Main and Greene Streets. At this meeting all members were present, and the 5th estimate of the Architect for work done on the Court House was allowed, making the total sum up to that time allowed the Contractors, $23,400.00. At this time, the foundation walls had been built and the iron for the first floor laid, and the broken ashlar work completed almost to the top of the first story windows, with the exception of the east wall.

George Little
Acting Secretary and
member of the Building
Commission

This is an extract from the report of the Courthouse Building Commission, signed by George Little, who was one of the commission members. The report indicates, among other work of the commission, that they had invited Lodge No. 49 of the FAM to take charge of the cornerstone laying ceremonies. (Courtesy of Greene County Archives—Time Capsule Document.)

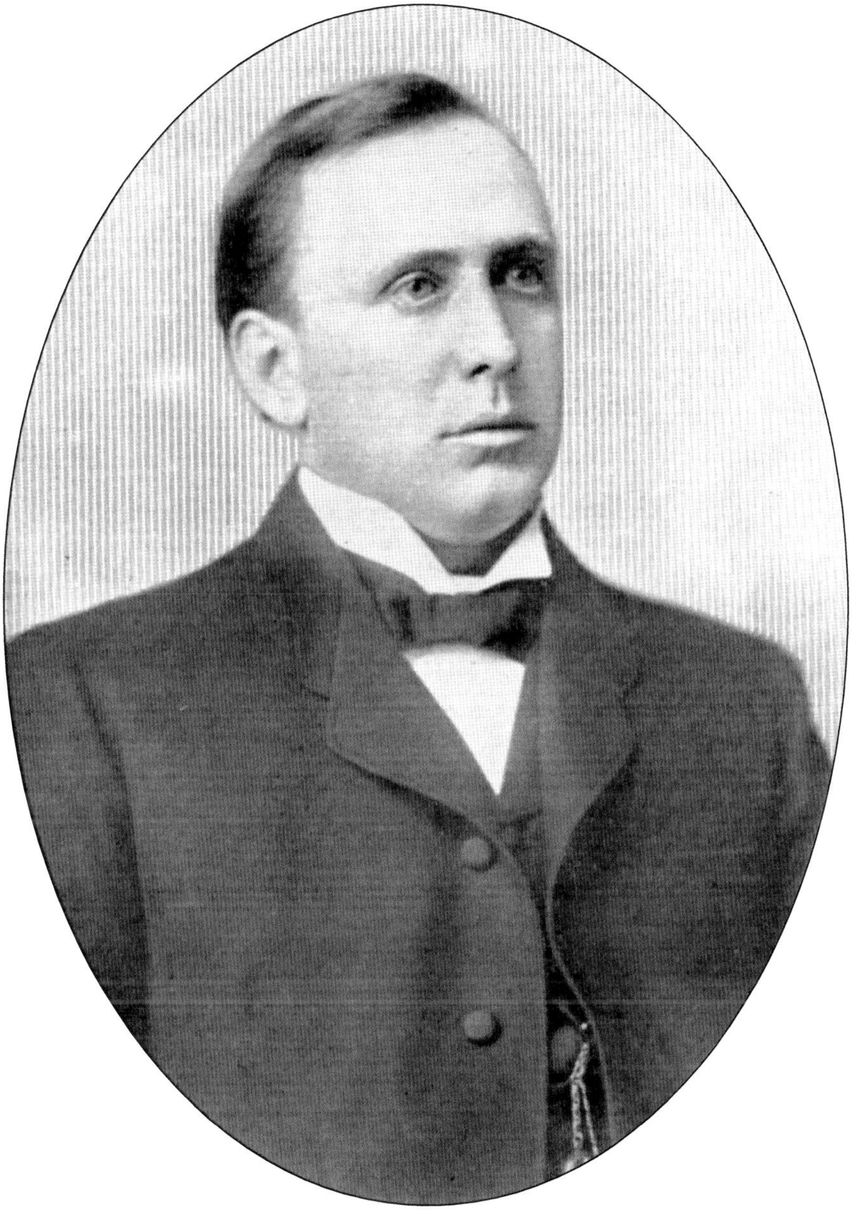

George Little, who replaced his father, John Little, on the Building Commission, following his father's death in 1900, was a member of the Greene County Bar Association, and a director of the Xenia National Bank. (Courtesy of Greene County Historical Society, Clevenger's *Xenia City Directory*, 1907.)

Xenia, O.

March, 15th, 1901.

Hanaford Son's
Architect's
Cincinnati, O.
John H. Dorman,
Sup't. Architect.

We the undersigned are employees of the Hennessy Bros & Evans Company, Contractors of the Green County COURT HOUSE,

Chas. Turner,	Wm. Jasper,	Clayton Howard,
Wm. Mc. Intosh,	Wm. Holtzapple,	James Whallen,
John Scanlon,	Ed. Jackson,	Ed. John,
Geo. Machay,	Frank Wright,	Joe. Munger,
Peter Yachley,	Richard Dean,	Tom Maloney,
Chas. Bortran,	James Winn,	Tom. Higgins,
WM. Herman,	Chas Justice,	John Roberts,
Chas. Buck,	Chas. Jenkins,	Tom. Adams,
Alex Frick,	Charles Greisbaum, Jr.	Wm. Anderson,
Charles Martindale,	Jerry Swable,	Jacob Green,
Henry Greisbaum,	James King,	Wm. Mc. Gran,
A. Mc. Claferty,	Charles Polley,	Geo. Rayner,
Alex Mackie,	Wm. Cline,	John Hamilton,
Newton Walley,	Milton King,	James Berry,
Geo. King,	Elijah Jasper,	Peter Lambert,
Mike Welch,	Arthur Phillips,	
Geo. Edwards,	James Daunton,	GEO. FRASER,
Tom. Buyssy,	Warner Peterson,	Sup't.
Pete Alexander,	Geo. Wright,	Henry Schlee,
		Time Keeper,

X-X-X-X-X-X-X-X-X-X-X-X-X-X-X-X-X-X-X-X-X-X-X-X-X-X-X-X-X-X-X-X-X-X-X-X

The HARDWARE was furnished by Mr. J.C. Conwell, Xenia, O.

Employees of whom are,

L.W. Cumberland,	Horace Oglesbe,
C.L. John,	A.D. Conklin,
C.B. Crane,	C.T. Rountree,

Samuel Hannaford and Sons, Architects of Cincinnati, Ohio, were awarded the contract to design the plans and specifications of the new courthouse. The firm had designed more than 300 structures in Ohio, Kentucky, Indiana, Tennessee, and West Virginia, including courthouses for Washington and Monroe counties in Ohio. Hennessey Brothers and Evans Company of Chicago won the bid for the construction work, and J.C. Conwell of Xenia furnished the hardware. (Courtesy of Greene County Archives—Time Capsule Document.)

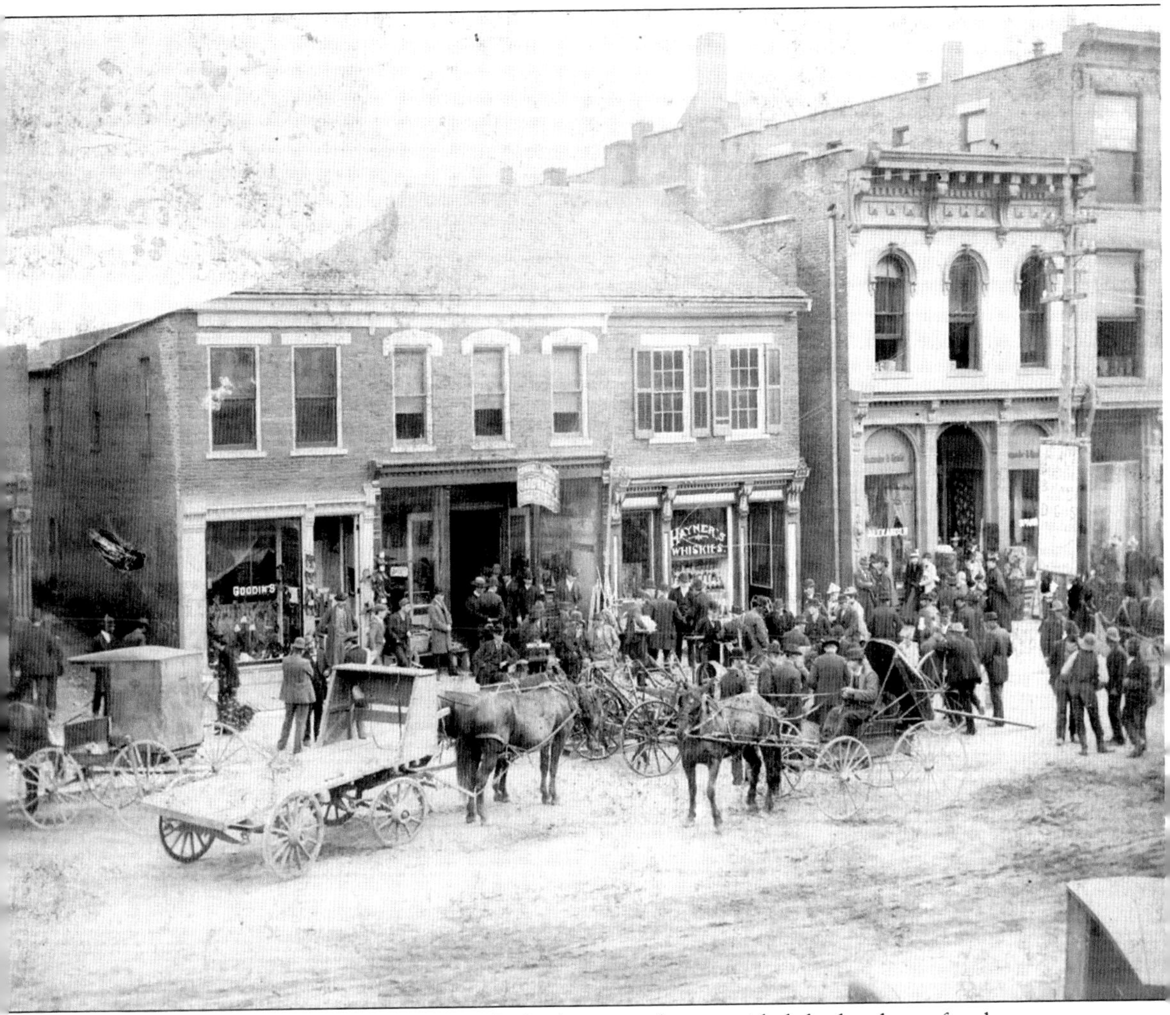

This is the hardware store of J.C. Conwell, the business that provided the hardware for the new courthouse. (Courtesy of Greene County Historical Society.)

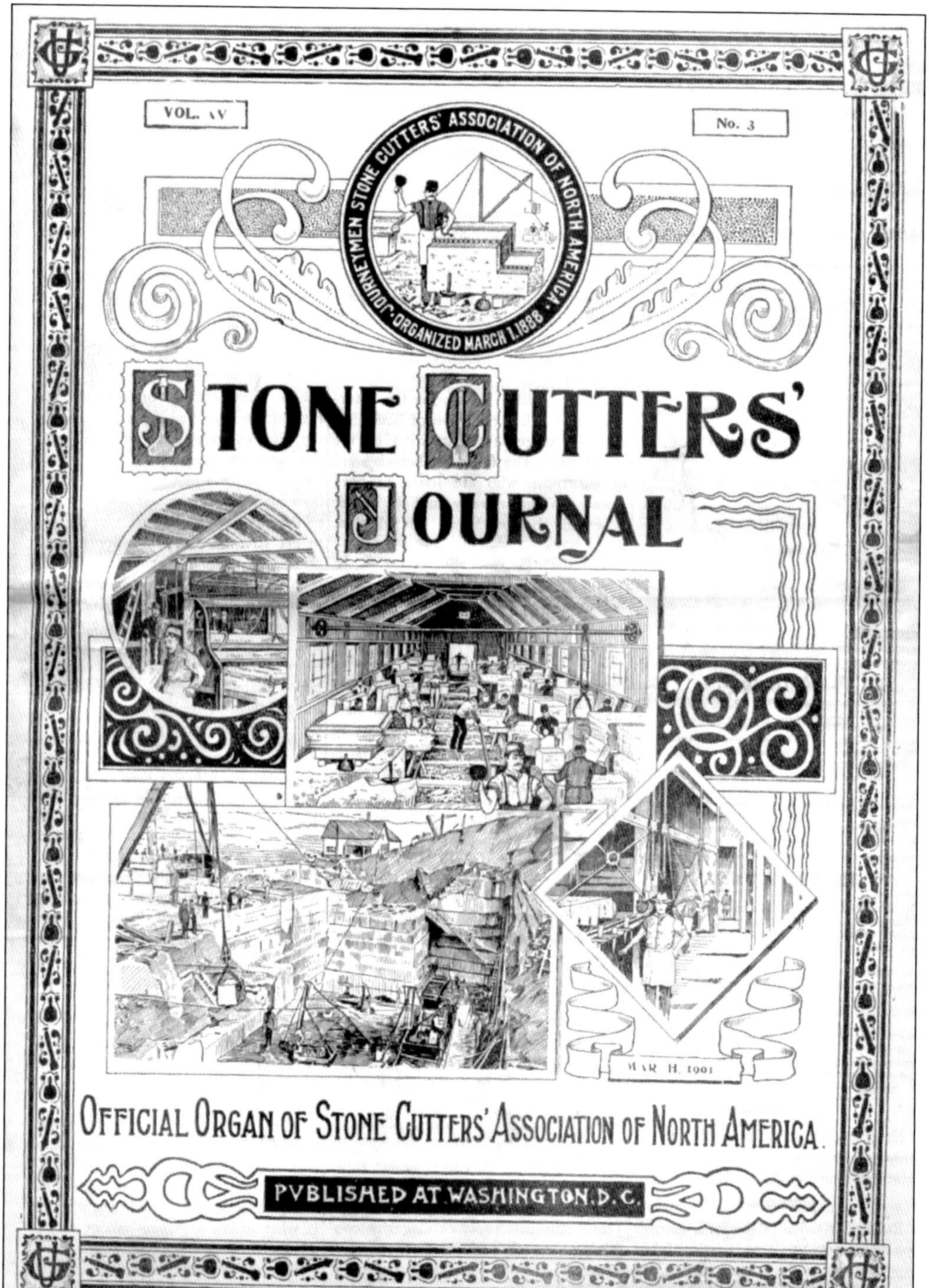

The stonecutters belonged to the Journeymen Stonecutters Association of North America, the oldest active union in North America, founded in 1853. A cover from one of their journals is shown here. The stonecutters' artwork was much valued on the buildings of the late 19th and early 20th century. (Courtesy of Greene County Archives—Time Capsule Document.)

Xenia, Ohio, Feb. 11.

JUST a few lines to let you know that our charter was hung in a manner that was a credit to ourselves and to the G. U. in general. We held a special meeting, christened the charter. Each member drank to its presence, and all hoping as our president, Thos. Keir, hung it on the wall that those who may come after us would be as enthusiastic in keeping it upon the wall as we were in hanging it there. We then threw open our doors, and the hanging of the charter of the Journeymen Stonecutters of Xenia, Ohio, will long be remembered by all those present. Songs, recitations, dances, cake-walks and refreshments filled the programme. The refreshments were donated mostly by M. J. Dugan, a member of the Pueblo branch of 1892, who is the proprietor of one of the finest wet goods emporiums in this city. We all stayed until the wee hours of the morning, every one feeling satisfied that the charter was hung as no one but stonecutters could hang it, and that we were the first to plant the emblem of unionism in Xenia. Then we went home.

GEO. McDONNELL, C. S.

This is the entry in the Stone Cutters' Journal from the Xenia Branch, published in March 1901. (Courtesy of Greene County Archives—Time Capsule Document.)

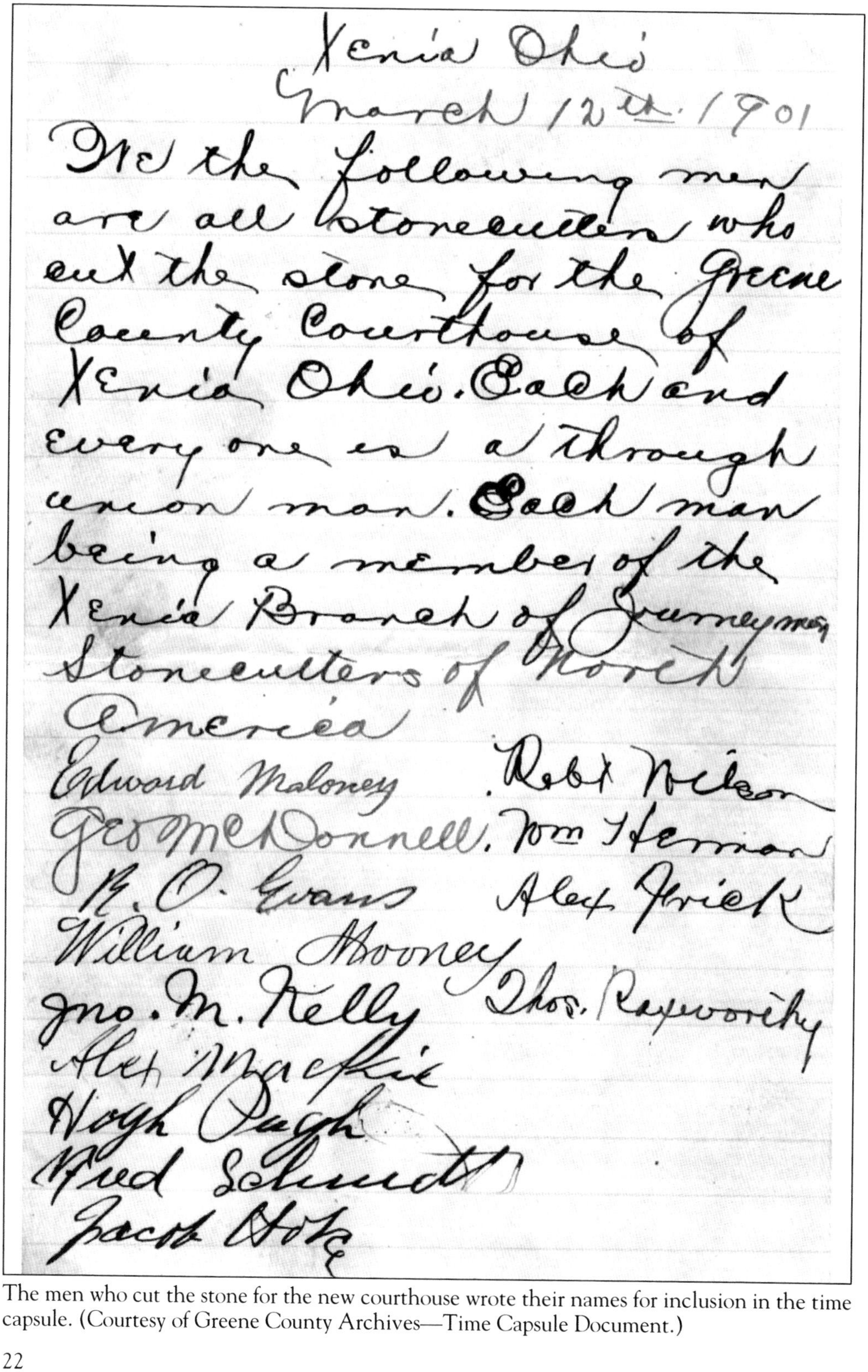

Xenia Ohio
March 12th 1901
We the following men
are all stonecutters who
cut the stone for the Greene
County Courthouse of
Xenia Ohio. Each and
every one is a through
union man. Each man
being a member of the
Xenia Branch of Journeymen
Stonecutters of North
America

Edward Maloney. Robt Wilson
Geo McDonnell. Wm Herron
R. O. Evans Alex Frick
William Mooney
Jno. M. Kelly Thos. Rayworthy
Alex Mackie
Hugh Pugh
Fred Schmidt
Jacob Holz

The men who cut the stone for the new courthouse wrote their names for inclusion in the time capsule. (Courtesy of Greene County Archives—Time Capsule Document.)

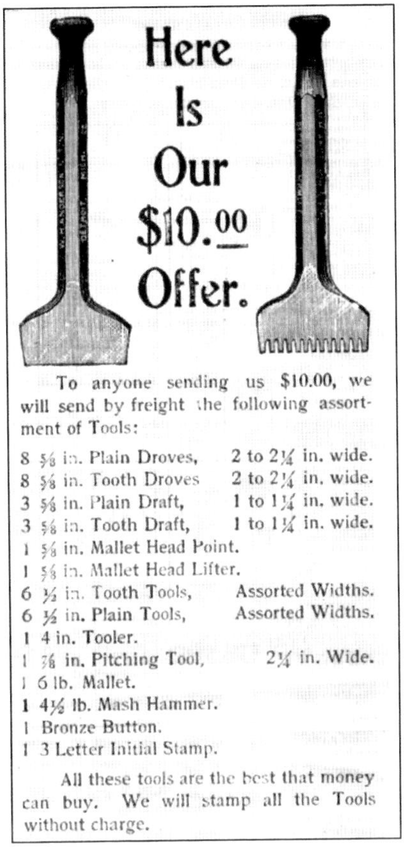

This advertisement from the copy of the Stone Cutters' Journal shows selections of stonecutters' tools for sale. (Courtesy of Greene County Archives—Time Capsule Document.)

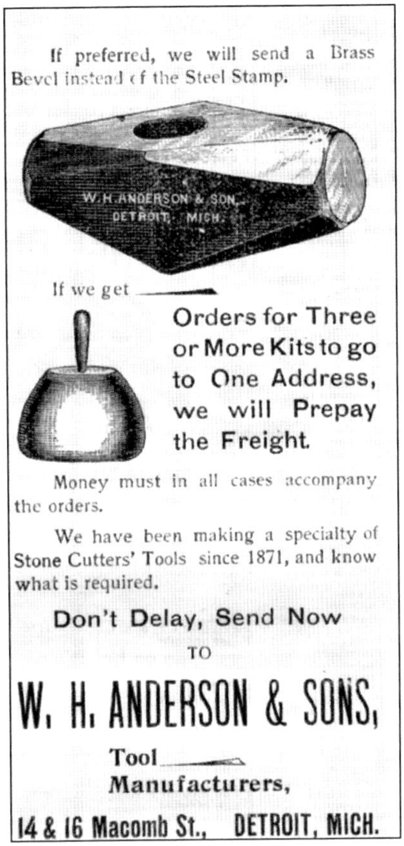

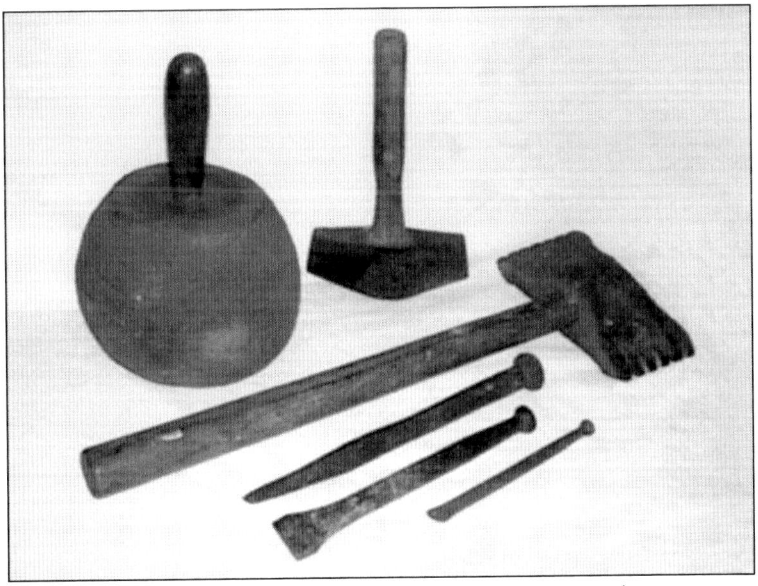

The mallet, chisels, and hammers shown here are some of the actual stonecutters' tools that were used to build the courthouse. They had belonged to George McDonnell, foreman of the stonecutters, who came to Xenia from Chicago for this purpose. (Courtesy of Greene County Historical Society.)

Brick Layer's International Union,

No. 16, Ohio.

Cyrus W. McIntosh
Rec. & Cor. Sec'y

TRADES COUNCIL
KUMP, PRINTER

Xenia Ohio, March 14th 1901

Bricklayers who constitute our union No 16 of Ohio

Chas Turner Pres.
T. P. Stratton Vice Pres. & Treasurer
Cyrus McIntosh Recording & Corres Sec
Emerson T Bingamon Fin-Sec.
Wm Stratton Door Keeper.
Wm McIntosh Deputy
Chas Buck
Chas Bertram
Thomas Staley
Joseph Griesbaum
George Fraser
George McKay
Wm Xanders
Peter Yeakley
Wm Felitz.

In union there is strength.

Organized November 27th 1893

Members of Branch No. 16, Ohio, of the Bricklayers and Masons International Union of America, signed their names for deposit in the time capsule. "In union there is strength." This union succeeded the Bricklayers International Union of America, the Xenia branch of which was founded in 1893. (Courtesy of Greene County Archives—Time Capsule Document.)

The Bricklayers and Masons International Union wished for the ceremonial laying of the cornerstone of the new courthouse to be recognized by union labor. (Courtesy of Greene County Archives—Time Capsule Document.)

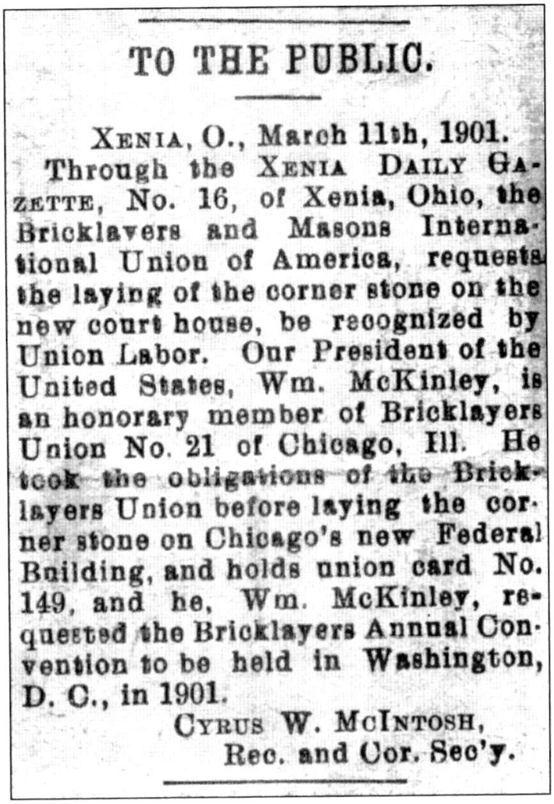

TO THE PUBLIC.

XENIA, O., March 11th, 1901.

Through the XENIA DAILY GAZETTE, No. 16, of Xenia, Ohio, the Bricklayers and Masons International Union of America, requests the laying of the corner stone on the new court house, be recognized by Union Labor. Our President of the United States, Wm. McKinley, is an honorary member of Bricklayers Union No. 21 of Chicago, Ill. He took the obligations of the Bricklayers Union before laying the corner stone on Chicago's new Federal Building, and holds union card No. 149, and he, Wm. McKinley, requested the Bricklayers Annual Convention to be held in Washington, D. C., in 1901.

CYRUS W. MCINTOSH,
Rec. and Cor. Sec'y.

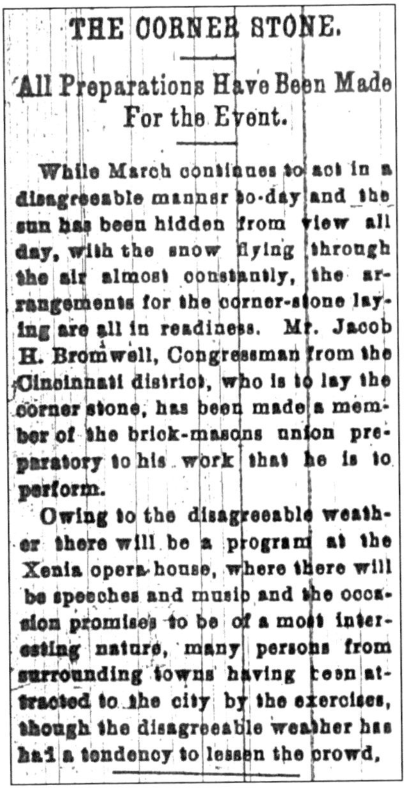

THE CORNER STONE.

All Preparations Have Been Made For the Event.

While March continues to act in a disagreeable manner to-day and the sun has been hidden from view all day, with the snow flying through the air almost constantly, the arrangements for the corner-stone laying are all in readiness. Mr. Jacob H. Bromwell, Congressman from the Cincinnati district, who is to lay the corner stone, has been made a member of the brick-masons union preparatory to his work that he is to perform.

Owing to the disagreeable weather there will be a program at the Xenia opera house, where there will be speeches and music and the occasion promises to be of a most interesting nature, many persons from surrounding towns having been attracted to the city by the exercises, though the disagreeable weather has had a tendency to lessen the crowd.

The *Xenia Daily Gazette* of March 15, 1901, indicated that Jacob H. Bromwell, Cincinnati district congressman, who was to perform the ceremonial laying of the cornerstone, was made an honorary member of the Bricklayers and Masons International Union of America. This was so the work could be performed by union labor. (Courtesy of Greene County Room, Greene County Public Library.)

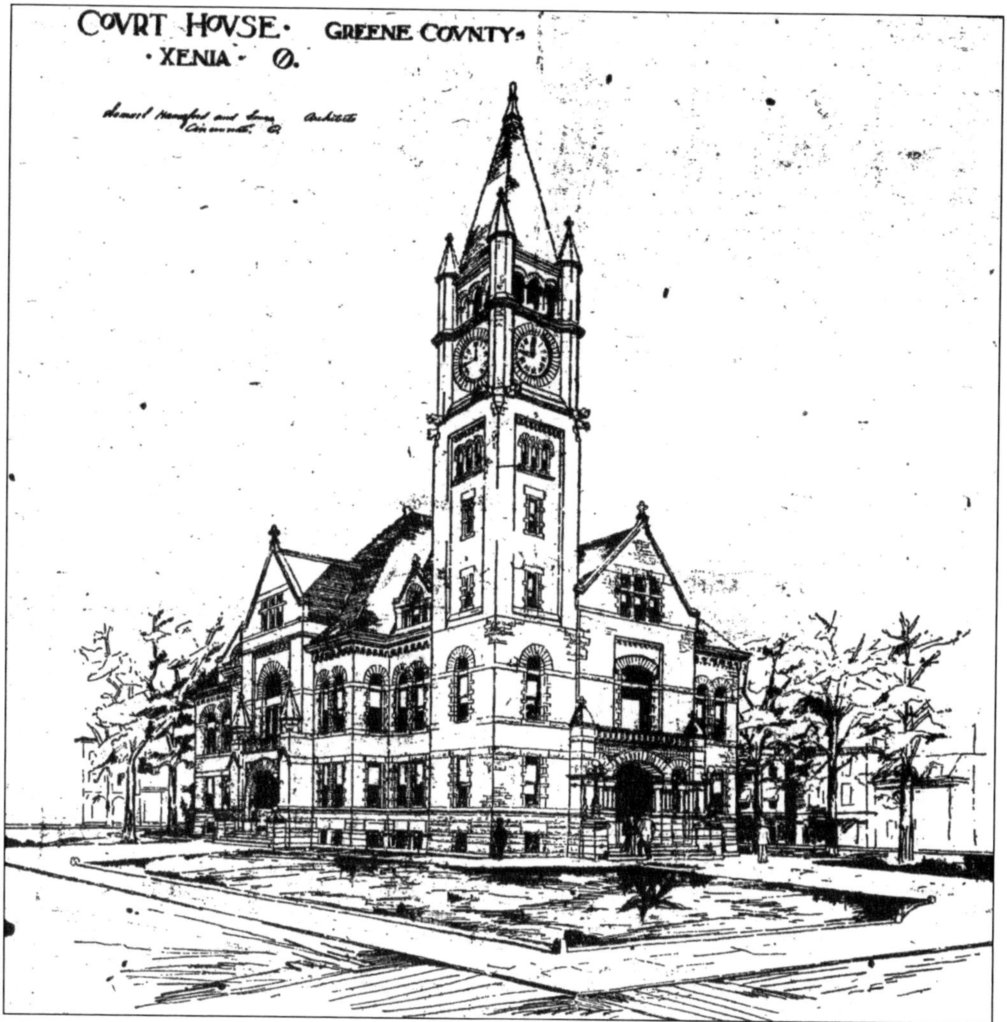

The *Xenia Semi-Weekly Gazette* of March 15, 1901, published this architect's rendition of how the finished courthouse would look. Note that, following the fashion of the time, it provides a remarkable architectural contrast to the classical building it was to replace. (Courtesy of Greene County Archives—Time Capsule Document.)

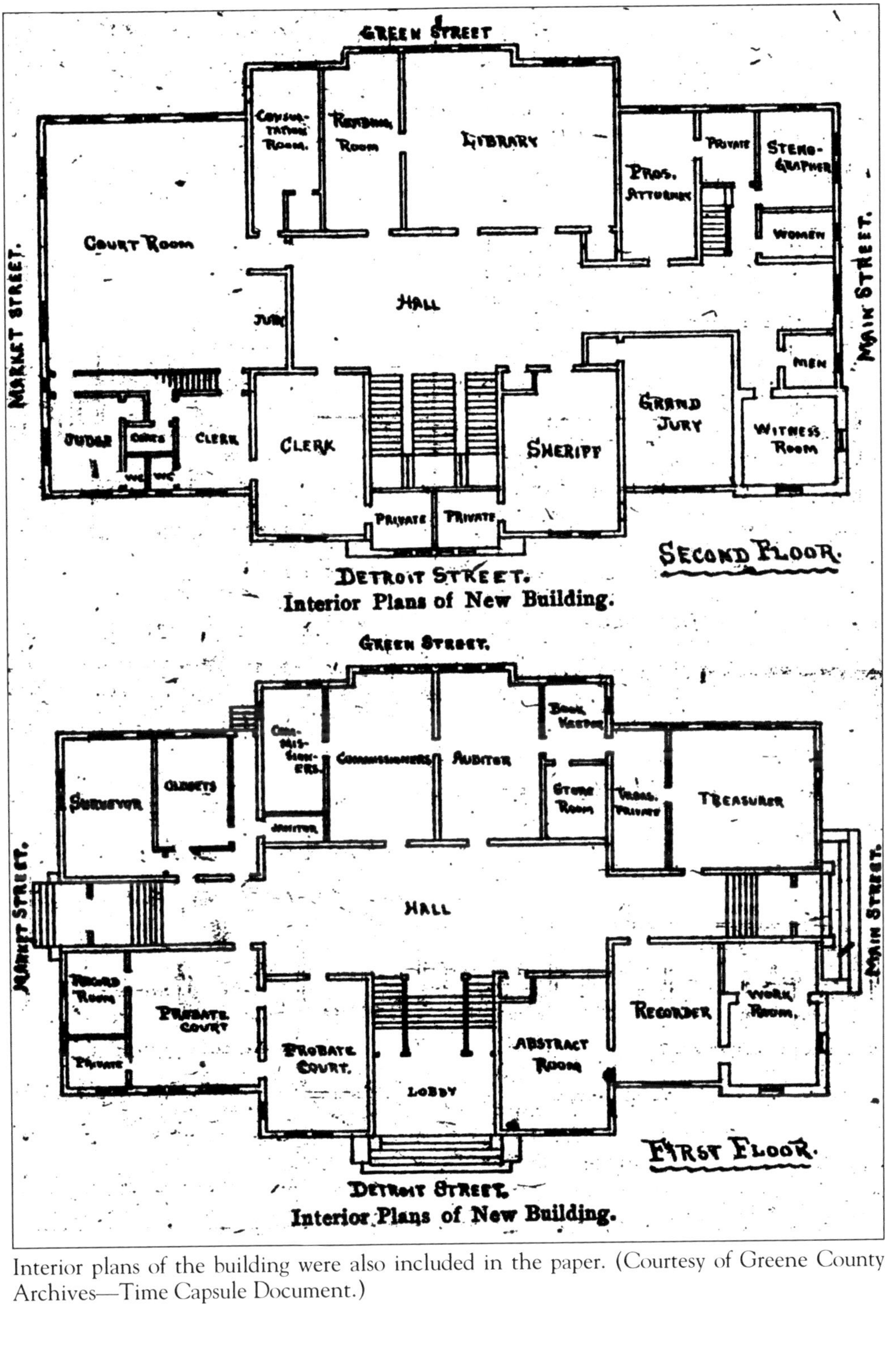

Interior plans of the building were also included in the paper. (Courtesy of Greene County Archives—Time Capsule Document.)

The Xenia Herald

L. H. WHITEMAN, Editor.

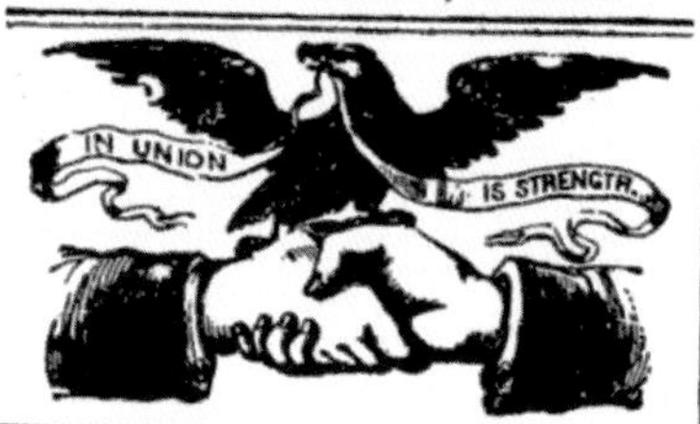

THURSDAY, FEBRUARY 28, 1901.

What Others Think.

. The following is from the Jamestown Press on Mr. Joseph Dean's effort to lay the corner-stone of the new court house.

But while the building progresses discussion is rife as to who should lay the corner stone. A little more than a year ago men were ready to fight the proposition of building a new court house in Greene county, and now some of these same citizens desire to lay the corner stone in this same objectionable structure. (Joe Dean will please notice.) Laying the corner stone was not thought of nor provided for till quite late in the winter. The interest then manifest was slight--a dormant spirit for the honors of the privilege—so the building commission decided to offer the honor to the Masonic fraternity and in an informal way it was accepted. Petitions have been circulated by Joe Dean asking that the soldiers be recognized. They are well worthy of this favor, if it is to be regarded such, and no one would have denied them the honor if it had been asked in time. But still another faction says, that not any order, party, church or class should be specially chosen and set aside for this work, but give it to the entire citizenship of the county—of course letting the representative citizens officiate in the ceremony. Withal it makes delicate diplomacy for the commissioner, who would be a candidate for remomination. What the outcome will be can not now be determined, but the tendency is for the commission to stand by their offer that was first accepted. Prominent Masons are as a matter of fact rather indifferent to the whole matter and would care but little to surrender the privilege, though they may hold to the prinple involved. The commission once having decided the matter, will not likely wish to raise more complications by taking it up again. Other matters of importance call for attention.

JOE DEAN'S anxiety to have the old soldiers association lay the corner-stone may be accounted for by the fact that he is the president of that body.

The Building Commission's decision to invite Lodge No. 49 of the FAM to organize the cornerstone laying ceremonies did not sit well with some. Judge Joseph Dean, for one, had other ideas, as this newspaper clipping attests. (Courtesy of Greene County Archives—Time Capsule Document.)

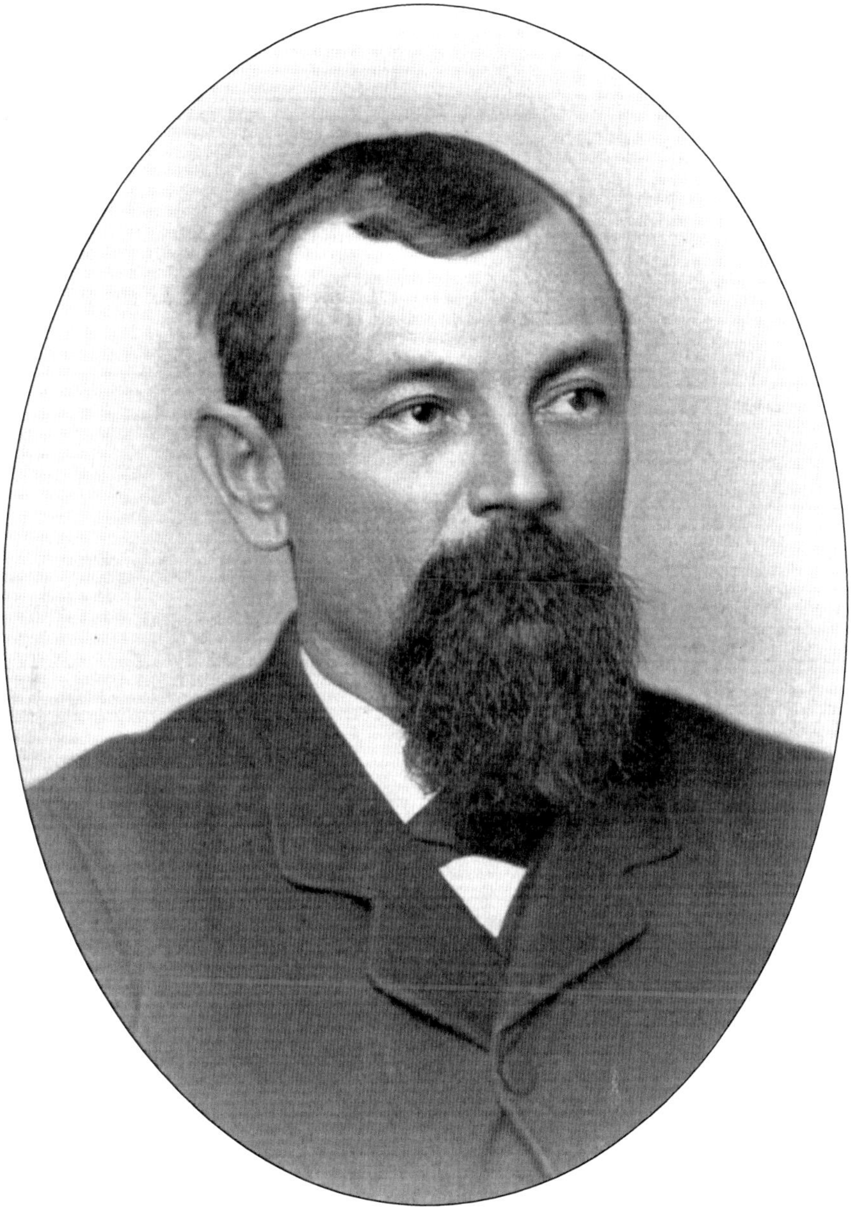

Joseph Dean was the judge of the Probate Court, and a member of the Greene County Bar Association. He had served in the Civil War and belonged to the Union Veteran Legion, the Grand Army of the Republic, and the Association of Ex-Soldiers and Sailors. A member of the United Presbyterian (UP) Church, he had also worked actively for the temperance movement. (Courtesy of Greene County Room, Greene County Public Library, Robinson's *History of Greene County, Ohio*, 1902.)

The Cedarville Herald.

CEDARVILLE, OHIO, MARCH 9, 1901.

Corner-stone of the New Court House.

Published by Request.

Mr. Editor of the Republican.

Some divison of opinion is entertained by our citizens concerning the laying of the corner-stone of the court-house. Some insist the Masons ought to lay it; others that the ex-soldiers, sailors and marines should conduct the exercises.

The executive commitee of the Association of Ex-soldiers, Sailors and Marine of Greene county, of which I am not a member, were called together to take some action in regard to it, and a committee of five was appointed by the chair to wait upon the Building Commission. I was one of that committee and found the facts to be these.

The Building Comission is composed of four men appointed by the court of Common Pleas and the county commissoners, who together constitute this Commission. The general public knew nothing about the proposition of the Commission to allow any order or class of individuals to lay the corner-stone until an invitaton was extended to the Masons to preform that function. They made mention of the matter to no one, and in that quiet condition of affairs the chairman of that body appointed a committeee of two, both being Masons, to invite their fellow Masons to lay the corner-stone.

Now we claim that was not fair to other associations and orders in Greene county who may be interested, and further that that action of the Commission, allowing the Masons to the corner-stone, ought to be rescinded under the circumstances just as courts do where judgments effecting the interests of others aro entered without notice, or in an exparte proceeding, as this was. The soldiers had talked about the corner-stone and had cherished the hope that permission would be granted them to lay it when the time came around, and that permission, I suggest, they ought to have. There can be no question why, appealing to the spirit of fairness which characterizes the Masonic fraternity, this should not be conceded to the ex-soldiers.

But some may say, the soldiers have no ritual. That is all nonsense. Churches and schools, or any society, can lay a corner-stone. Is it possible that intelligence enough cannot be found among all the soldiers of Greene county te have an appropriate ceremonial on such an occasion? It is not only fitting; it is proper that the ex-soldiers should lay the corner-stone, symbolizing the loyality of this people to the government, and it must be conceded that they are far more representative of the people that are the Masons, very many of whom are old soldiers themselves. The Masonic fraternity does not represent a single principle attaching to the court-house, or any other in this country; no more even than to a court-house in Spain or France. while the ex-soldiers are liv-exponents of the distinctive principles of the people of the county and their loyalty to the constitution.

The Masonic lodge in Xenia has 207 members, 42 of whom reside out of the county, some in other states and others in foreign lands. This leaves only 165, which includes 23 who do not attend the lodge at all. There are 49 mem-of the Yellow Springs lodge, with 15 livin out of our county. Burlington lodge has a membership of 44, with 14 out o the county, an Jamestown 89, with 23 out of the county, leaving only 307 including about fifty who do not attend the lodge meeting at any time. So the fact remains that if the stone is laid by the Masons only about 550 residents will be able to attend. If more attend they must come from other counties.

Then it must be considered that the corner-stone cannot be laid by the Masons of Greene county, so far as the chief actor in the scene is concerned.

Lew Whiteman, Worshipful Master of the lodge here cannot lay it. The Grand Master of the state must act according to the rules of the order, upon whom it devolves to select a committee for that purpose. Our boys would only be permitted to march around on that occasion, possibly a few being selected to help the Grand Master.

With the ex-soldiers all would be different. We would do it all ourselves. In our association we have 900 ex-soldiers, 1800 sons of veterans and 145 veterans of the Spanish war, there being over 3000 in the association, representing almost every interest, profession and industry in the county. Our chaplain is Dr. Irons, Professor in the Theological Seminary, who is ably fitted for the undertaking. Just let us try it.

Something has been said of me personally; that it was in bad taste for me to represent the association of ex-soldiers, having fought the court-house when it was before the people. This, I confess, is true. When the first proposition for building a court-house was precipitated I then voted against it, but in so doing I was only in accord with the voters of the county, who were overwhelmingly opposed to the plan then proposed, and upon that proposition no court-house could have been built. Two meetings of citizens were held in my office to consider the second proposition.

At these meetings I took the consensus of opinion of those present and drew up a resolution, expressing their views, which provided for a court-house Commission of five persons, to be named in a special statute, independent of the commissioners, under whom the court house was to be constructed. Walder Williamson was chairman of both meetings, and they were well attended. No others had taken any steps whatever in the matter. A day was proposed for a mass meeting of citizens to consider the resolution, and in that meeting and before, pending the discussion of the subject, a different resolution was prepared by Mr. Frank McGervey, engrafting the views of both parties, which provided that four citizens be selected by the Common Pleas Judge, to act in construction with the county commissioners. This was presented to the meeting and unanimously adopted. Without the steps being taken as first above stated, we would have had no new court-house today. Thus I certainly did as much as I could toward bringing the subject up in an acceptable manner before the people.

Much has been said about the interest I am taking in the matter, and some insist that I am working for my own self aggrandizement, and to further my political interest. My record in putting myself forward in the chair is not before you; neither is it true, I always avoid such conspicuity. I do not believe that it conduces to one's political advantage. In the position which I now occupy I feel that I can serve my comrades and the loyal people of this county; and I propose to do my whole duty in the matter. We know there are persons who object to our views in this matter, but their objections are not well taken, and we propose therefore to overrule them so far as we can.

Whatever may be said of the people of this county becoming tired of the old soldiers, as some would have you believe, this, to any great extent, is not true. Whatever may pervade the minds of a few individuals concerning certain matters in which the ex-soldiers are interest, I am nevertheless persuaded that the people of Greene county are just as loyal to the soldier today as they were when the first gun was fired on Sumpter. They stand by to support us still. Then let us not displease any of our good and loyal friends of the county when we insist upon laying the corner-stone of the new court-house; for the principle of justice are with us, and we propose to maintain our right to the end.

J. N. DEAN.

Joseph Dean's account of the reasoning behind the request to have the ex-soldiers organization, rather than the Masons, perform the cornerstone celebration, was published in the *Cedarville Herald*, March 9, 1901. (Courtesy of Greene County Archives—Time Capsule Document.)

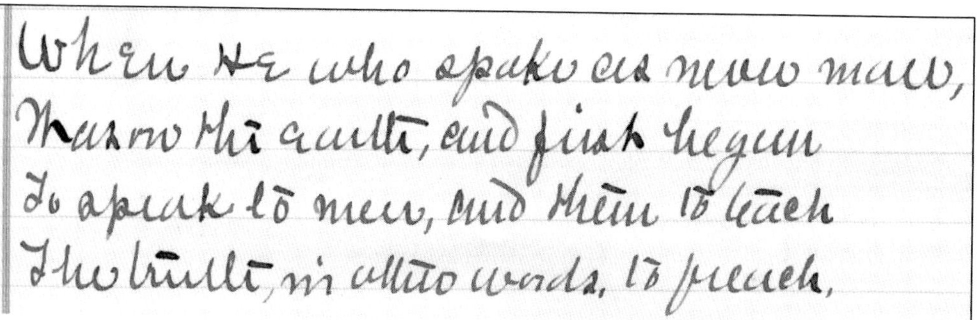

When He who spake as never man,
Was on the earth, and first began
To speak to men, and them to teach
The truth, in other words, to preach,

He ran across a certain sect
Who then and there did loud object
To every thing He said and did,
Because, they said, some things were hid.-
Were done in secret like a lodge,
The idle curious ones to dodge,
And that offended those U.P.s,
Then called United Pharisees,
And from that day to the present time,
In every land and every clime,
Whenever anything is done,
No matter what, by anyone
If these U.P.s. are not let in
They're sure to raise a mighty din.
They then united with the Jews,
Who kept pawn shops and sold old shoes
And a lot of tramps who carried the
hod
And they crucified the Son of God.
And from that time to the present day
Those same U.P.s want to have a say
In every little thing that's done,
Even such as laying a cornerstone,
And if they do not have their way,
And leave things done just as they say.
They threat to bring down the chastening rod
As they did when they killed the Son of God.
Even now in the County of Greene
Our Judas Iscariot Joseph Dean
Is trying to rally this U.P. clan
And to muster them, every woman and man
To come to his aid and see if they can,
By hook or crook or by singing and praying
Put a stop to the Court House corner stone laying,
By the Masons invited by the Court House Committee
Which Joe Dean thinks would be a great pity,
And he has tried to get things in a muddle
And thinks he's all the duck in the puddle.
But the Masons will lay that corner stone,
And to judge by the past it will be rightly done,
For they are old hands and know how to do it,
And when it is all over Joe Dean will rue it
That even he had a word to say
For he'll be a dog that has had his day.

By W.A. Paxson,
Jamestown Ohio

W.A. Paxson, the bar association's poet, composed this poem. In surprisingly offensive language, it describes the Masons' reaction to Judge Dean's attempts to deprive them of their prominent role in the ceremonies. The first four lines show the appearance of the original document but, as the handwriting is hard to read, the rest of the poem is shown in transcription. Paxson's use of the term "UP," supposedly refers to United Presbyterian, the church Joseph Dean attended. Joseph Dean held a meeting for the citizens of Greene County in the council chambers on Saturday, March 9, 1901, to consider the Building Commission's action. (Courtesy of Greene County Archives—Time Capsule Document.)

Joe Dean's. Indignation Meeting.

On Saturday — Mr Joseph Dean
Thought the Masons he would fix;
But it was wrong — his little scheme
A yaller dog — and only six,

But poor Joe and his party of six,
And the reputed little yaller dog,
Found the whole plan had gone to sticks,
When longing eyes, cleared from the fog,

But on the fifteenth day of March,
In the year nineteen-hundrd-one
The Masons to the place did march,
And truly laid the corner-stone,

Alas! this indignation meeting,
Of history has become a part,
Although dear Joseph's heart was beating,
He never, never threw a dart,

Waldo D. Edenburn,

First year High-School,

The *Xenia Herald* of March 14, 1901, pronounced Joseph Dean's protest meeting a failure, as so few people showed up, despite his attempts to draw spectators in from the street outside the meeting place. High School student, Waldo Edenburn, commemorated the meeting in this poem. (Courtesy of Greene County Archives—Time Capsule Document.)

XENIA DAILY GAZETTE
AND TORCHLIGHT.
...AR. XENIA, OHIO, SATURDAY EVENING MARCH 16, 1901.

CEREMONIES

AT CORNER STONE LAYING

Were Witnessed By Several Thousand People and Were Most Impressive.

List of Articles Placed in the Corner Stone and the Persons Officiating.

In the midst of the falling snow and in the presence of a crowd of five thousand people which packed the public square, the corner stone of Greene county's new court house was laid yesterday afternoon with solemn and impressive ceremonies. March was in one of her disagreeable moods and the morning broke with lowering clouds and almost all day long the snow came sifting down, melting almost as fast as it fell and making it disagreeable to get about. But even the March weather could not keep the crowd at home and they began to come into the city early in the morning from all the surrounding towns. Then the Masons from all the surrounding cities were attracted by the event and as two o'clock approached the time for the ceremony, all about the north-east corner of the building all the available standing place was taken and there was a struggle for good positions.

The ceremonies were in charge of Xenia Lodge, No. 49, F. & A. M. and prior to the corner stone laying the Masons met in the lodge room and the grand lodge was constituted. Then the procession was formed by the Master of Ceremonies, T. A. Fravell, and the members repaired to the scene of the exercises. Some 250 Masons were at the lodge room meeting and the procession was further increased by being joined by a number of Masons on the street. The S. of V. band furnished the music and the members made a fine appearance as they appeared in the insignia of the order.

The list of Grand officers of the order in the laying of the corner stone was as follows:

Jacob H. Bromwell......Grand Master
O. C. Baker....Deputy Grand Master
M. J. Hartley..Senior Grand Warden
E. B. Reynolds...Jr. Grand Warden
E. H. Hart..........Sr. Grand Deacon
S. D. Wolf...........Jr. Grand Deacon
Allen Andrews..........Grand Orator
H. H. Eavey..........Grand Treasurer
W. A. Galloway.....Grand Secretary
T. J. Kennedy.....Sr. Grand Steward
Charles Fetz.......Jr. Grand Steward
Jno. J. McCabe.......Grand Chaplain
Marcus Shoup..........Grand Marshal
S. B. Evans..................Grand Tyler

The Masons assembled on the first floor of the court house surrounding the corner stone and the ritual was performed in a most impressive manner, Grand Master, Jacob Bromwell, having charge of the exercises at the corner stone laying. The proclamation was made by Marcus Shoup, grand marshall of the occasion and this was followed by the invocation delivered by the acting grand chaplain, Rev, J. J. McCabe, of Dayton. The presentation of the trowel to Grand Master Jacob Bromwell, was made by Mr. L. H. Whiteman. Mr. H. H. Eavey, as deputy grand treasurer, was the custodian of the small copper box which contained the documents to be placed in the corner stone. After the reading by him of a list of the articles which the box contained there was a song by the triple quartette from Trinity M. E. church and the high honor of placing the box in the corner was then performed by Mr. Eavey with due dignity and impressiveness and the corner stone was lowered to its resting place. Then followed the trial of the stone by means of the plumb, level and square. To deputy grand master, Orin C. Baker, was given the square, deputy grand senior warden, M. J. Hartley, was given the level and the plumb was given to deputy grand junior warden, Dr. E. Reynolds, who each stepped forward and made the test of the stone, pronouncing it square, level and plumb. Then followed the ceremony of scattering the corn and pouring the wine and oil over the stone, this duty being performed by Grand Master Jacob Bromwell, the following words being uttered by him as he performed the work:

"I scatter this corn as an emblem of plenty. May the blessings of heaven be showered upon us and upon all like undertakings, and inspire the hearts of the people with virtue, wisdom and gratitude.

I pour this wine as an emblem of joy and gladness. May the Great Ruler of the Universe bless and prosper our National, State and Municipal Governments, preserve the Union of the states, and may their Union be a bond of friendship and brotherly love that shall endure through all time.

I pour this oil as an emblem of peace. May the blessing of peace abide with us continually, and may the Grand Master of Heaven and Earth shelter and protect the widow and orphan; shield and defend them from the trials and vicissitudes of the world, and so bestow His mercy upon the bereaved, the afflicted, and the sorrowing, that they may know sorrow and trouble no more."

Concluding this ceremony he made the following invocation: May the all-bounteous author of nature bless the inhabitants of this place with an abundance of the necessaries, conveniences and comforts of life; assist in the erection and completion of this building; protect the workmen against every accident; long preserve the structure from decay; and grant to us all a supply of the corn of nourishment the wine of refreshment and the oil of joy.

The grand marshall, Marcus Shoup, then made the proclamation declaring the corner stone laid and the grand master delivered the following words of the ritual: Brethren, the work of the day is done. In the deep foundation of this structure we have placed our memorial. Here we have with becoming ceremonies laid the corner stone of a magnificent temple, to be devoted to the material interests of the people of this enlightened, cultured and highly favored community. The generations yet to come will gaze with pride upon this noble pile, and under its shelter prosecute the work appropriate to its several apartments The enterprise, liberality and wisdom of the men of to-day will not be forgotten. Future generations will pay due homage to your memories for this invaluable inheritance, and it will stand as a glorious monument of the estimate put by you upon the value of education, morality, refinement, justice and religion, and may the Great Architect of the Universe shape their minds to a still higher appreciation of these sublime themes.

Owing to the disagreeable weather which prevailed, the exercises which followed the corner stone laying took place in the Xenia opera house, and one of the largest crowds which ever assembled there was present to listen to the addresses. Every seat from pit to dome was packed and the aisles were crowded and many persons were unable to get in. The opening address was delivered by Hon. Jacob Bromwell. Past Grand Master, Allen Andrews, of Hamilton, followed by an eloquent address containing many fine thoughts, delivered in an entertaining manner and holding the closest attention of his audience from start to finish. He was followed by Mr. George Little, in behalf of the building commission, and his address is highly complimented on all hands. At the exercises at the opera house the music was furnished by the male voices from Trinity church, and by the S. of V. band, and at the conclusion, "America," was sung by a large number of the children of the public schools.

As a close to the exercises of the day the Masonic Lodge at night held a meeting and performed work in the Master Mason degree, a large number of visitors being present from all the surrounding towns and cities. A fine banquet was served and a number of interesting addresses were made, Prof. E. B. Cox acting as toastmaster for the occasion.

Altogether the laying of the corner stone was a most memorable occasion. Nearly every business house in the city closed its doors while the ceremonies were in progress and the schools were dismissed at noon, hundreds of the children watching the interesting ceremonies which will make a lasting impression on their minds. On the two exposed sides of the corner stone is engraved simply the date of its being laid, March 15, 1901.

NOTICE—The Court House Daily (Thursday's) though we printed one thousand extra, are all sold.

The March 16, 1901, edition of the *Xenia Daily Gazette* published an account of the cornerstone laying ceremonies. Although the poor weather necessitated some of the ceremonies be moved to the Xenia Opera House, rather than remain outdoors, there seem to have been no further conflicts that day. (Courtesy of Greene County Room, Greene County Public Library.)

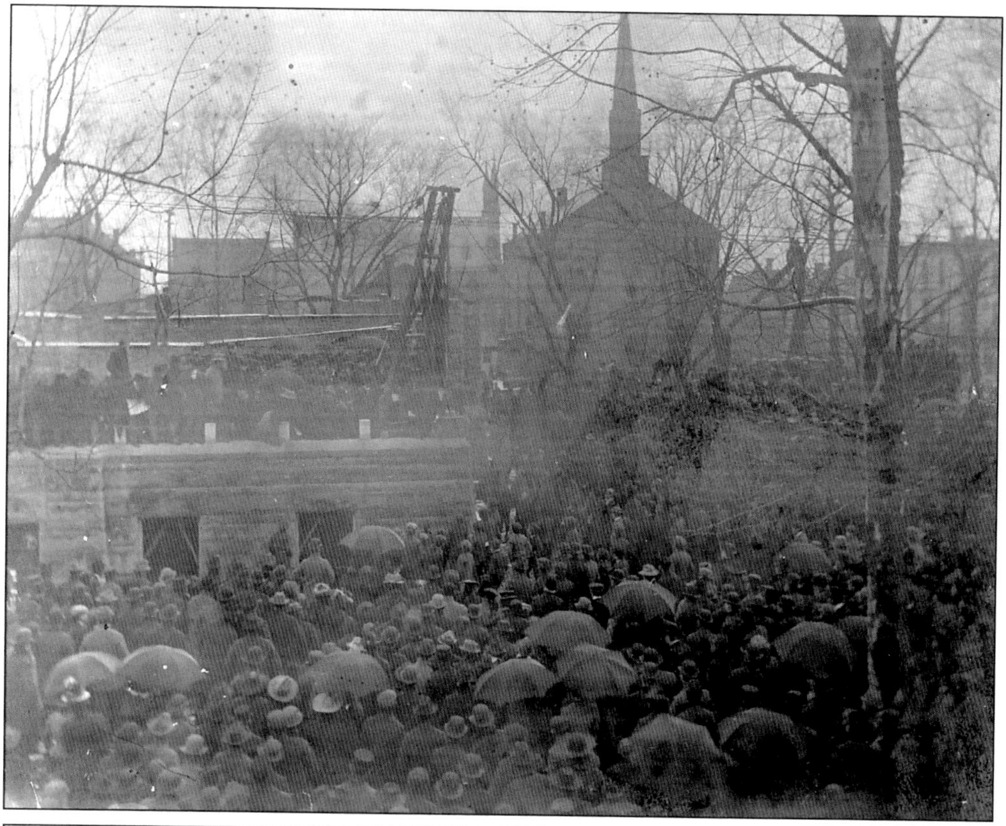

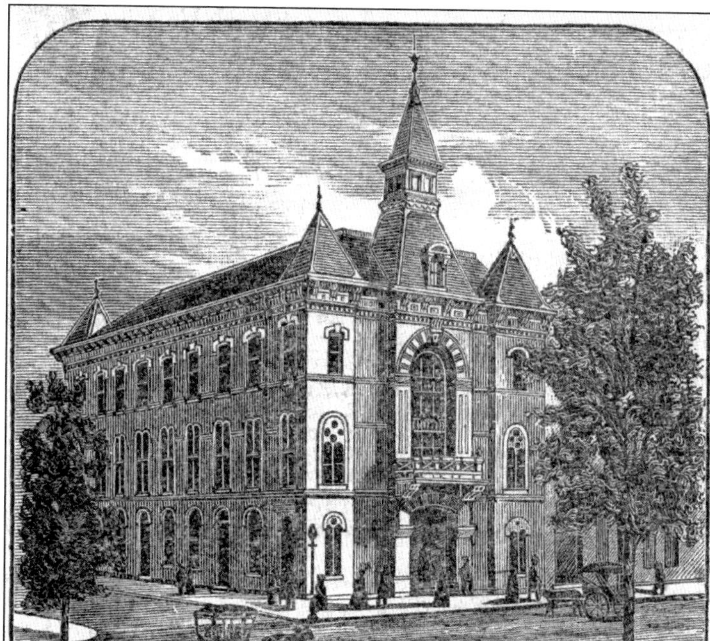

Xenia City Building and Opera House.

The umbrellas everywhere attest to the bad weather on the day of the cornerstone laying. Approximately 5,000 people showed up to view the ceremonies. (Courtesy of Greene County Room, Greene County Public Library.)

The Xenia Opera House is where the cornerstone laying festivities continued after the outdoor work was done. The Opera House was used for many ceremonial activities, including high school graduations. (Courtesy of Greene County Archives—Time Capsule Document.)

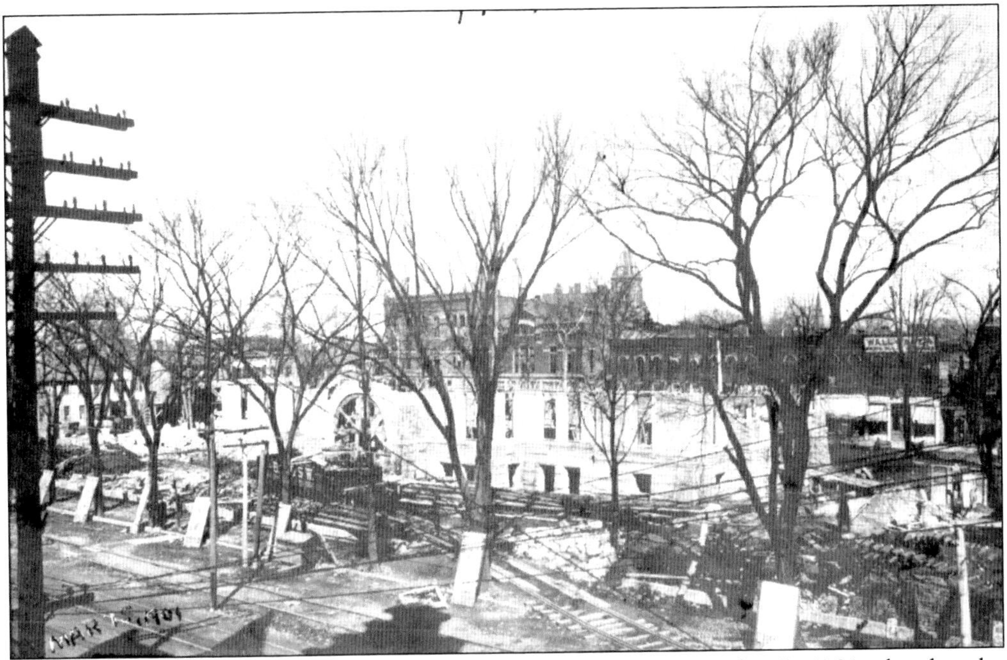

This view of the courthouse construction site was taken on March 15, 1901, the day the cornerstone was laid. (Courtesy of Greene County Historical Society.)

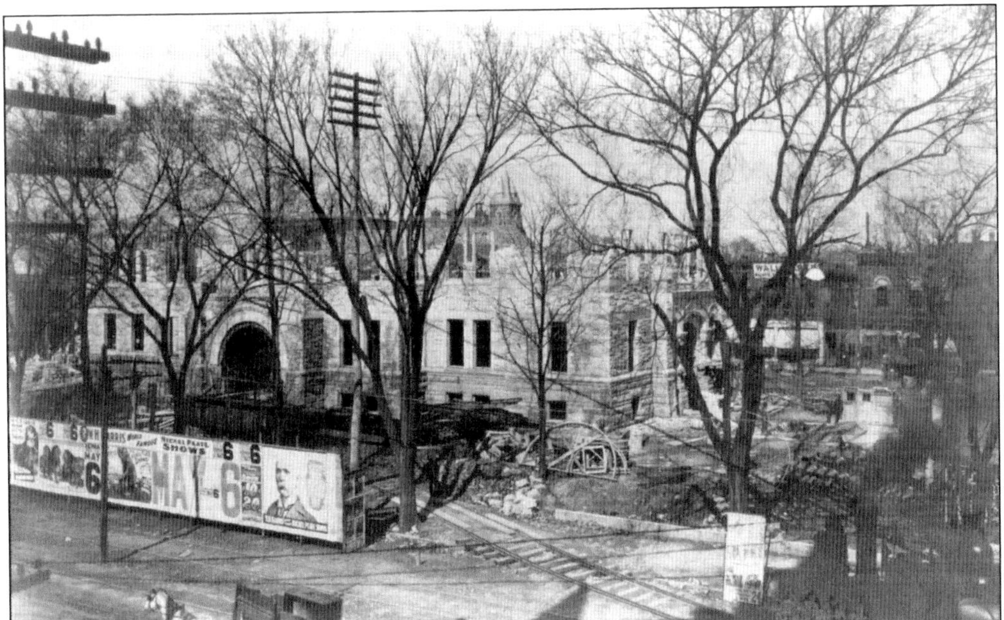

Here is a later view of the courthouse construction. The placards surrounding the site advertise the Harris Nickel Plate Circus, which was one of the best known small shows at this time. It was to visit Xenia in May of 1901. (Courtesy of Greene County Historical Society.)

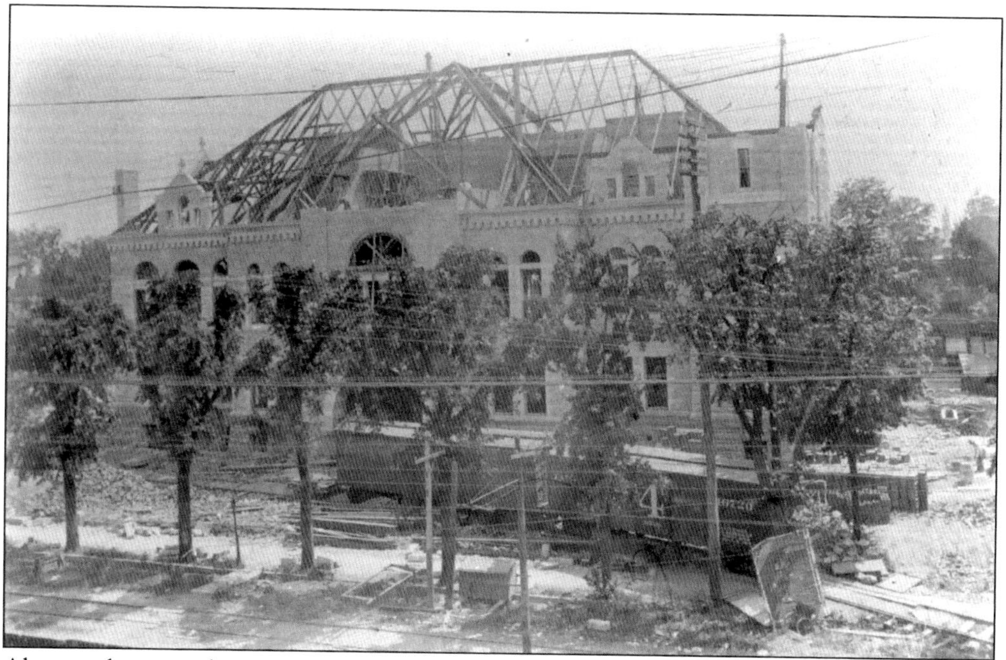

Above, the courthouse is now close to completion. (Courtesy of Greene County Historical Society.)

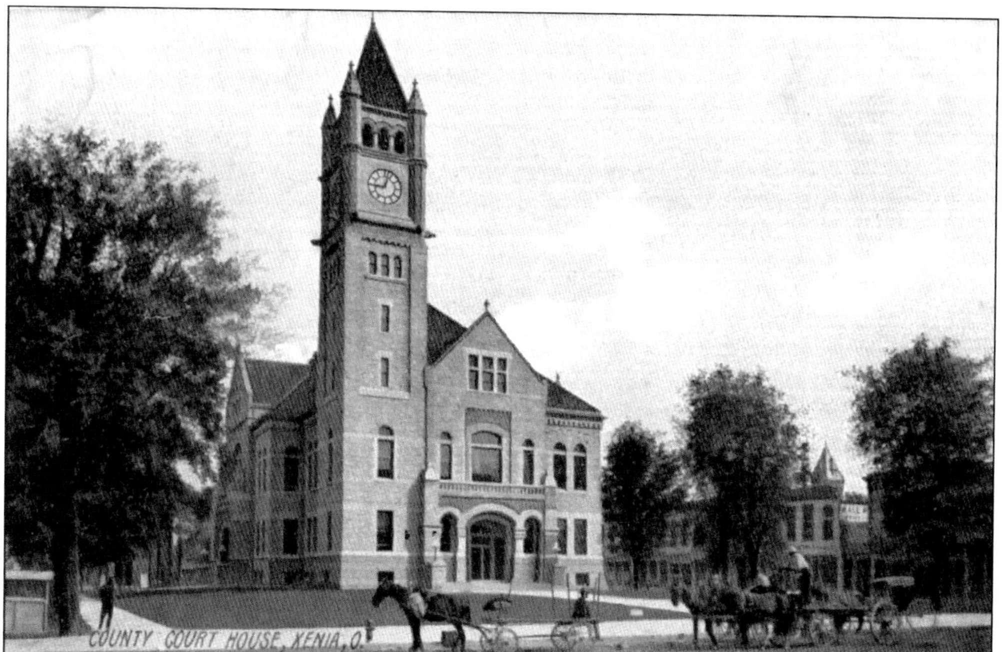

A popular postcard from the days soon after the new courthouse was finished shows the view from Main Street. (Courtesy of Greene County Room, Greene County Public Library.)

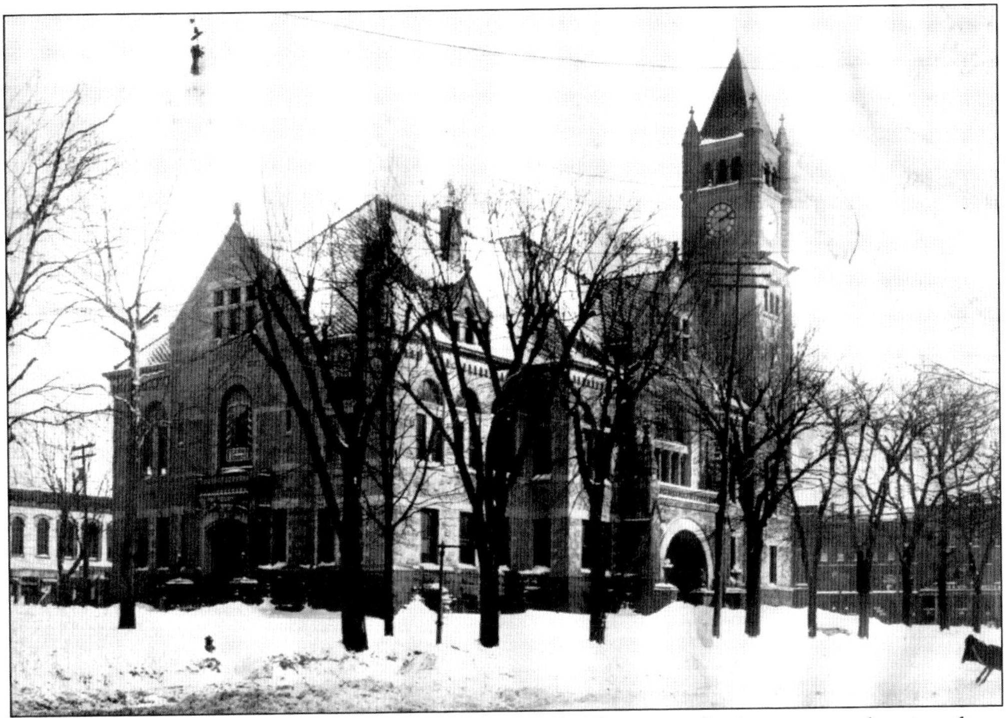

A winter scene, again showing the courthouse shortly after it was built, captures the view from Detroit Street. (Courtesy of Greene County Room, Greene County Public Library.)

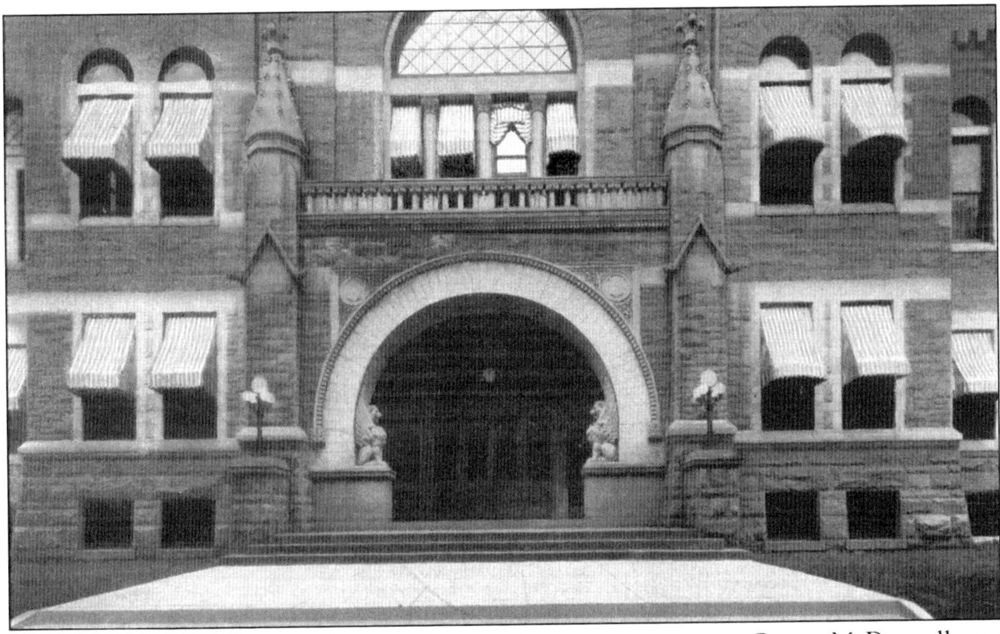

Here is a close up of the winged lions at the courthouse's east entrance. George McDonnell, one of the traveling stonecutters who came to Xenia for the purpose of working on the courthouse, designed them. He stayed in Xenia and other examples of his work survive in the area. (Courtesy of Greene County Room, Greene County Public Library.)

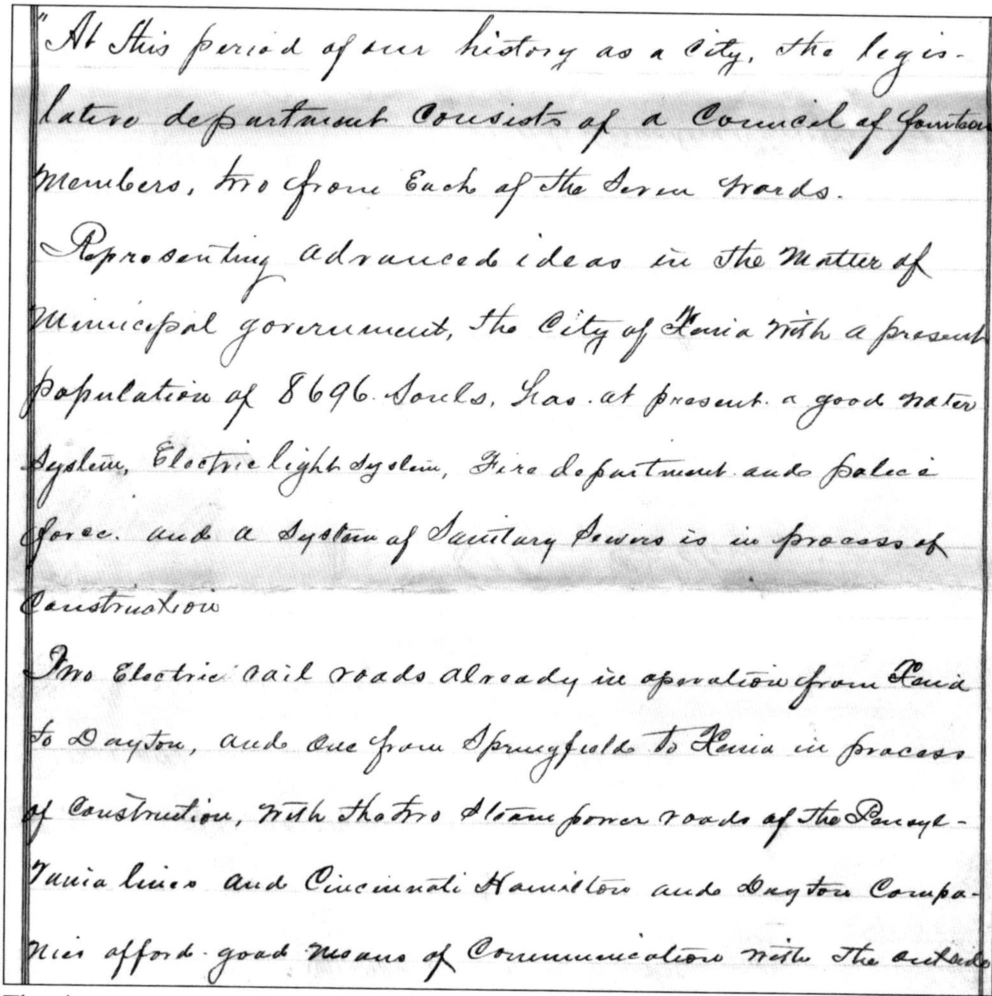

"At this period of our history as a City, the legislative department Consists of a Council of fourteen members, two from Each of the Seven wards.

Representing advanced ideas in the matter of municipal government, the City of Xenia with a present population of 8696 Souls, has at present a good water system, Electric light system, Fire department and police force. and a System of Sanitary Sewers is in process of Construction

Two Electric rail roads already in operation from Xenia to Dayton, and One from Springfield to Xenia in process of Construction, with the two Steam power roads of the Pennsylvania lines and Cincinnati Hamilton and Dayton Companies afford good means of Communication with the outside

This document, written by a municipal councilor and enclosed in the time capsule, describes the City of Xenia in March of 1901. The extract above reads:

> *At this period of our history as a city, the legislative department consists of a council of fourteen members, two from each of the seven wards.*
>
> *Representing advanced ideas in the matter of municipal government, the City of Xenia with a present population of 8696 souls, has at present a good water system, electric light system, Fire department and police force and a system of Sanitary Sewers is in process of construction.*
>
> *Two Electric rail roads already in operation from Xenia to Dayton, and one from Springfield to Xenia in process of construction, with the two steam power roads of the Pennsylvania lines and Cincinnati Hamilton and Dayton Companies afford good means of communication with the outside world.*

(Courtesy of Greene County Archives—Time Capsule Document.)

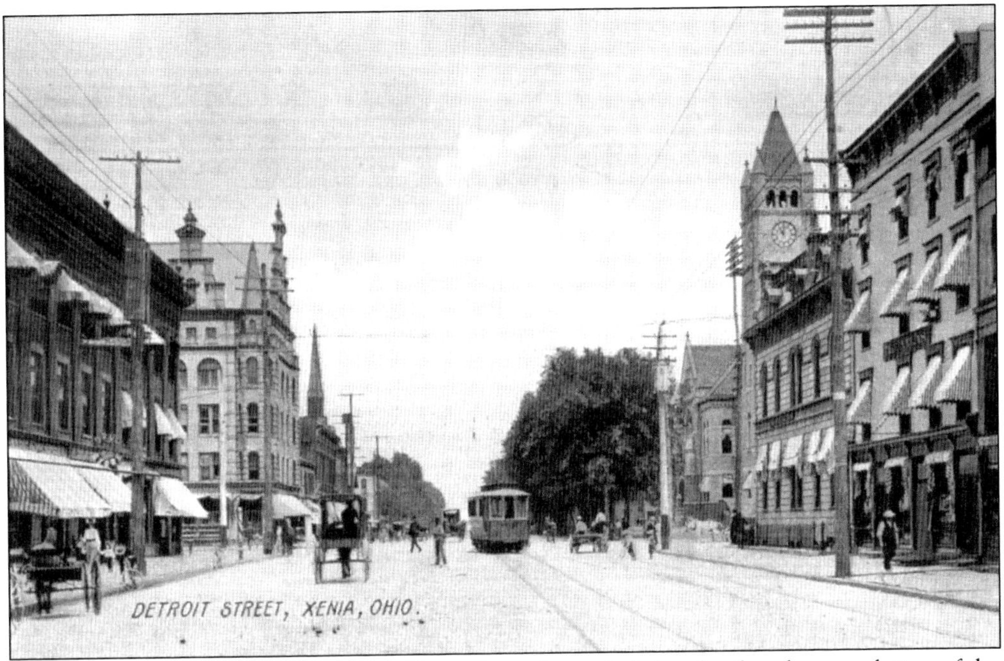

This postcard depicts a street scene in Xenia from the period shortly after the completion of the new courthouse. (Courtesy of Greene County Room, Greene County Public Library.)

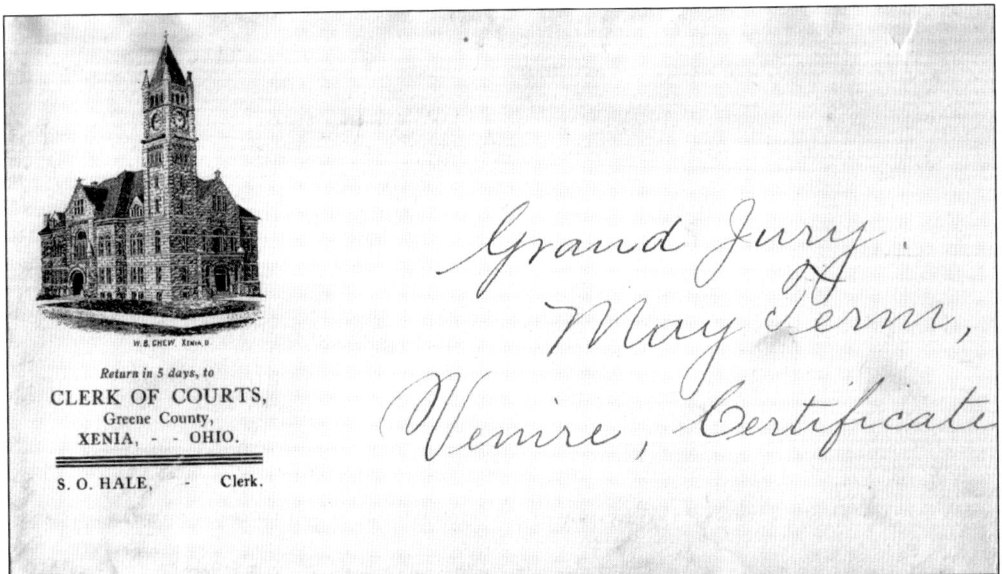

The new courthouse soon came to be used as the logo on county stationery, as this envelope shows. S.O. Hale served as Clerk of Courts from 1900 to 1909. (Courtesy of Greene County Archives.)

The Xenia Semi Weekly Gazette.
AND TORCHLIGHT.
VOLUME 33. XENIA, OHIO, FRIDAY, MARCH 15, 1901. NUMBER 31.

LOOKING FORWARD

A HUNDRED YEARS HENCE.

A Visit to the City of Xenia When the Corner Stone is Opened in the Year 2001.

The place is the great city of Xenia and the time is 2001.

Along the streets there rise great, tall buildings of stone and iron, sky-scrapers, of peculiar construction. On every hand there is bustle and confusion for men are still in pursuit of the almighty dollar and the marts of trade still draw forth strife in the struggle for supremacy.

The city has broadened out in its boundaries and a bird's eye view taken from the top of a twenty story building shows building, as far as the eye can reach. There are great factories, modeled after new patterns, where new and strange products are turned out. There are no tall chimneys sending forth great volumes of black smoke, for the wheels and spindles are driven by a new and improved motive power. But while the men labor, as of old, it is under different conditions which make them better and happier. Handsome homes abound along wide boulevards, all of stone or other material for wood is now a scarce article, the supply long since having become exhausted.

There is no longer any night—for science has turned it into day and when the sun sinks in the west other great lights, made by artificial means, flash up in the sky, and the passing of the sun is not noted. There are no longer any extremes of heat and cold, for men have learned to control the temperature and the fierce rays of the midsummer sun are made mild and pleasant as a balmy day of spring. Xenians no longer have to go down in their pockets to pay coal bills, for the city government looks after the matter of modifying the cold. But there are "kickers" just as there were a hundred years ago when people burned coal and the fellow who is at the head of the city government has a hard time trying to hold his job and at the same time make the temperature exactly right for all the inhabitants. A few of the little country towns and villages still use electricity for light and heat, but they are rapidly doing away with it for the new methods.

Distance has been conquered. Xenians now eat their dinners at their homes and take supper and attend the theatre in New York and San Francisco. Flying machines are to be seen everywhere. Entire families enter these models of elegance and sail slowly along, the passengers casting languid glances down at the busy towns and cities over which they are speeding. Races are held by these chariots of the air and thousands of persons float around and watch the swift and noiseless contests. In a room of curios on Green street there are to be seen some relics of Xenia's early days and one of them is Jake Baldner's automobile, the first one that ever appeared on the streets of the city. People stand around and view it curiously and wonder how people ever got around by such antiquated means. Then there is another relic there known as the electric car, which was used many years ago for passenger traffic between Xenia and Dayton. The cars of the present day speed through the air almost with lightning speed.

The Xenia business man now talks all over the world by means of the telephone, the wires of which are under the sea and knit the continents together. The Xenian sits in his handsomely furnished office and calls up London or Rio Janeiro and orders goods to be brought to his door the following day. Then he calls up the pretty telephone girl at "central" and makes love to her, though she is in New York. And he never says a word about being married.

About a hundred years ago there was a man named Tesla, who invented what was known as wireless telegraphy and this has been developed until it has brought the planets into communication. By means of it Xenians can talk to the inhabitants in Mars and Charlie Greenlease, Carl Beall, Geo. Grottendick and some of the other young men who have been flirting with the young ladies on that planet are impatiently waiting for means to be effected by which they can pay their friends in that far-a-way world a visit. Already there is a possibility that the moon may be visited within the next few years.

Down along Shawnee run there is a big factory going night and day and we step inside and ask to be shown through. Machines are clicking noisily and some distance ahead we see a chute from which little round white globes are falling by the hundreds. A close examination shows them to be eggs, which are now turned out by machinery. The hen lost her job many years ago and the forlorn expression of some of our east end friends is now easily accounted for.

Over on the west side of the city there is an establishment for turning out fruits and vegetables, literally forcing them out of the soil day after day. When you want a gallon of great ripe strawberries all the fellow in charge has to do is to start his machine in motion and your bucket is soon filled.

Medicine and surgery have made wonderful progress and unknown diseases no longer baffle the physicians. A remedy has been found for them all and man lives out his days and dies at length from old age.

In the center of the city men are busy at work tearing down an old stone building. It is the "old" court house built in the year 1901. The massive stones show evidence of disintegration and are discolored and moss covered. The great iron beams are twisted and the great stones are being thrown down from the walls in a ruthless manner.

Suddenly at the north-east corner of the wall there is a lull in the work of the men and all are gathered around a small copper box. The corner stone of the old building has been reached and the curious crowd awaits eagerly while the sealed lid is being carefully removed. Through a hundred years of darkness and silence, while mighty events have been transpiring throughout the world, the contents of this small box have lain untouched and unseen. And on a warm balmy day in spring, in the year 2001, these old and faded documents are brought forth into the light and sunshine. Men always handle such documents with a certain awe and as they are carefully unfolded the crowd stands around in silence and looks eagerly at the old papers.

Down among the documents are copies of the DAILY and SEMI WEEKLY GAZETTE published away back in 1901. What queer looking old papers they are, to be sure! The print is odd and the spelling is so funny. How do you suppose people ever were accustomed to such printing and spelling? There are all sorts of queer items about people of whom we never heard or dreamed. And the merchants have advertisements of queer things that are never used in this day and age of the world.

But the "oldest inhabitant" looks over the paper and glances his eye along the list of carriers for the DAILY GAZETTE and he remembers several of them. One was a banker of forty years ago. Another one was years ago the leading merchant in the city and still another one grew up, was elected to congress and finally became president (which one will it be, boys?) Another one grew up and was married and never did anything but discuss politics and growl at the weather man and his wife couldn't even take in washing because of the progress of the world.

And so the old papers are filed away in the Green street museum, telling their story long after the persons who wrote it, and the printers who set it up and the publishers who sent it on its way, have passed to their final slumber.

This newspaper article predicts how the people of Xenia in 1901 imagined the Xenia of 2001. In some ways it is remarkably prophetic, but in others it falls far short of the current reality. (Courtesy of Greene County Archives—Time Capsule Document.)

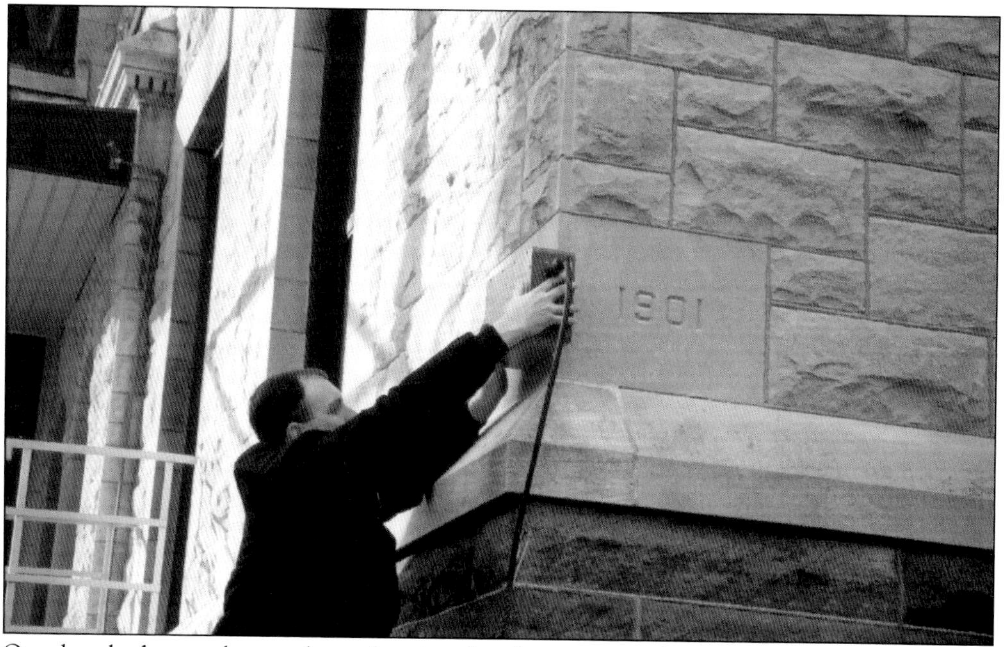

One hundred years later, when planning for the centennial celebrations, Greene County employees set to work to attempt to find the time capsule. Here, Marcus Lehotay is shown using a metal detector in an attempt to determine the exact location of the box. (Courtesy of Greene County Historical Society.)

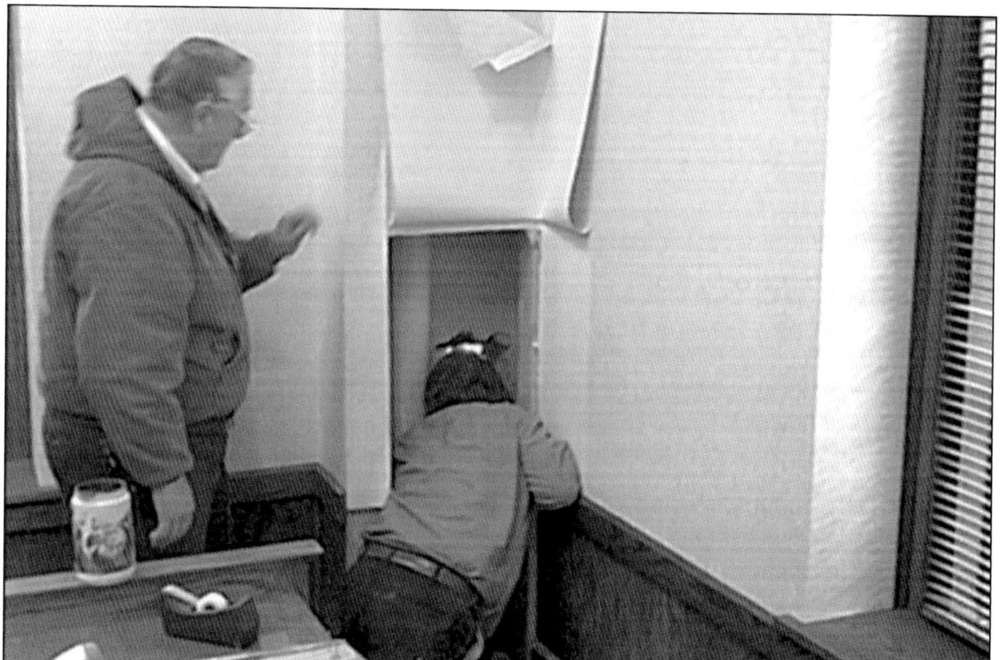

Work continued from the inside of the building. County employees, Joe Macik and Jeff Damrell, are shown here digging into the corner of Judge Robert Hagler's meeting room. (Courtesy of Greene County Archives.)

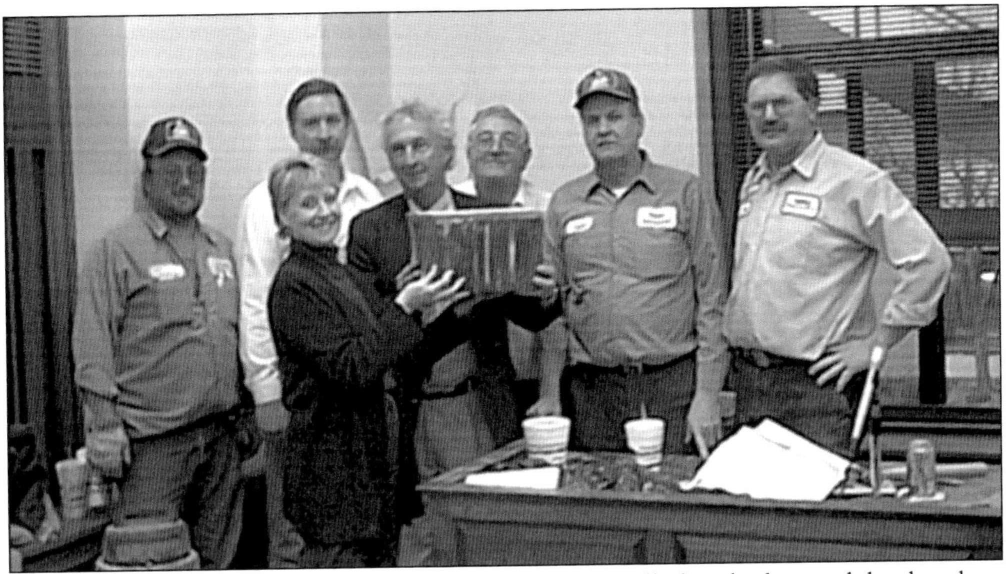

There was great excitement when the time capsule was actually found, after much hard work, at close to 7:00 P.M. on Friday, February 23, 2001. Pictured from left to right are county employees Rick Brooks, Kiser Brown, Archivist Gillian Hill, Commissioner W. Reed Madden, Joe Macik, Buford Hale, and Dona Reed. (Courtesy of Greene County Archives.)

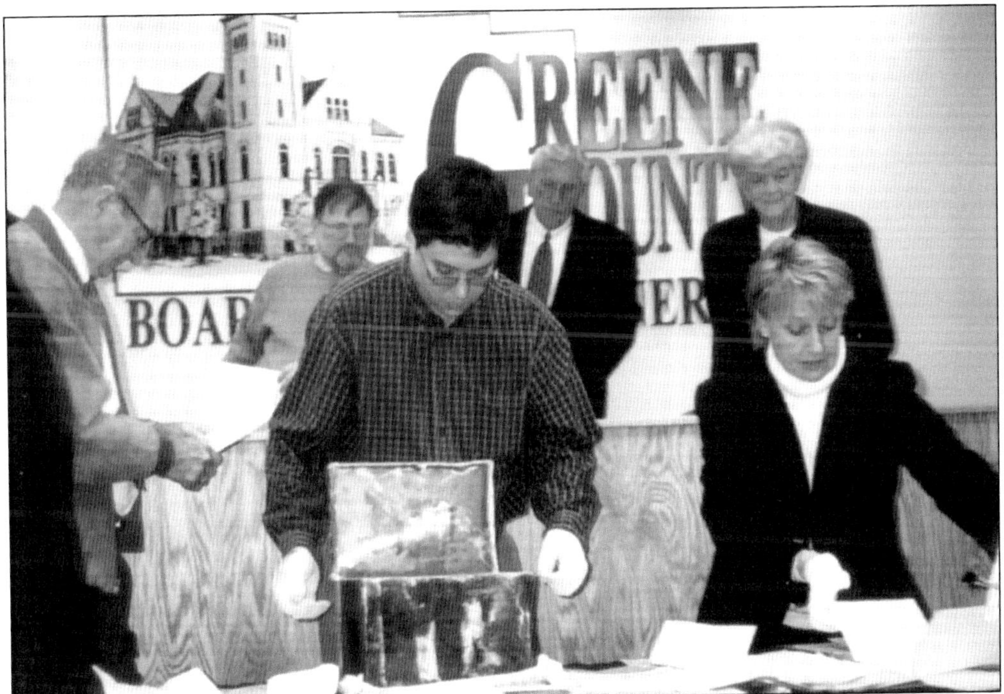

The capsule was opened at a public meeting of the Commissioners on Tuesday, February 27, 2001. Pictured from left to right are Delmer Bone, retired county commissioner; Steve Haller, counsel to the Commissioners; Chris Wydman, assistant archivist; Ralph Harper, President of the Board of County Commissioners; Kathryn Hagler, county commissioner; and Gillian Hill, archivist. (Courtesy of Greene County Historical Society.)

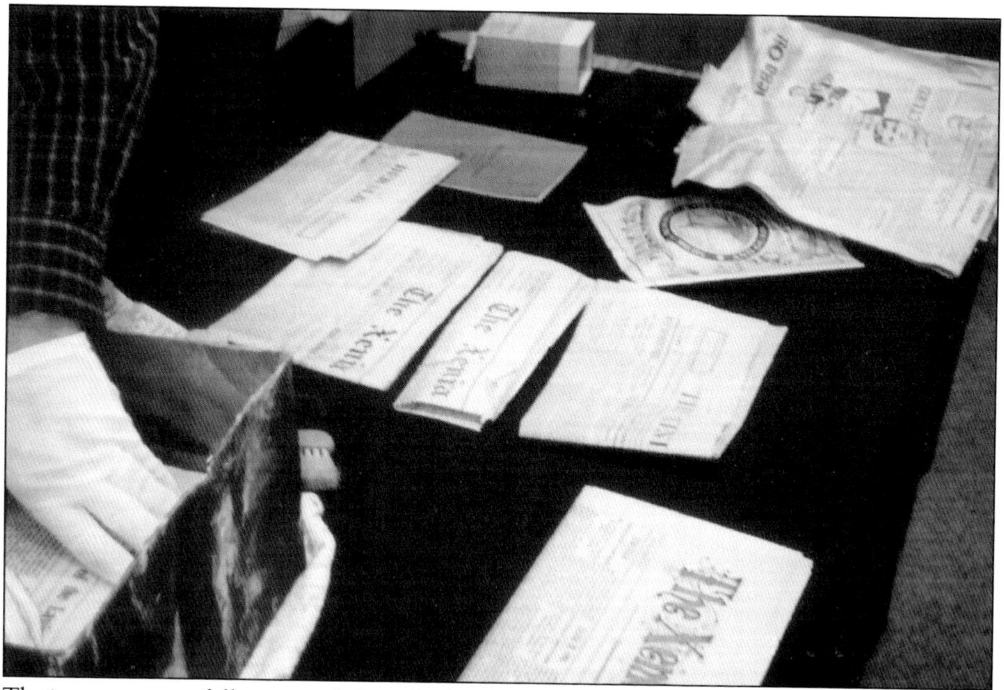

The items were carefully removed, described to those people present at the meeting, and placed on a display table for the press to photograph. (Courtesy of Greene County Historical Society.)

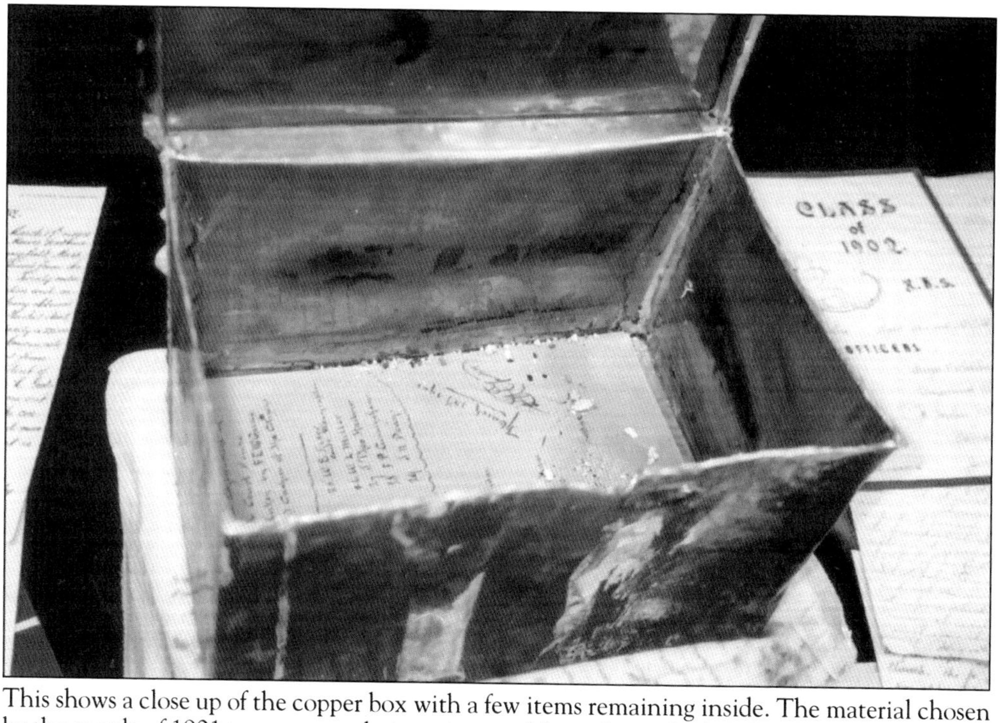

This shows a close up of the copper box with a few items remaining inside. The material chosen by the people of 1901 to represent their society could now be studied and analyzed. (Courtesy of Greene County Historical Society.)

Two

CHURCHES

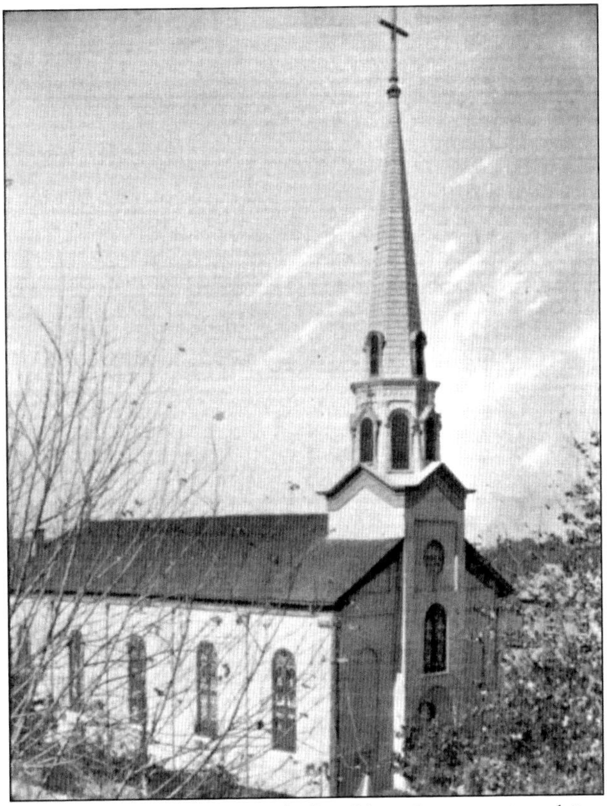

This photograph of St. Brigid's Roman Catholic Church was printed in a souvenir booklet that was published in 1898 and enclosed in the time capsule. (Courtesy of Greene County Archives—Time Capsule Document.)

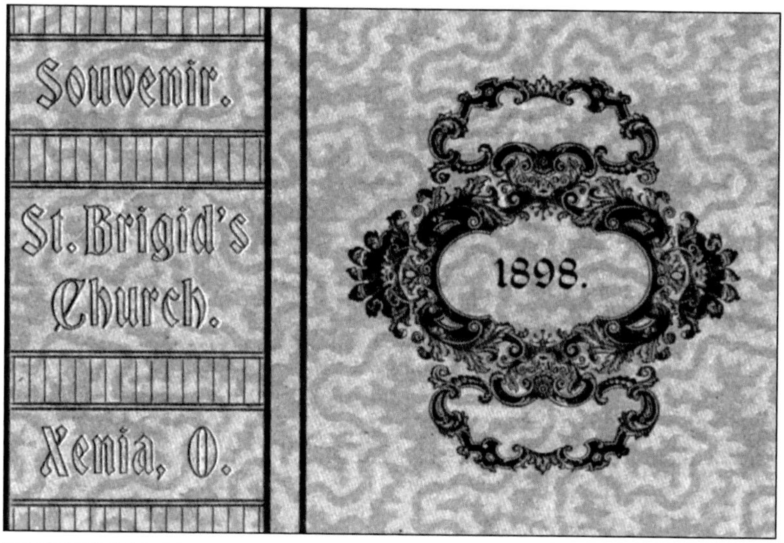

The souvenir booklet from St. Brigid's Roman Catholic Church was a wonderful source of photographs and commercial advertisements from local merchants. (Courtesy of Greene County Archives—Time Capsule Document.)

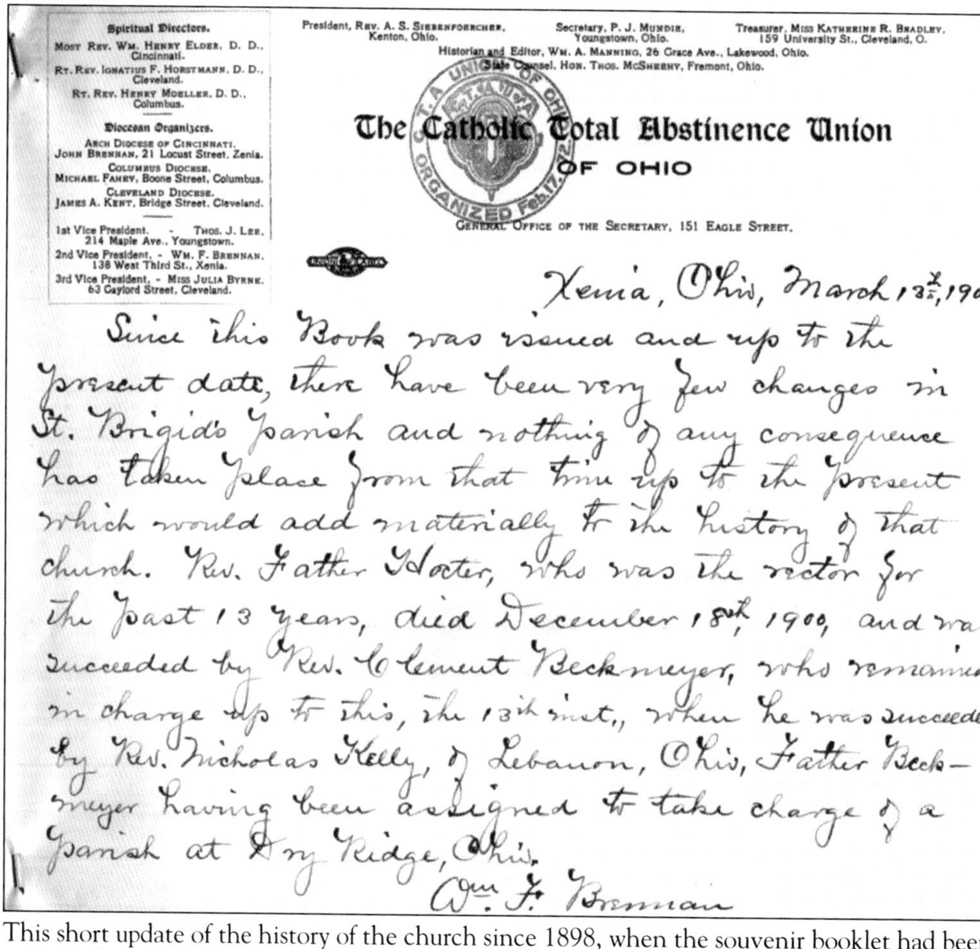

Spiritual Directors.
Most Rev. Wm. Henry Elder, D. D., Cincinnati.
Rt. Rev. Ignatius F. Horstmann, D. D., Cleveland.
Rt. Rev. Henry Moeller, D. D., Columbus.

Diocesan Organizers.
Arch Diocese of Cincinnati. John Brennan, 21 Locust Street, Zenia.
Columbus Diocese. Michael Fahey, Boone Street, Columbus.
Cleveland Diocese. James A. Kent, Bridge Street, Cleveland.

1st Vice President. - Thos. J. Lee, 214 Maple Ave., Youngstown.
2nd Vice President, - Wm. F. Brennan, 138 West Third St., Xenia.
3rd Vice President, - Miss Julia Byrne, 63 Gaylord Street, Cleveland.

President, Rev. A. S. Siebenfoercher, Kenton, Ohio. Secretary, P. J. Mundie, Youngstown, Ohio. Treasurer, Miss Katherine R. Bradley, 159 University St., Cleveland, O.
Historian and Editor, Wm. A. Manning, 26 Grace Ave., Lakewood, Ohio.
State Counsel, Hon. Thos. McSheehy, Fremont, Ohio.

The Catholic Total Abstinence Union OF OHIO

General Office of the Secretary, 151 Eagle Street.

Xenia, Ohio, March 13th, 1901.

Since this Book was issued and up to the present date, there have been very few changes in St. Brigid's parish and nothing of any consequence has taken place from that time up to the present which would add materially to the history of that church. Rev. Father Hocter, who was the rector for the past 13 years, died December 18th 1900, and was succeeded by Rev. Clement Beckmeyer, who remained in charge up to this, the 13th inst., when he was succeeded by Rev. Nicholas Kelly, of Lebanon, Ohio, Father Beck-meyer having been assigned to take charge of a parish at Dry Ridge, Ohio.

Wm. F. Brennan

This short update of the history of the church since 1898, when the souvenir booklet had been published, was pinned inside the back cover. (Courtesy of Greene County Archives—Time Capsule Document.)

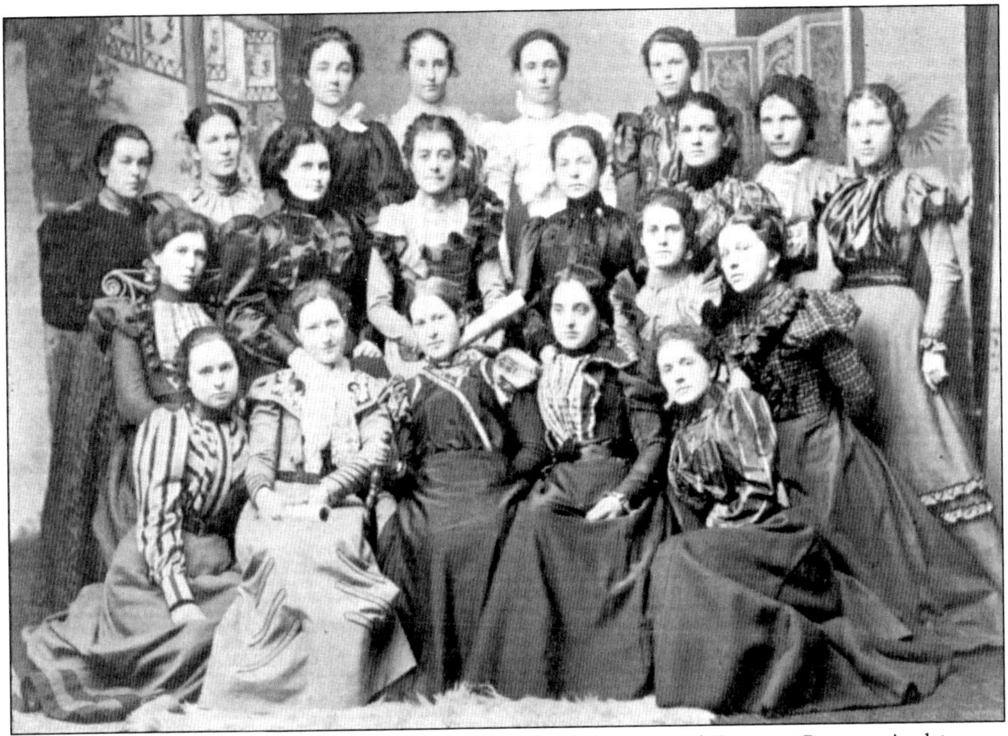

Pictured is the senior choir of St. Brigid's Church. (Courtesy of Greene County Archives—Time Capsule Document.)

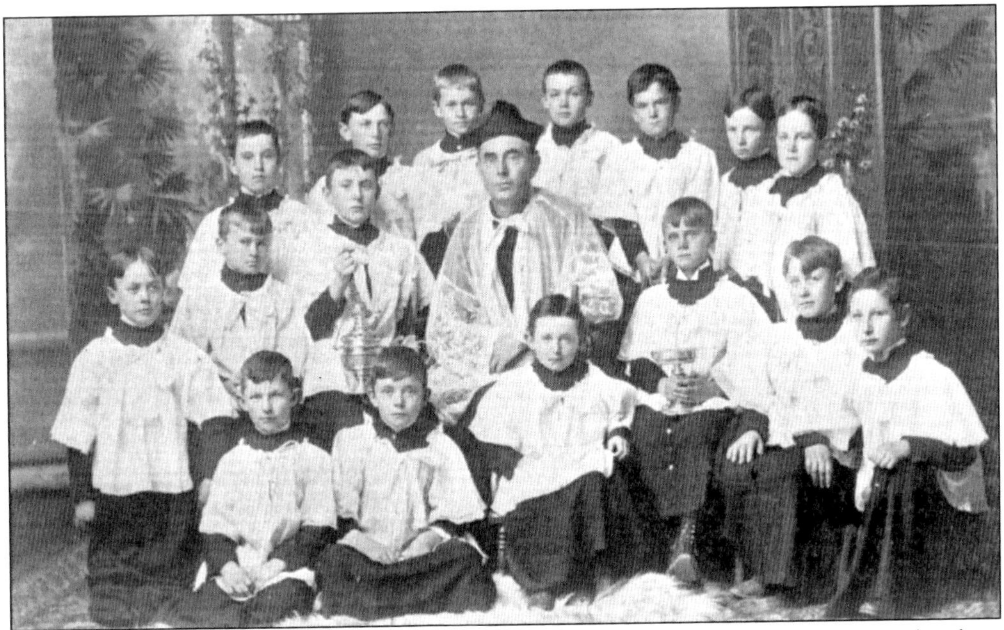

To the left of Father Isaac Hocter, the rector from 1887 until his death in 1900, is altar boy, Charles A. Carrol. He was the father of Charles R. Carrol, Ph.D., who is the present historian of St. Brigid's. Dr. Carrol identified his father in this photo. (Courtesy of Greene County Archives—Time Capsule Document.)

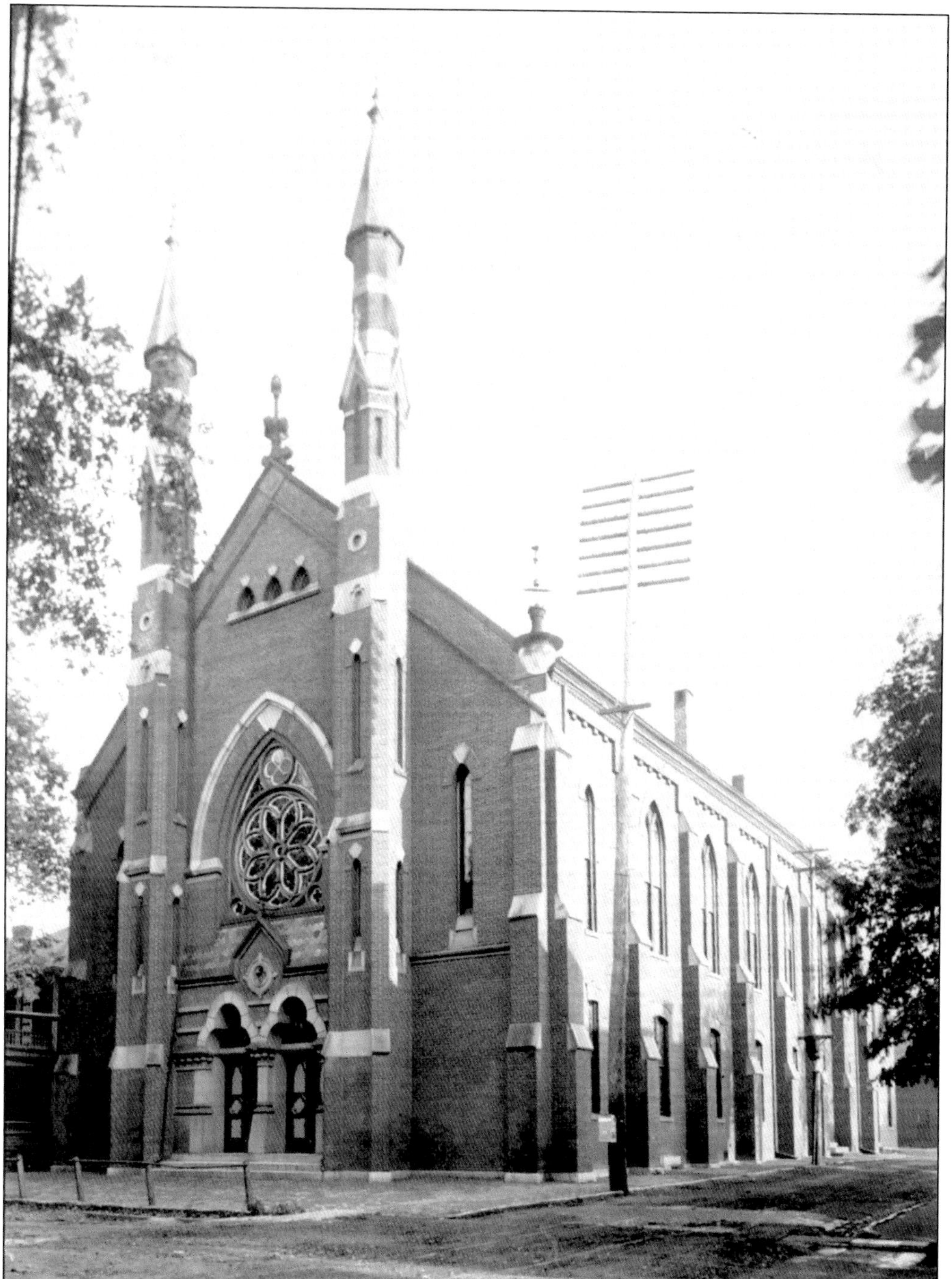

The First Presbyterian Church was located on the southeast corner of Market and King Streets in Xenia. (Courtesy of Greene County Historical Society.)

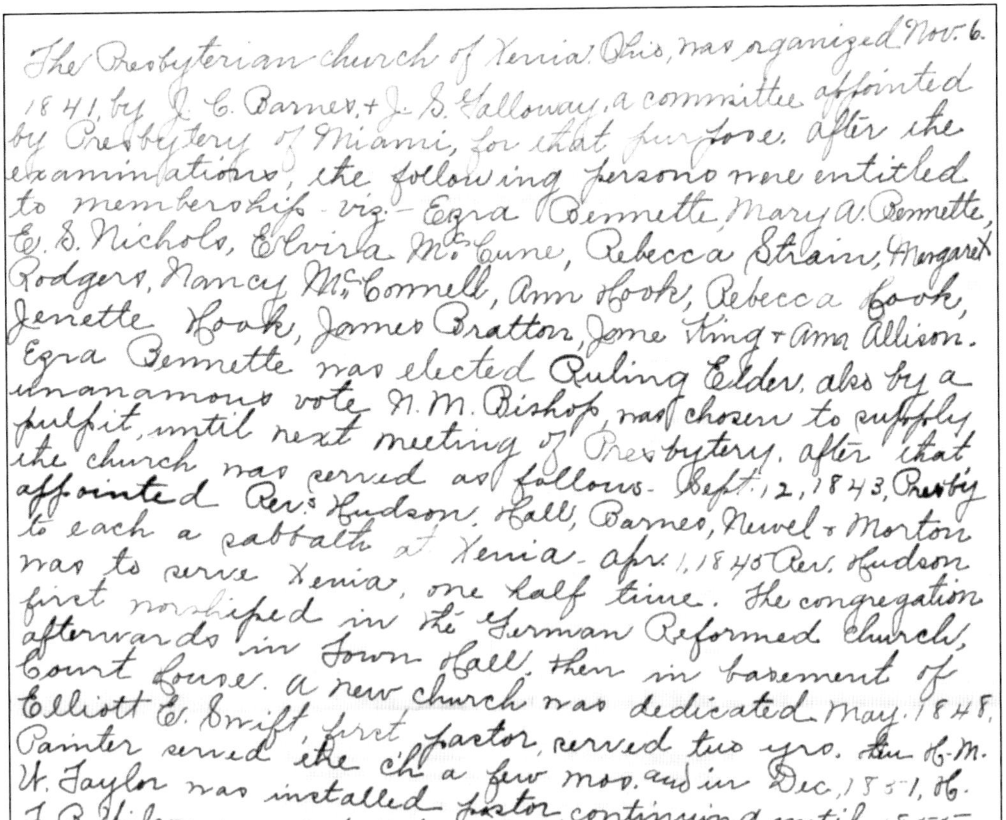

The Presbyterian church of Xenia Ohio, was organized Nov. 6. 1841, by J. C. Barnes, + J. S. Galloway, a committee appointed by Presbytery of Miami, for that purpose. After the examinations, the following persons were entitled to membership - viz - Ezra Bennette, Mary A. Bennette, E. S. Nichols, Elvira McCune, Rebecca Strain, Margaret Rodgers, Nancy McConnell, Ann Hook, Rebecca Hook, Jenette Hook, James Bratton, Jane King + Ann Allison. Ezra Bennette was elected Ruling Elder. also by a unanamous vote N. M. Bishop, was chosen to supply pulpit, until next meeting of Presbytery. After that the church was served as follows - Sept. 12, 1843, Presby appointed Revs Hudson, Hall, Barnes, Newel + Morton to each a sabbath at Xenia - Apr. 1, 1845 Rev. Hudson was to serve Xenia, one half time. The congregation first worshiped in the German Reformed Church, afterwards in Town Hall, then in basement of Court House. A new church was dedicated May 1848. Elliott E. Swift first pastor, served two yrs. Rev H. M. Painter served the ch a few mos. and in Dec. 1851, H. W. Taylor was installed pastor, continuing until 1855. J. B. Wilson was installed pastor 1855, served until his death in Sept. 1858. In April 1859 J. E. Arman was called who served a few mos. then W. J. Findley served 9 yrs - J. H. Montgomery served 2 yrs, + W. W. Ralston 2 yrs - J. M. Hopkins from Apr. 1876 until 1881. J. M. Wood stated supply 2 yrs, then Chas. Axtele from 1883 to 1886. - J. C. Ely from 1886 until 1897 - J. E. McGee from Nov. 1897 to Apr. 1899 - J. S. Edenburn from Sept 1899 until present time - present membership 517 - Officers - Elders, E. C. Fleming, David Watt, A. C. Messenger, Ora Whittington, C. M. Galloway, James Stewart - C. N. Lupton + J. A. Hutchinson - Deacons - Chas Johnson, W. E. Clark, O. C. Baker, R. D. Adair, P. R. Madden, Robt. Williamson + Albert Woodrow. E. C. Fleming Supt S. School - R. C. West Assist Supt. S. S.

Written March - 14 - 1901 - by Mrs A. C. Messenger.

Included in the manual of the First Presbyterian Church was this handwritten history, with a list of the pastors since 1841, when the church was first organized in Xenia. (Courtesy of Greene County Archives—Time Capsule Document.)

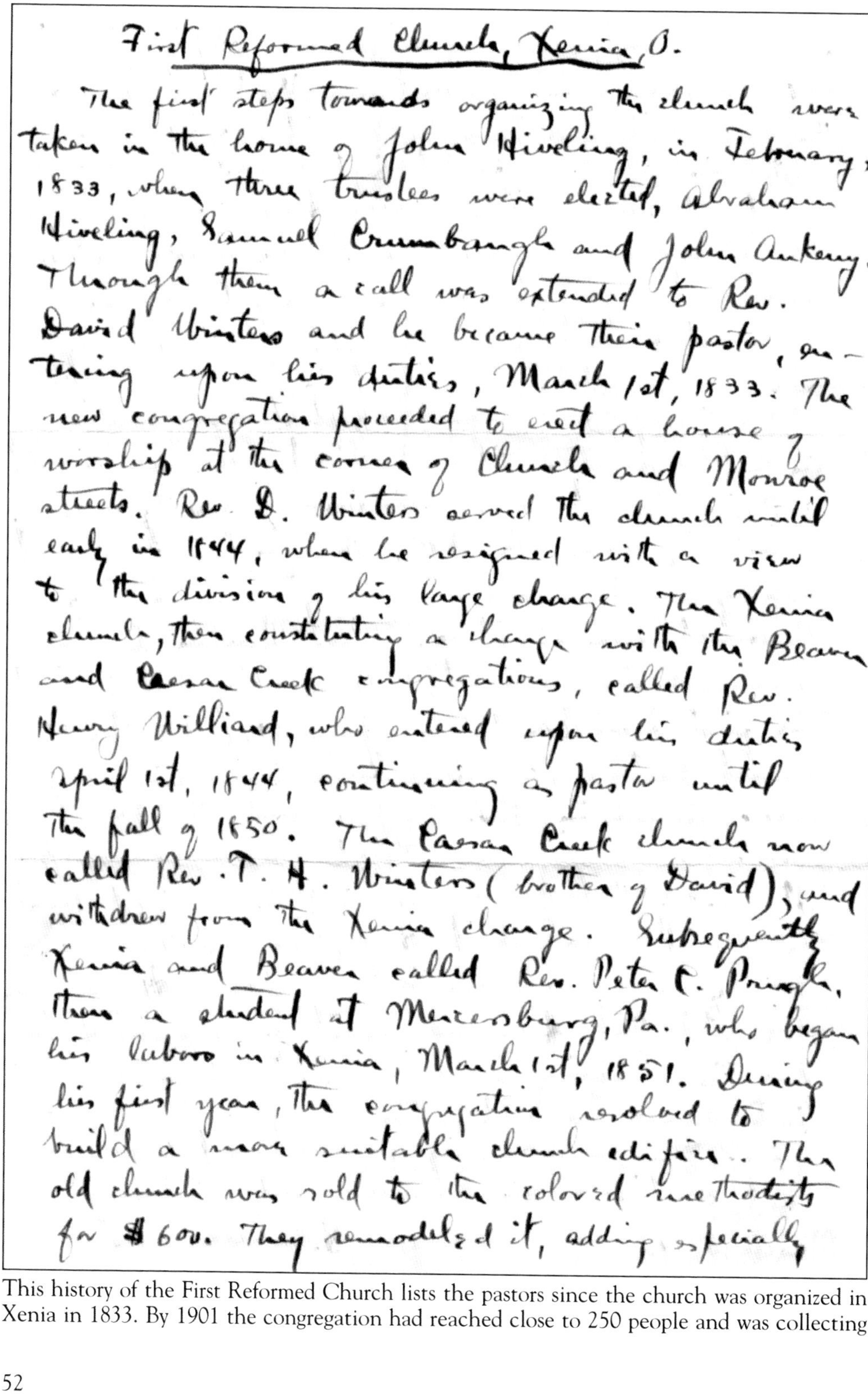

First Reformed Church, Xenia, O.

The first steps towards organizing the church were taken in the home of John Hivling, in February, 1833, when three trustees were elected, Abraham Hivling, Samuel Crumbaugh and John Ankeny. Through them a call was extended to Rev. David Winters and he became their pastor, entering upon his duties, March 1st, 1833. The new congregation proceeded to erect a house of worship at the corner of Church and Monroe streets. Rev. D. Winters served the church until early in 1844, when he resigned with a view to the division of his large charge. The Xenia church, then constituting a charge with the Beaver and Caesar Creek congregations, called Rev. Henry Williard, who entered upon his duties April 1st, 1844, continuing as pastor until the fall of 1850. The Caesar Creek church now called Rev. T. H. Winters (brother of David), and withdrew from the Xenia charge. Subsequently Xenia and Beaver called Rev. Peter C. Prugh, then a student at Mercersburg, Pa., who began his labors in Xenia, March 1st, 1851. During his first year, the congregation resolved to build a more suitable church edifice. The old church was sold to the colored methodists for $600. They remodeled it, adding especially

This history of the First Reformed Church lists the pastors since the church was organized in Xenia in 1833. By 1901 the congregation had reached close to 250 people and was collecting

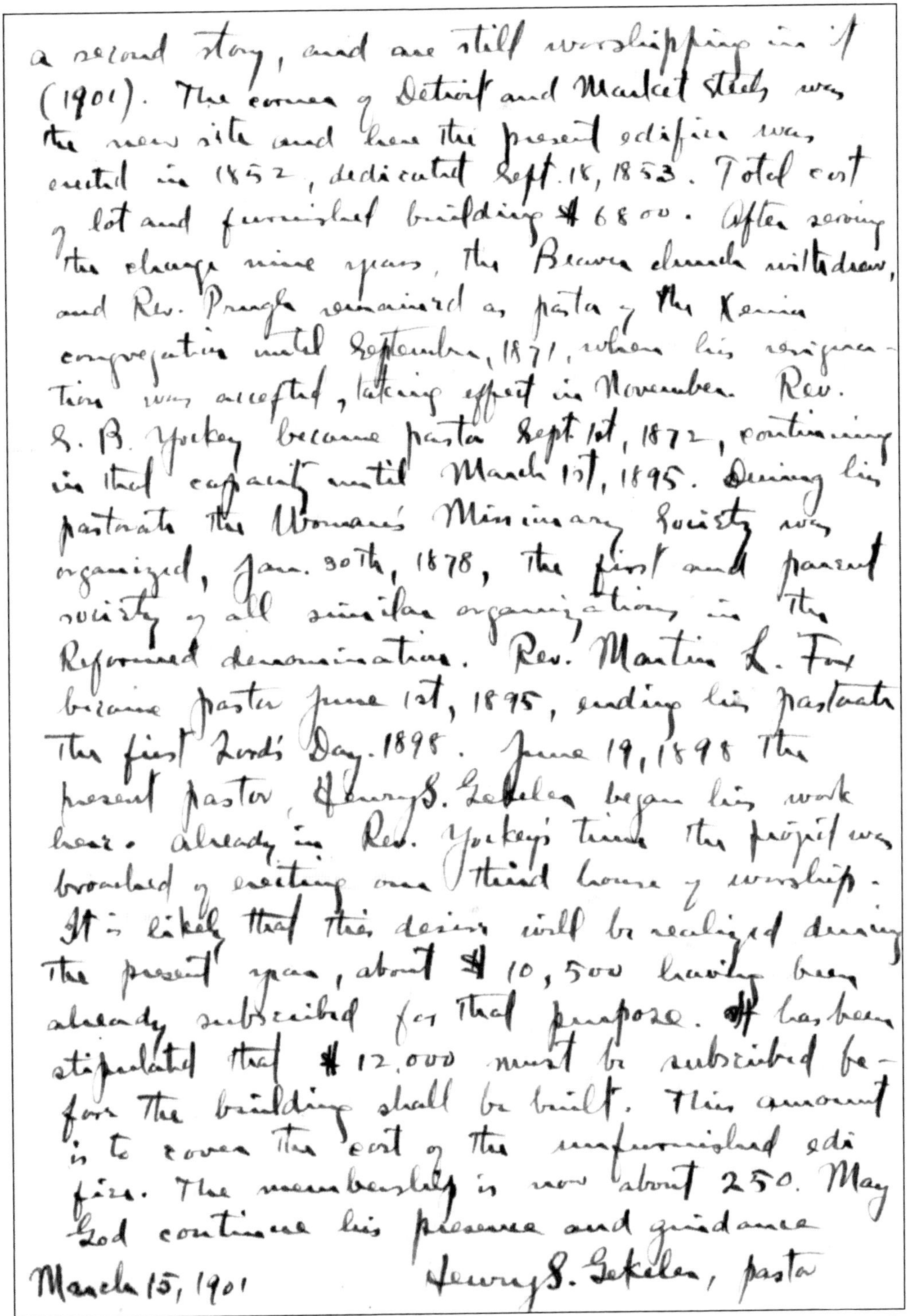
a second story, and are still worshipping in it
(1901). The corner of Detroit and Market streets was
the new site and here the present edifice was
erected in 1852, dedicated Sept. 18, 1853. Total cost
of lot and furnished building $6800. After serving
the charge nine years, the Beaver church withdrew,
and Rev. Pringle remained as pastor of the Xenia
congregation until September, 1871, when his resigna-
tion was accepted, taking effect in November. Rev.
S. B. Yockey became pastor Sept 1st, 1872, continuing
in that capacity until March 1st, 1895. During his
pastorate the Woman's Missionary Society was
organized, Jan. 30th, 1878, the first and parent
society of all similar organizations in the
Reformed denomination. Rev. Martin L. Fox
became pastor June 1st, 1895, ending his pastorate
the first Lord's Day. 1898. June 19, 1898 the
present pastor Henry S. Gekeler began his work
here. Already in Rev. Yockey's time the project was
broached of erecting our third house of worship.
It is likely that this desire will be realized during
the present year, about $10,500 having been
already subscribed for that purpose. It has been
stipulated that $12,000 must be subscribed be-
fore the building shall be built. This amount
is to cover the cost of the unfurnished edi-
fice. The membership is now about 250. May
God continue his presence and guidance

March 15, 1901 Henry S. Gekeler, pastor

funds for a new church building. (Courtesy of Greene County Archives—Time Capsule Document.)

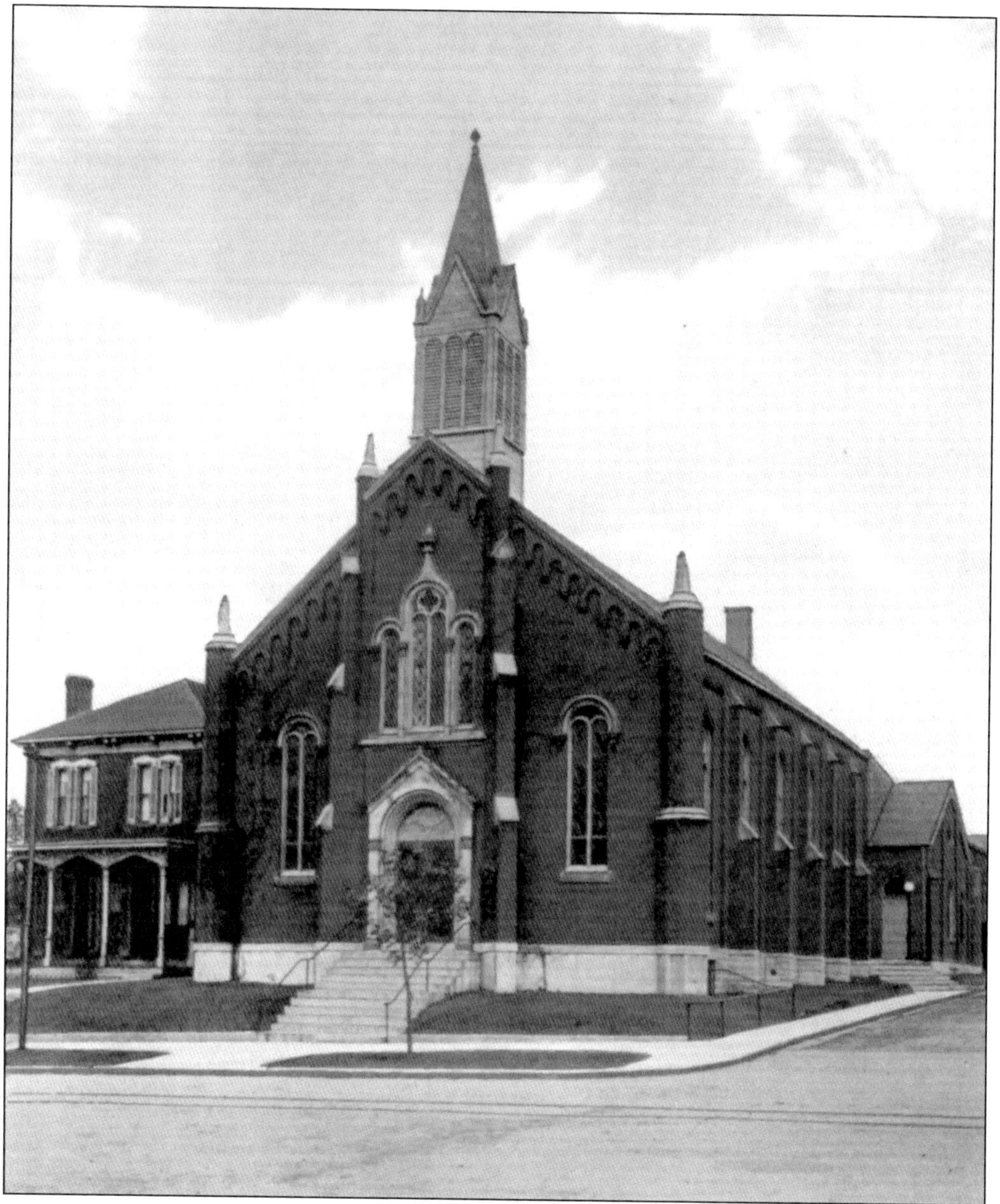

Pictured is Trinity Methodist Episcopal Church at its location on the corner of Main and Monroe Streets in Xenia. (Courtesy of Greene County Historical Society.)

History of Trinity M. E. Church.

Trinity Church was organized from the membership of the First M. E. Church. At the first Quarterly-Conference of the First Church held Nov 14 - 1863, Rev. Louis J. Fee being pastor, the first steps were taken to build a new Church. The following board of Trustees was appointed Alfred Trader, Wm Sweeney, Alfred Thirkield, Moses D. Gatch, Chas. R. Merrick, Wm F. Pelham, Sam'l Newton, John L. Connable, Henry Barnes.

The corner stone was laid May 14 - 1864. The Church membership was formally organized in Sep. 1864 when the Conference appointed Rev. Geo. C. Crum D.D. as the pastor. 119 Came by transfer from the First Church and 9 by letter, making a membership of 128. As the church building was not yet completed the new congregation held services in the chapel of the College building. The lecture room of the church was dedicated by Rev. J. L. Grover D.D. on Nov. 30 - 1864. The audience room was completed the next year and dedicated on Oct. 1st 1865 by Dr. I. W. Wiley D.D. afterward Bishop.

The following pastors have been appointed to the charge by the conference.

'64-'65-'66 Rev. Geo. C. Crum D.D.
'67-'68- Rev. John W. Fowble,
'69-'70- Rev. John W. Cassatt,
'71-'72- Rev. M. Dustin.
'73-'74- Rev. D. J. Starr.
'75-'76 Rev. Geo. C. Crum D.D.
'77-'78-'79 - Rev. W. N. Broadbeck
'80-'81-'82 - Rev. S. Weeks. D.D.
'83-'84-'85 - Rev. David W. Clark D.D.
'86 - '90 (five years) Rev. A. N. Spahr
'91-'92-'93 Rev. D. C. Vance.
'94 - '98 - (five years) Rev. C. M. Van Pelt
'99 - 91 Rev. Merrick E. Ketcham.

The present membership of the Church is 405 full members and 50 probationers. The Official Board at present is constituted as follows.

Chairman Rev. Merrick E. Ketcham.
Local Preacher Rev. Irving F. McKay.
Stewards, S. B. Cornwell, E. H. Piper, S. B. LeSourd, G. W. Ebright, C. W. Trader, Geo. A. Thompson, Geo. C. Stokes, J. L. McGarvey, J. P. Chew, Abraham Newton, Wm H. King, H. H. Conklin, Emery Beal,
Trustees, Lester Arnold, W. R. McGarvey, H. W. Owens, F. E. McGarvey, W. B. Chew, W. F. Trader, F. D. Alexander, Geo. L. White, A. J. Chatfield.
Class Leaders. Geo. C. Stokes, Wells Shipley, Mr. Jas. L. McGarvey, T. A. Edwards.
Pres. of Epworth League. Miss Emma Ebright.
Supt. of Junior League, Mrs. Jas. L. McGarvey.
Sup. of S. School Mr. Geo. W. Ebright.
Asst. Supt. Mr. Geo. A. Thompson

Merrick E. Ketcham
Pastor.

The pastor of Trinity Methodist Episcopal Church, Merrick E. Ketcham, submitted this history of his church. (Courtesy of Greene County Archives—Time Capsule Document.)

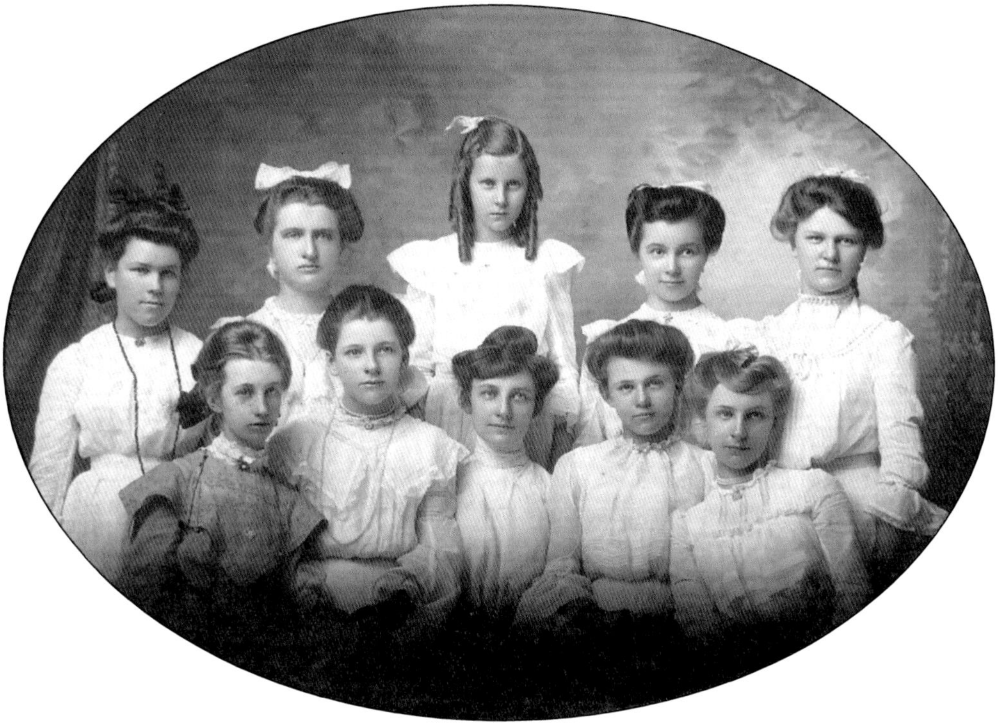

This photograph of Mae Peterson's Sunday School Class at Union Church, although undated, indicates that many of these children belonged to the families mentioned in the church history, which was enclosed in the time capsule. Pictured from left to right are (front row) Bertha Sellars, Bessie Michener, Mae Watkins, Lula Watkins, and M. Whitacre; (back row) Marie Elam, Mabel Davis, Helen Maxey, Ella Resfarme, and Edith Watkins. (Courtesy of Greene County Room, Greene County Public Library.)

"Old Union Church."

March 12th 1901.

Old Union Church is situated two-and one half miles south of Xenia Greene Co. Ohio. The first settlers at this point in 1805 were most of them from "Old Virginia" of Methodist stock.

They came to get a way from slavery some of them owning slaves, and giving them their freedom for conscience sake.

After building their log cabins and clearing a few acres, it being there an unbroken wilderness. not forgetting to meet at their different homes for the worship of God. Feeling the need of a public place of worship, by a united effort they hewed the logs and erected a good log church, covered with a clapboard roof, warmed with a huge fire place, in one end. and lit with tallow dips made and donated by the sisters.

In the course of years, when the people became more prosperous, the log house gave way to a frame building on the same spot. This has been a noted place for sending out ministers of the Gospel, could name more than a dozen. After the frame building began to get out of repair, too small for the congregation, some time in the fifties, a commodious brick edifice took its place. At the present time we have a flourishing congregation, largely made up of the third and fourth generations of those good old people, most of them professed christians. The first settlers were the Watsons, Heaths, Bonners, Sales, Pelhams, Scarffs, Butlers, Wrights, Maxeys, Loyds, Smiths, Davises, Stowes, Owens, Andersons, Reeds, Goodes, Bells, Liles. In 1901 they are Maxeys, Ledbetters, Davises, Elams, Curls, Watkins, Bells, Stowes, Liles, Barrows, Whitackers, Goodes, Spahrs, Benders, Reeds, Sellars, Barnes, St. Johns, Boots, Watsons, Grants, Hufmans.

S. A, Stowe

Mrs. S. A. Stowe.

The history of the Old Union Church is shown here partially in manuscript and partially in transcription. Formerly Methodists from Virginia, the community settled south of Xenia in 1805. Their history lists some of the founding families and also the names of the families who belonged to their church in 1901. (Courtesy of Greene County Archives—Time Capsule Document.)

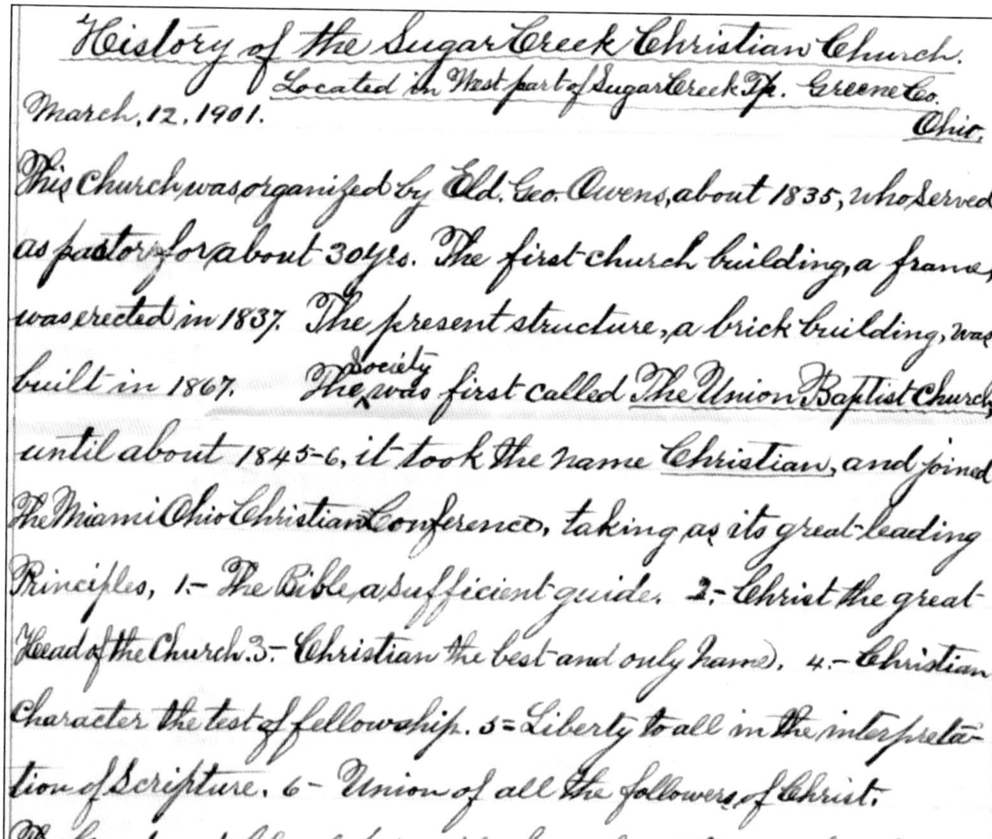
History of the Sugar Creek Christian Church.
Located in West part of Sugar Creek Tp. Greene Co. Ohio.
March, 12, 1901.

This Church was organized by Eld. Geo. Owens, about 1835, who served as pastor for about 30 yrs. The first church building, a frame, was erected in 1837. The present structure, a brick building, was built in 1867. The society was first called The Union Baptist Church, until about 1845-6, it took the name Christian, and joined the Miami Ohio Christian Conference, taking as its great leading Principles, 1- The Bible a sufficient guide. 2- Christ the great Head of the Church. 3- Christian the best and only name. 4.- Christian Character the test of fellowship. 5= Liberty to all in the interpretation of Scripture. 6- Union of all the followers of Christ. These broad and liberal principles have characterized this Church for more than half a Century. The following ministers have served as pastors:- Geo. Owens; Jos. Weeks; P. McCullough; T.A. Brandon, A.L. McKinney; C.C. Phillips; Richard Brandon; P. Banta; C.T. Emmons; H.Y. Rush; B.F. Vaughan; J.F. Ullery, C.W. Garroutte; C.J. Jones; A.L. Ferguson; A. Dunlap; S.D. Bennett; A.W. Hook; H.E. Butler; R.H. McDaniel; H.A. Smith; W.D. Samuel; O.P. Furnas the present Pastor.

The present number of members is 95. The church maintains regular preaching all the year, Sunday school, and a Missionary Society. Signed by B.F. Vaughan Church Clerk.

B.F. Vaughan, the church clerk of Sugarcreek Christian Church in Sugarcreek Township, submitted this handwritten history and the tenets of his church for the time capsule. (Courtesy of Greene County Archives—Time Capsule Document.)

Three

EDUCATION

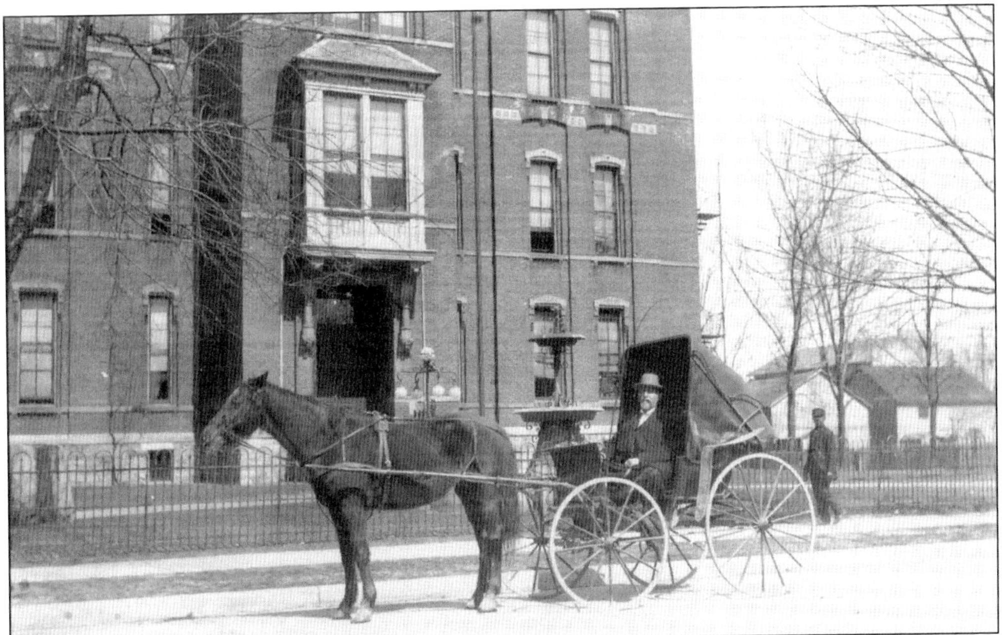

Edwin B. Cox served as superintendent of Xenia Schools for 31 years. The students affectionately knew him as "Daddy" Cox. He is shown here outside the Xenia High School in his famous horse and buggy. (Courtesy of Greene County Room, Greene County Public Library.)

XENIA PUBLIC SCHOOLS.

Organization for the year 1900- 1901.

BOARD OF EDUCATION.

Mr. R. D. Adair, president	term	expires	1902.
Mr. B. Schlesinger, clerk	"	"	1902.
Mrs. Mary E. Moore, treasurer	"	"	1901.
Mrs. E. H. Carruthers	"	"	1901.
Mr. J. E. Jones	"	"	1903.
Mr. J. Kany	"	"	1903.

TEACHERS.

Central Building, East Market Street.

Edwin B. Cox	Superintendent	Salary	$1800.
A. F. Maynard	Sup'v'r of Music	"	750.
C. C. Buckles	Truant Officer	"	600.

Central High School.

G. J. Graham	Principal-Latin	"	1200.
Mary Wilgus	Mathematics	"	1000.
Anna MacCracken	History and Latin	"	800.
Jean B. Elwell	English and Elocution	"	800.
S. W. Collett	Science	"	800.
Jessa J. Pearson	German and Civ. Gov.	"	750.

Grammar and Primary Grades.

Anna Galloway	Eighth-year Grade	"	650.
Margaret Clark	Eighth " "	"	650.
Laura B. McElwain	Seventh " "	"	500.
Anna J. Conner	Seventh " "	"	500.
Clara Martin	Sixth " "	"	450.
May M. Harper	Sixth " "	"	450.
Ella Ambuhl	Fifth " "	"	450.
Rose M. Case	Fourth " "	"	400.
Mae Prugh	Third " "	"	400.
Florence Whitmer	Second " "	"	400.
Leila Quinn	First " "	"	500.
Cora Williams	Substitute	"	
W. H. King	Janitor	"	900.

West Market Street Building.

Fannie K. Haynes, Prin.	Fifth-year Grade	"	500.
Mae Stevenson	Fourth " "	"	400.
Clara McCarty	Third " "	"	400.
Ella Hudson	Second " "	"	400.
Luella Baker	First " "	"	500.
Carrie Ray	Substitute	"	
W. W. Marshall	Janitor	"	300.

Cincinnati Ave. Building.

Harriet Scarff, Principal	Fifth--year Grade	"	500
Mary Gretsinger	Third " "	"	400.
Edith Marshall	Second " "	"	400.
Anna B. Morrow	First " "	"	500.
Wm. Maxwell	Janitor	"	240.

XENIA PUBLIC SCHOOLS.

Spring Hill Building, Chestnut and High Streets.

Olga Schlesinger, Prin. –	Seventh and Sixth Grades,	Salary	$550.
Letitia Dillencourt	Fifth and Fourth "	"	450.
Rachel Maxwell	Third and Second "	"	400.
Laura Loyd	First-year "	"	500.
A. B. Rowe	Janitor	"	400.

East Main Street High School. (Colored.)

T. D. Scott, Principal, –	Latin and Science	"	1100.
Laura V. Phelps	English and Mathmetics	"	700.
Kate Schweibold	German and Science	"	700.
Lucretia Willis	Eighth- year Grade	"	600.
Mrs. Wm. Cosby	Janitor	"	240.

East Market Street Building. (Colored.)

Lucy J. Meredith, Prin. –	Sixth-year Grade	"	500.
Selena C. Gaines	Seventh " "	"	500.
Mattie P. Cruisman	Fifth " "	"	450.
Carrie E. Butler	Fourth " "	"	400.
Eva A. Nichols	Third " "	"	400.
Osee Towles	Second " "	"	400.
Amanda C. Brinson	First " "	"	450.
Lydia A. Scott	First " "	"	500.
Emma J Williams	Night School	"	120.
Mamie Harris	Substitute	"	
David Lee	Janitor	"	480.

Statisics and Notes.

Enumeration of School Youth, May 1900.	2276
Enrollment in Pulic Schools, for the year,	1579.
Enrollment, February 1901,	1393.
Attendance, February 1901, (Much sickness)	1245.
Number of School Houses	6.
Population of city, (Census of 1900)	8696.

Xenia City School District embraces considerable territory beyond the city limits.

An addition of four rooms was this year built to the Spring Hill School Building, making it a modern and beautiful eight room house.

By action of the board of education on March 11th, 1901, the proposition to build a large new school house in the west part of the city is to be submitted the electors of the district April 1st, 1901. Also the proposition to build a new school house for the accommodation of the small children of Orient Hill.

The above facts about the public schools of Xenia were prepared and arranged by the superintendent,

EDWIN B COX.

Superintendent Cox wrote this report on the current status of the schools. Particularly interesting are the names of teachers and other school employees, with their salaries listed. (Courtesy of Greene County Archives—Time Capsule Document.)

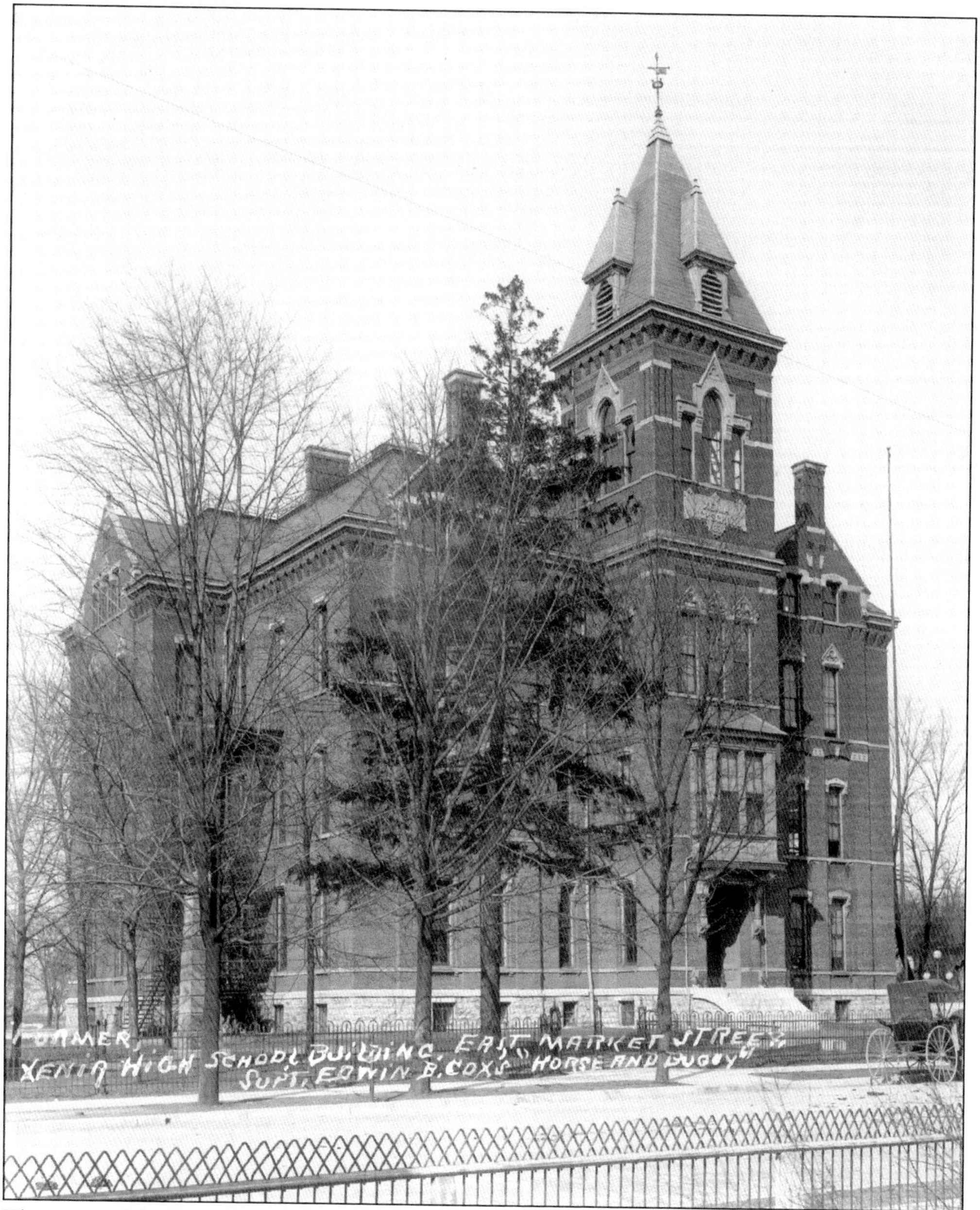

This view of the Xenia High School includes the horse and buggy used by Superintendent Cox. (Courtesy of Greene County Room, Greene County Public Library.)

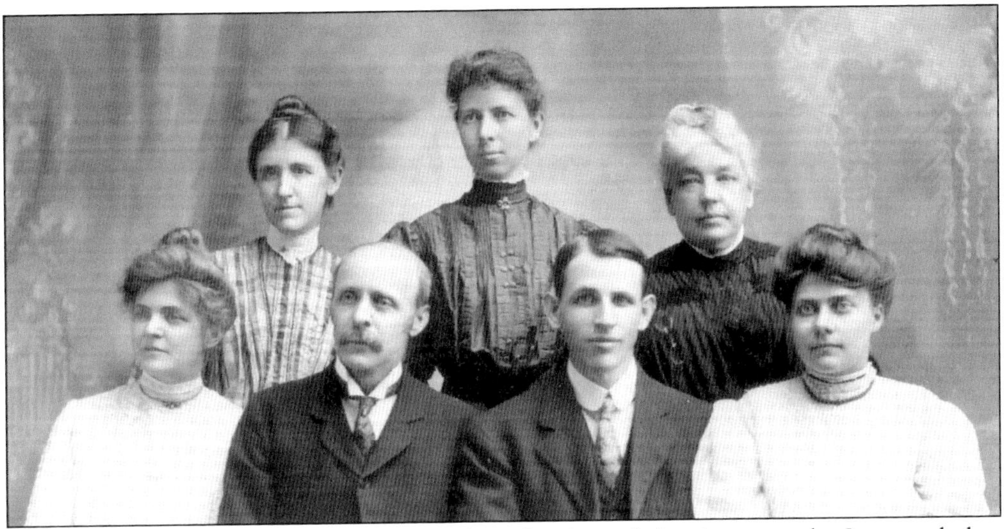

This photograph was taken a little later than the date of the time capsule. It nevertheless portrays several of the teachers mentioned in Superintendent Cox's report. Shown from left to right are Jean Elwell, Mary Wilgus, G.J. Graham, Jessa Pearson, Mr. Buck (not on list), Anna McCracken, and Anne Bailey (not on list). (Courtesy of Greene County Room, Greene County Public Library.)

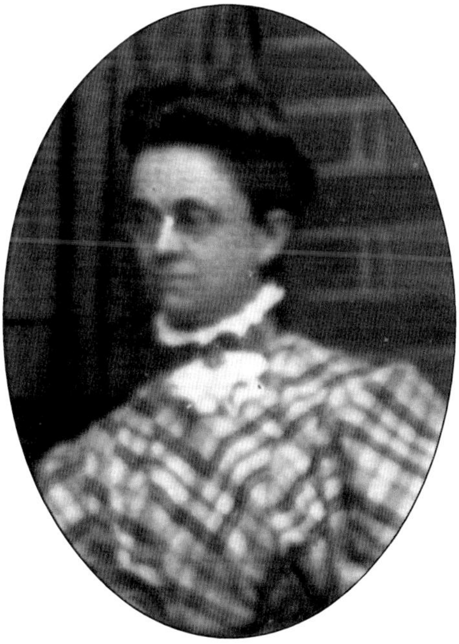

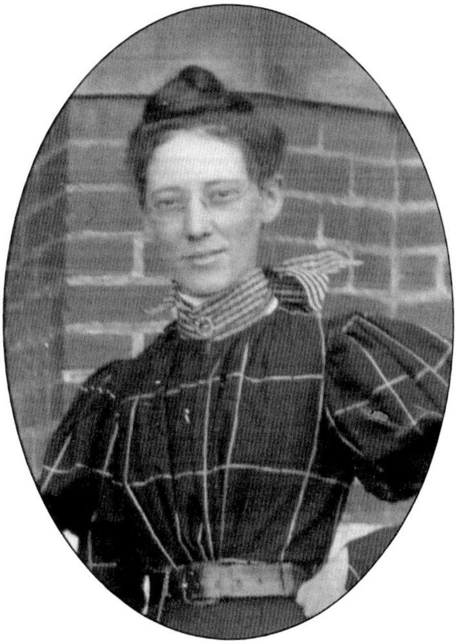

Left: Miss Clara Martin taught sixth grade for the 1900–1901 school year.
Right: Miss Mae Stevenson taught fourth grade at the West Market Street school building for the 1900–1901 school year. (Courtesy of Greene County Room, Greene County Public Library.)

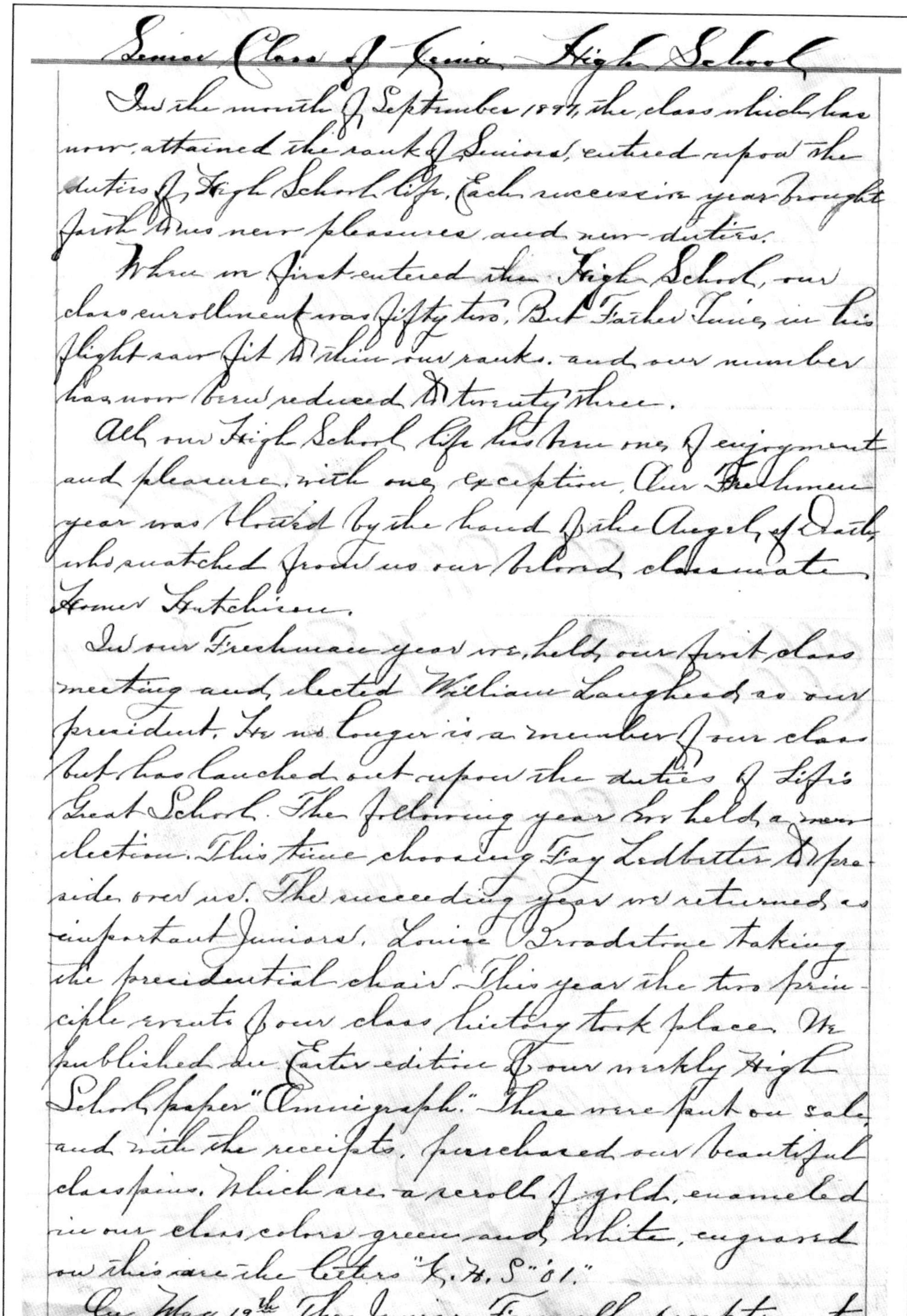
Senior Class of Xenia High School

In the month of September 1897, the class which has now attained the rank of Seniors, entered upon the duties of High School life. Each successive year brought forth thus new pleasures and new duties.

When we first entered the High School, our class enrollment was fifty two. But Father Time, in his flight saw fit to thin our ranks, and our number has now been reduced to twenty three.

All our High School life has been one of enjoyment and pleasure, with one exception. Our Freshmen year was clouded by the hand of the Angel of Death, who snatched from us our beloved classmate Homer Hutchison.

In our Freshman year we held our first class meeting and elected William Laughead as our president. He no longer is a member of our class but has lanched out upon the duties of Life's Great School. The following year we held a new election. This time choosing Fay Ledbetter to preside over us. The succeeding year we returned as important Juniors, Louise Broadstone taking the presidential chair. This year the two principle events of our class history took place. We published an Easter edition of our weekly High School paper "Omnigraph." These were put on sale, and with the receipts, purchased our beautiful class pins. Which are a scroll of gold, enameled in our class colors green and white, engraved on this are the letters "X. H. S." '01.

On May 19th. The Junior Farewell reception to

The senior class of Xenia High School donated this report of their high school years. It ends: "And it is with mingled joy and regret that we look forward to June, for after that we can do no more than follow our class motto 'Advance and Conquer.'"

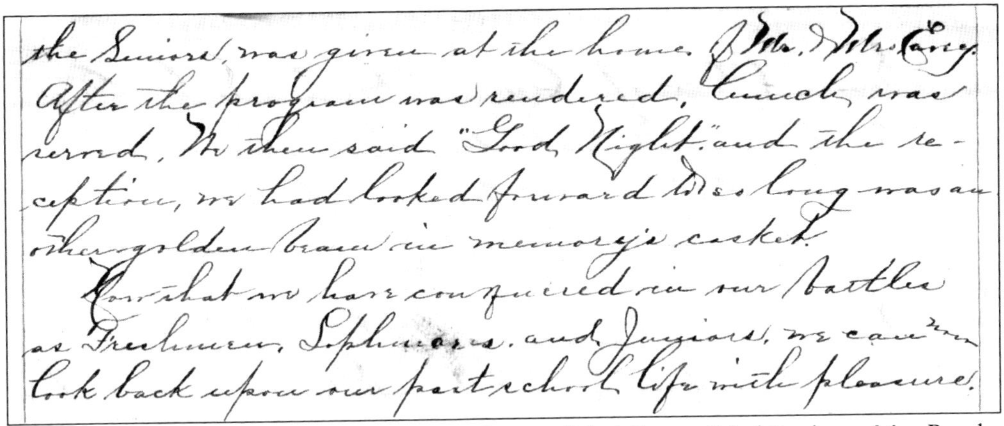

the Seniors, was given at the home of Mr. & Mrs. Carey.
After the program was rendered, lunch was
served. We then said "Good Night" and the re-
ception, we had looked forward to so long was an
other golden beam in memory's casket.
Now that we have conquered in our battles
as Freshmen, Sophomores, and Juniors, we can
look back upon our past school life with pleasure.

The document lists the names of the class officers—Ethel Evans, Ethel Rayburn, May Bundy, and Charles Fulkerson; followed by the class roll—Viola Orr, Louise Broadstone, Ethel Evans, Mary Harper, Nellie Johnson, Julia McCormick, M. Fay Ledbetter, Edna McClellan, Florence Wright, Euretta Meredith, Florence Schnebly, Opal Mallow, Chas Clark, Mae Bundy, Chas Fulkerson, M. Gertrude Labron, Lena Hetsel, Alice Marshall, Anna Linkhart, Clara Dillingham, W. Fleming Watt, Margaret McConnell, and Olive McConnell. (Courtesy of Greene County Archives—Time Capsule Document.)

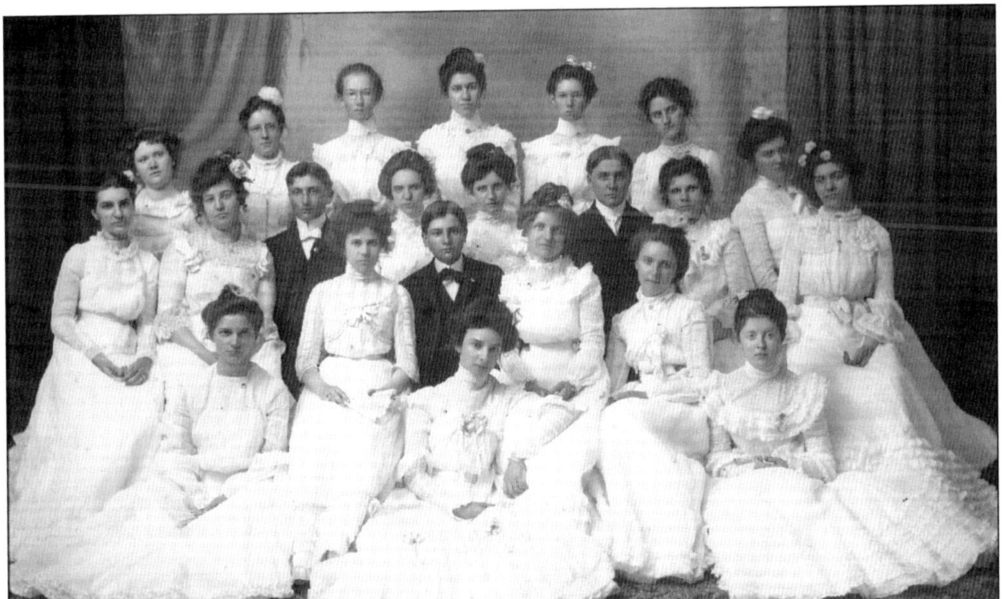

This beautiful photograph of the Xenia High School Class of 1901 pictures those students listed on the roll. Unfortunately, the students could not be individually identified. (Courtesy of Greene County Historical Society.)

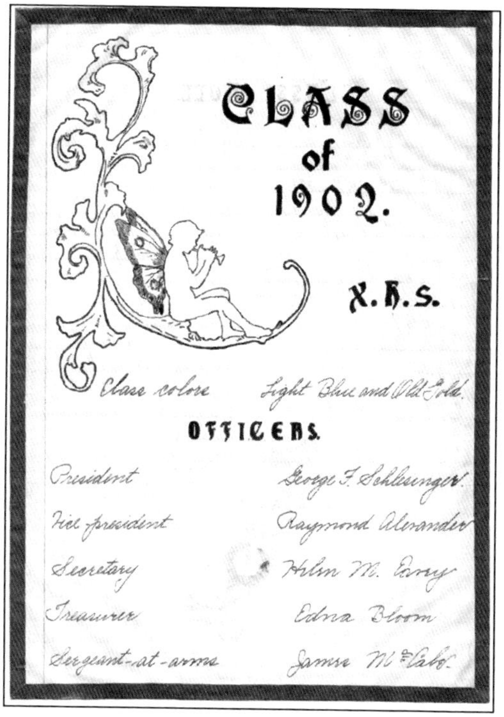

CLASS of 1902.

X. H. S.

Class colors Light Blue and Old Gold.

OFFICERS.

President	George F. Schlesinger
Vice president	Raymond Alexander
Secretary	Helen M. Davy
Treasurer	Edna Bloom
Sergeant-at-arms	James McCabe

The Xenia High School Class of 1902 also included their names for posterity. (Courtesy of Greene County Archives—Time Capsule Document.)

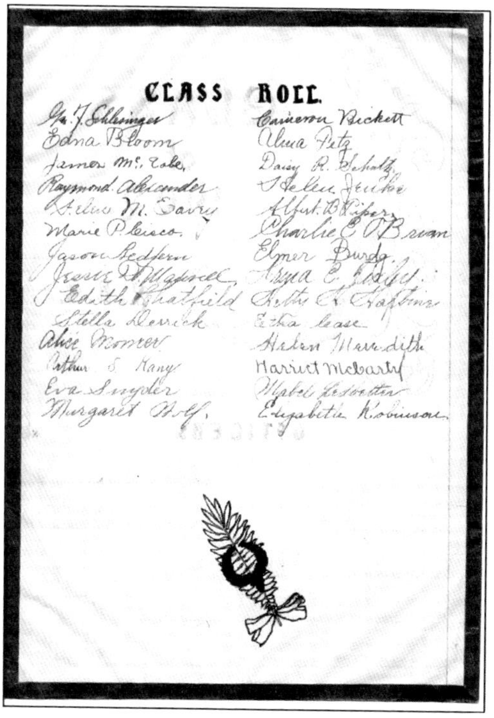

CLASS ROLL.

Geo. F. Schlesinger	Cameron Beckett
Edna Bloom	Alma Fetz
James McCabe	Daisy R. Schultz
Raymond Alexander	Helen Jenkins
Helen M. Davy	Alfert B. Piper
Marie P. Cisco	Charlie E. O'Brian
Jason Redfern	Elmer Burdg
Jessie [illegible]	[illegible]
Edith [illegible]field	[illegible]
Stella Derrick	Etha Lease
Alice Monroe	Helen Meredith
Arthur S. Kany	Harriet McCarty
Eva Snyder	Mabel [illegible]
Margaret Wolf	Elizabeth Robinson

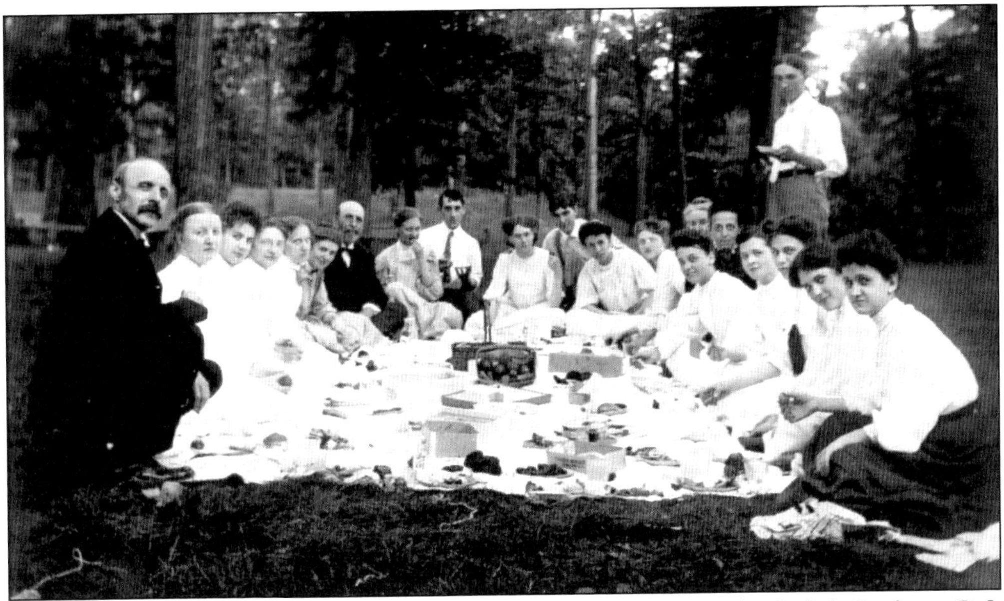

The Xenia High School Class of 1902 at a picnic. Identified are, on the far left, Professor G. J. Graham, the principal of the high school; to the left rear, Professor E.B. Cox, the superintendent of the Xenia Schools; Arthur Kany, one of the two male students seated at the rear; and, standing at the right, Thearl White, a former student. (Courtesy of Greene County Room, Greene County Public Library.)

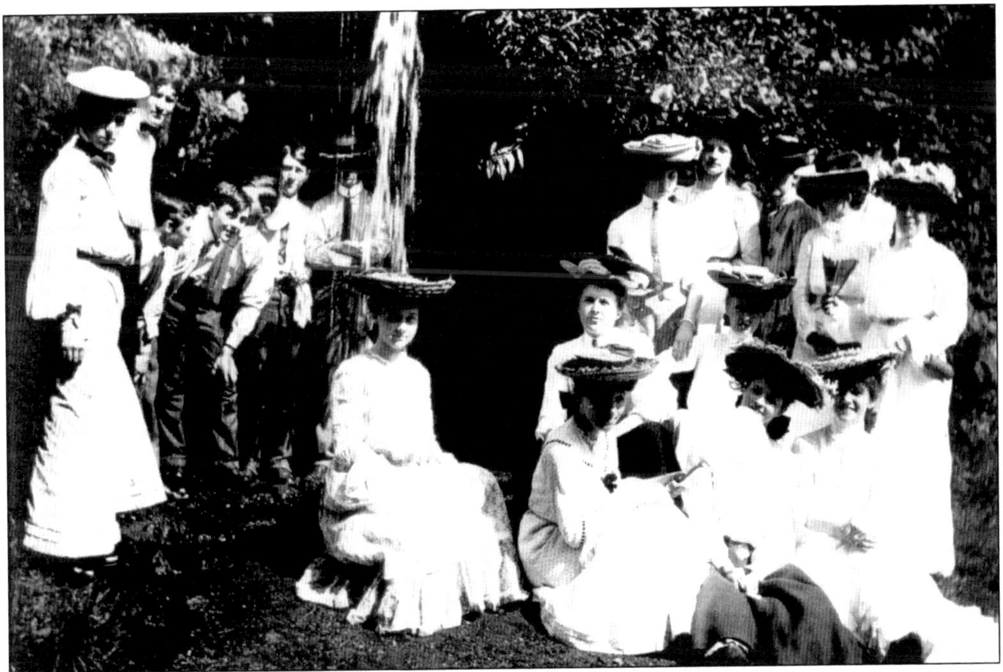

In this photograph of some of the class of 1902, teacher Miss Jessa Pearson is pictured standing on the left; in the middle, seated, is student Edna Bloom; and at the rear, standing second from the left, is student Irma Finley. Both Edna and Irma were later to become teachers in the Xenia school system themselves. (Courtesy of Greene County Room, Greene County Public Library.)

In Memory of the Sophomore Class of Xenia High School.

Class of 1903.

March 15, 1901.

Our motto. "Amoses interse amaniis".

Class History of 1903.

History, says a Sophomore, is a "record of disturbances". Hence it must be confessed that the aggregation of poets, preachers, doctors, and Philosophers, composing this class, have no history, and the Board will agree that we have made few disturbances, and the ones we made were crisp and to the point.

As a rule, however we have been unusually well-behaved and our winning ways have taken the hearts of all. What the future will bring forth we know not. But whatever our fate, we leave this monument of our iniquity to be a model for future classes.

Now good friends remember our good deeds and us.

While we lie sleeping under the dust.

Colors of the class;

Old rose

And

White.

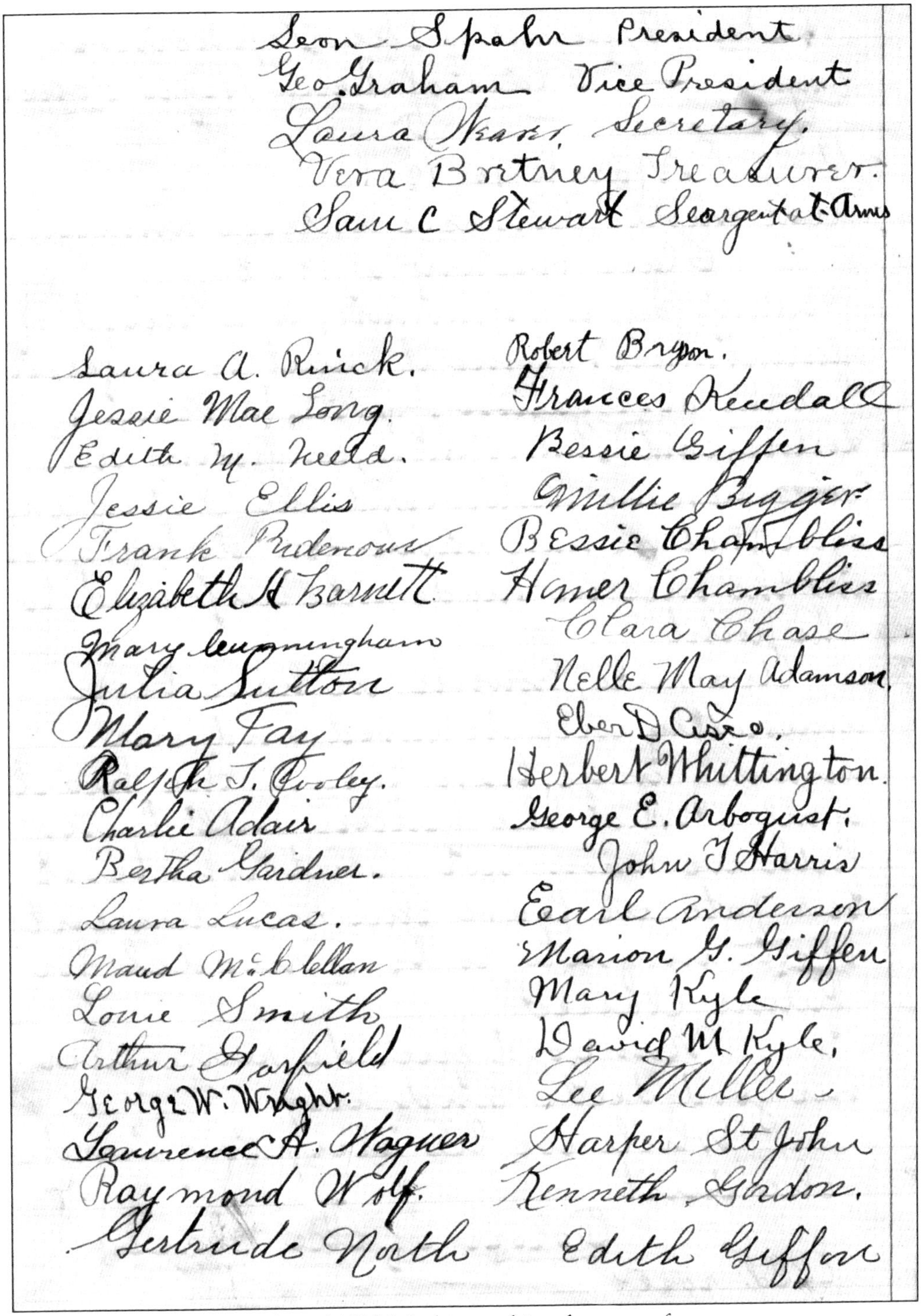

Leon Spahr President
Geo. Graham Vice President
Laura Kearr, Secretary.
Vera Britney Treasurer.
Sam C Stewart Seargent at Arms

Laura A. Rinck.	Robert Bryon.
Jessie Mae Long.	Frances Kendall
Edith M. Reed.	Bessie Giffen
Jessie Ellis	Millie Bigger.
Frank Ridenour	Bessie Chambliss
Elizabeth A Barnett.	Homer Chambliss
Mary Cunningham	Clara Chase
Julia Sutton	Nelle May Adamson
Mary Fay	Eber D Cox.
Ralph T. Cooley.	Herbert Whittington.
Charlie Adair	George E. Arboguist.
Bertha Gardner.	John T Harris
Laura Lucas.	Earl Andersen
Maud McClellan	Marion G. Giffen
Louie Smith	Mary Kyle
Arthur Garfield	David M Kyle.
George W. Wright.	Lee Miller.
Lawrence A. Wagner	Harper St John
Raymond Wolf.	Kenneth Gordon.
Gertrude North	Edith Giffen

The Xenia High School Class of 1903 left this touching document for us:
Now good friends remember our good deeds and us
While we lie sleeping under the dust.
(Courtesy of Greene County Archives—Time Capsule Document.)

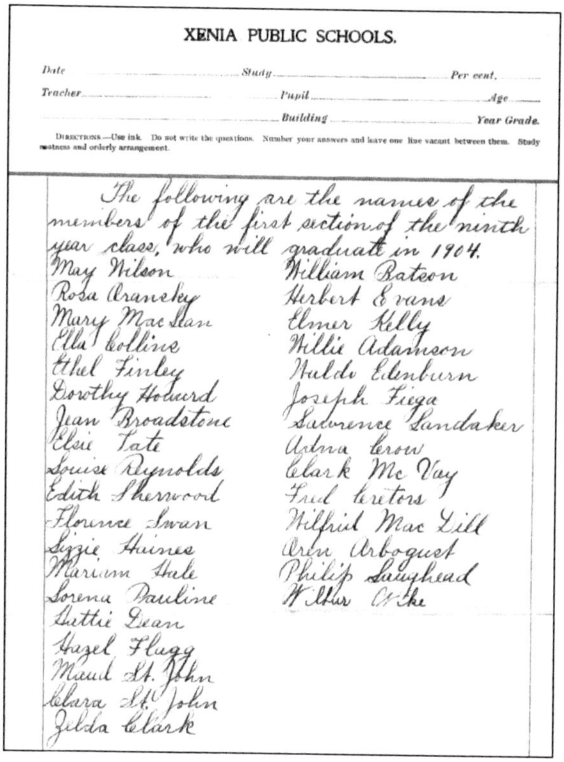

XENIA PUBLIC SCHOOLS.

Date ______ Study ______ Per cent. ______
Teacher ______ Pupil ______ Age ______
______ Building ______ Year Grade.

DIRECTIONS.—Use ink. Do not write the questions. Number your answers and leave one line vacant between them. Study neatness and orderly arrangement.

The following are the names of the members of the first section of the ninth year class, who will graduate in 1904.

May Wilson	William Bateon
Rosa Aransky	Herbert Evans
Mary MacLean	Elmer Kelly
Ella Collins	Willie Adamson
Ethel Finley	Waldo Elenburn
Dorothy Howard	Joseph Fiega
Jean Broadstone	Lawrence Landaker
Elsie Tate	Adna Crow
Louise Reynolds	Clark McVay
Edith Sherwood	Fred Ceretors
Florence Swan	Wilfried MacLill
Lizzie Haines	Oren Arbogust
Mariam Hale	Philip Laughead
Lorena Pauline	Wilbur Oke
Lettie Dean	
Hazel Flagg	
Maud St. John	
Clara St. John	
Zelda Clark	

The two freshman classes, due to graduate in 1904, also signed their names. This is the first section. (Courtesy of Greene County Archives—Time Capsule Document.)

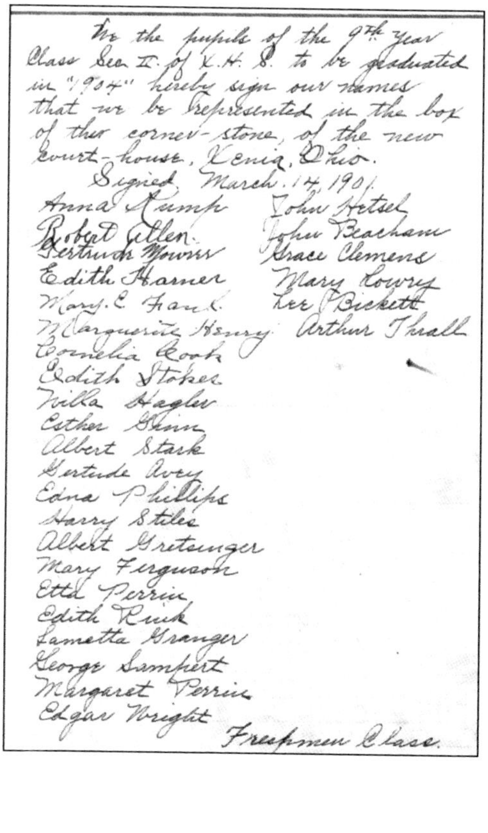

We the pupils of the 9th year Class Sec II. of X. H. S. to be graduated in "1904" hereby sign our names that we be represented in the box of the corner-stone, of the new court-house, Xenia, Ohio.
Signed, March. 14, 1901.

Anna Rump	John Hetsel
Robert Allen	John Beacham
Gertrude Mowrer	Grace Clemens
Edith Harner	Mary Lowry
Mary E. Frank	Lee Bickett
Marguerite Henry	Arthur Thrall
Cornelia Cook	
Edith Stokes	
Nilla Hagler	
Esther Glenn	
Albert Stark	
Gertrude Avey	
Edna Phillips	
Harry Stiles	
Albert Gretsinger	
Mary Ferguson	
Etta Perrin	
Edith Rink	
Lametta Granger	
George Sampert	
Margaret Perrin	
Edgar Wright	

Freshmen Class.

This is the second section of the freshman class. (Courtesy of Greene County Archives—Time Capsule Document.)

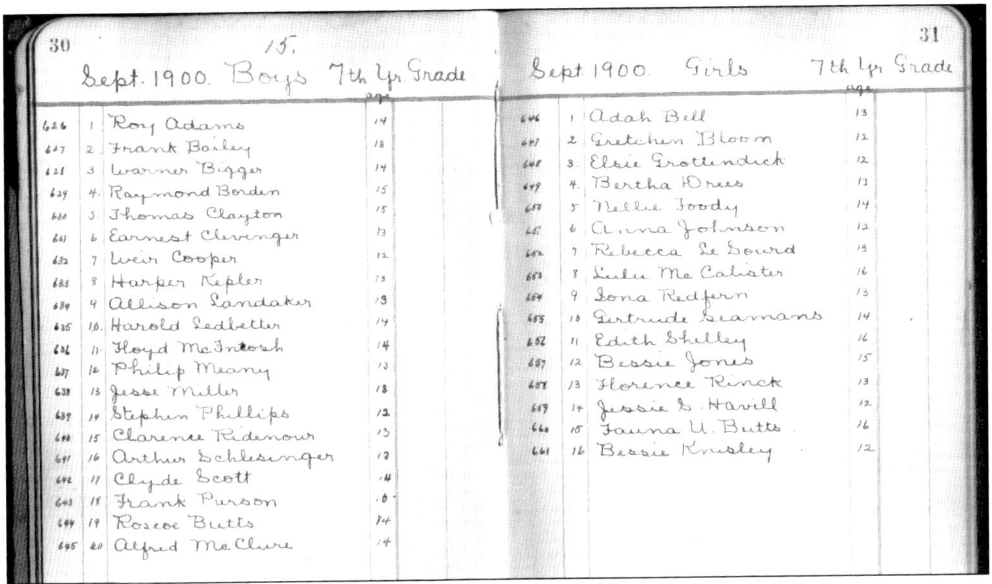

30 15.

Sept. 1900. Boys 7th Yr. Grade

			age
626	1	Roy Adams	14
627	2	Frank Bailey	13
628	3	Warner Bigger	14
629	4	Raymond Borden	15
630	5	Thomas Clayton	15
631	6	Earnest Clevenger	13
632	7	Weir Cooper	12
633	8	Harper Kepler	13
634	9	Allison Landaker	13
635	10	Harold Ledbetter	14
636	11	Floyd McIntosh	14
637	12	Philip Meany	13
638	13	Jesse Miller	13
639	14	Stephen Phillips	12
640	15	Clarence Ridenour	13
641	16	Arthur Schlesinger	12
642	17	Clyde Scott	14
643	18	Frank Purson	16
644	19	Roscoe Butts	14
645	20	Alfred McClure	14

31

Sept. 1900. Girls 7th Yr. Grade

			age
646	1	Adah Bell	13
647	2	Gretchen Bloom	12
648	3	Elsie Grottendick	12
649	4	Bertha Drees	11
650	5	Nellie Foody	14
651	6	Anna Johnson	12
652	7	Rebecca Le Sourd	13
653	8	Lulu McCalister	16
654	9	Iona Redfern	13
655	10	Gertrude Seamans	14
656	11	Edith Shelley	16
657	12	Bessie Jones	15
658	13	Florence Rinck	13
659	14	Jessie S. Havill	12
660	15	Fauna U. Butts	16
661	16	Bessie Knisley	12

Teacher Miss Laura McElwain kept a roster of all the students who passed through her classes from 1886 to 1914. Many of the high school students named in the reports they submitted for the time capsule can be found at an earlier stage of their schooling in the pages of Miss McElwain's notebook. This extract shows the students of her seventh grade class from the 1900–1901 school year. (Courtesy of Greene County Room, Greene County Public Library.)

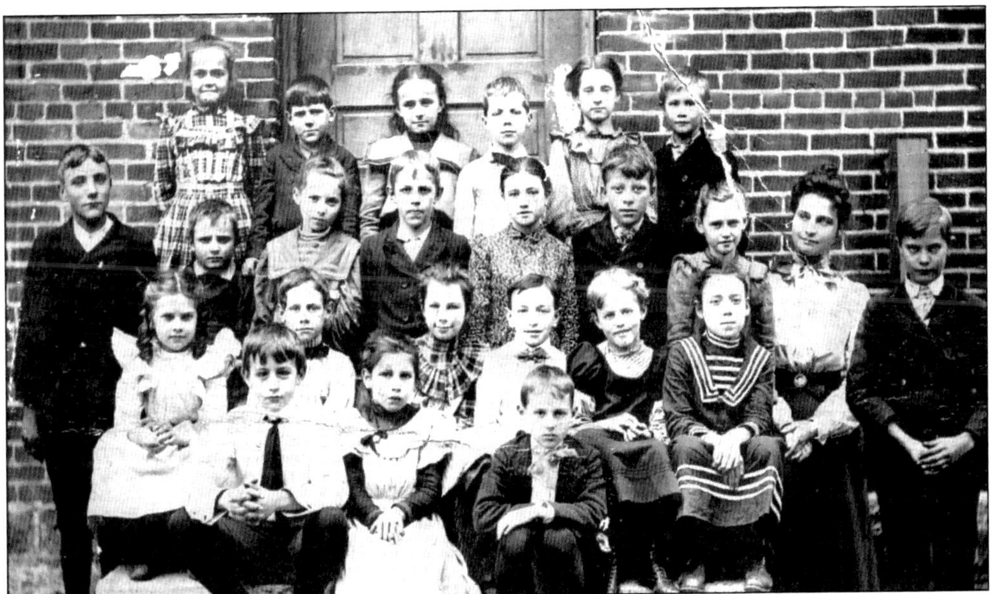

This is Clara McCarty with her third grade class at the West Market Street school in 1901. Pictured from left to right are (front row) Howell Garfield, unidentified, and Fred Hunt; (second row) Margaret Howard, Charles Galloway, Karleen McCarty, Louis F. Clark, Evelyn Galloway, and unidentified; (third row) Walter Blackmore, John Bath, Bessie Gorham, Sherman Robinnet, ? Blackburn, ? Tracy, Zoe Sedman, Miss McCarty, and Forest Kester; (fourth row) Mary Kyle, Homer Rudic, Gertrude Hager, Allen Thompson, Louella Lucas, and George Kester. (Courtesy of Greene County Historical Society.)

Class of 1901.

1. Charles Clarke, Electrical Engineer, 1010 Ridgway Ave., Chicago, Ill.
2. Charles Fulkerson, Physical Instructor, Joliet, Ill.
3. Fleming Watt, Creamery, City.
4. Louise Broadstone, Mrs. John Dillencourt, 2019 Oakland Ave., Minneapolis, Minn.
5. Mae Burdg, Cartersville, Ga.
6. Ethel Evans, Mrs. George Hamilton, 338 E. Jefferson St., Springfield, O.
7. Mary Harper, Teacher in Spring Valley, near City.
8. Lena Hetsel, near City.
9. Nellie Johnson, near City.
10. Gertrude Labron, Mrs. Wilbur Mills, 925 Chicago Ave., Minneapolis, Minn.
11. Fay Ledbetter, Stenographer, City.
12. Anna Linkhart, Chief Operator, Bell Telephone Co., City.
13. Euretta Meridith, Teacher, Springfield, O.
14. Alice Marshall, Mrs. Carl Downing, City.
15. Julia McCormick, Proof-Reader, Xenia Gazette, City.
16. Edna McClellan, Mrs. Ralph Ferguson, near City.
17. Olive McConnel, Teacher, City.
18. Margaret McConnel, Teacher in country near City.
19. Bertha Patterson, Mrs. Earnest Hutchison, near City.
20. Florence Schnebley, Teacher in country, City.
21. Florence Wright, Mrs. Ralph Neeld, City.
22. Clara Dillingham, Mrs. Geo. Sheets, City.

This extract from the Annual Report of the Xenia Public Schools, published in 1909, lists some of the students from the class of 1901 who wrote their names for the time capsule. It gives an interesting glimpse of how their lives were progressing. (Courtesy of Greene County Room, Greene County Public Library.)

Class of 1901.

1. James Love, Medical Student, Meharry Medical College, Nashville, Tenn.
2. Hermann Messenger, City.
3. Joel Miles, Barber, Pueblo, Colo.
4. Lucy Butler, Mrs. Louis Harding, City.
5. Clara Maxwell, Mrs. Algernon A. Owens, Detroit, Mich.
6. Rosa McCann, Dressmaker, City.
7. Fannie Saunders, Mrs. Charles Galloway, City.

The 1909 Annual Report of the Xenia Public Schools also lists the progress of the Class of 1901 from the East Main Street High School for African-American students, included in Superintendent Cox's report for the time capsule. (Courtesy of Greene County Room, Greene County Public Library.)

The Ohio Soldiers' and Sailors' Orphans' Home (OS&SO Home) provided housing and schooling for almost 1,000 children of deceased servicemen. The children received education through high school and, from age 14 on, they were required to learn a trade. (Courtesy of Greene County Archives—Time Capsule Document.)

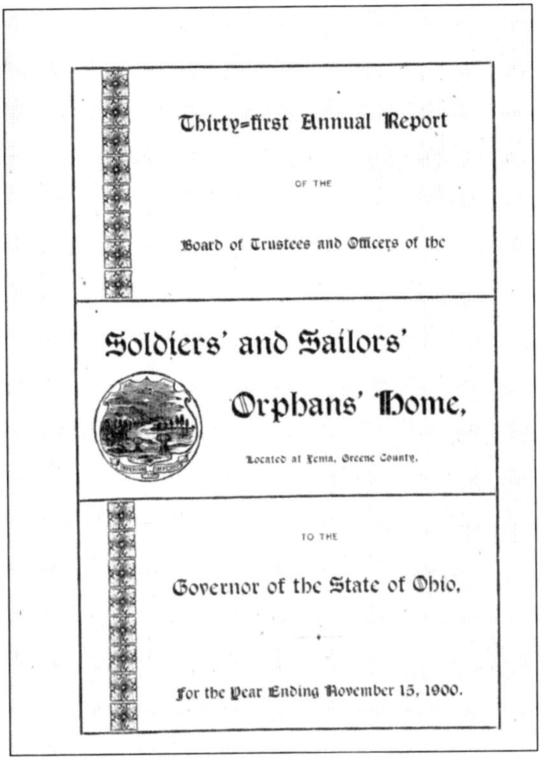

Thirty-first Annual Report

OF THE

Board of Trustees and Officers of the

Soldiers' and Sailors' Orphans' Home,

Located at Xenia, Greene County,

TO THE

Governor of the State of Ohio,

For the Year Ending November 15, 1900.

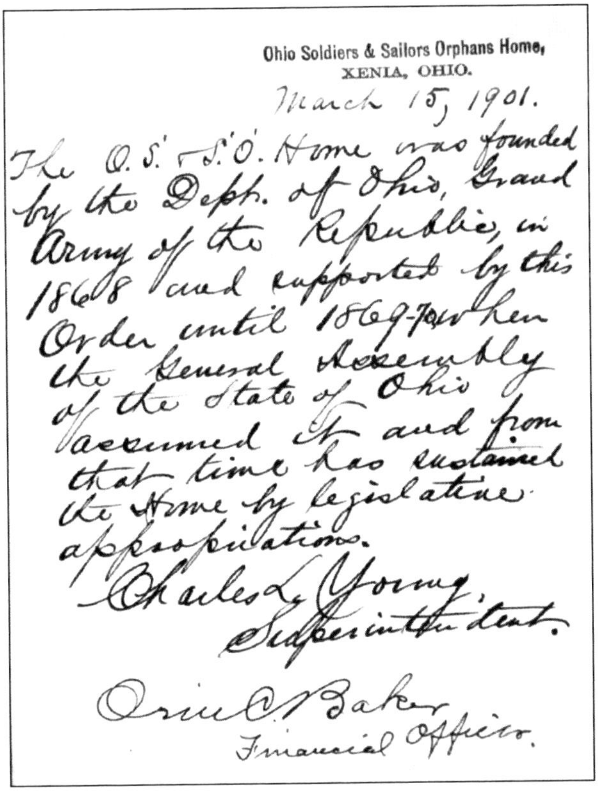

Ohio Soldiers & Sailors Orphans Home,
XENIA, OHIO.

March 15, 1901.

The O.S.' & S.'O. Home was founded by the Dept. of Ohio, Grand Army of the Republic, in 1868 and supported by this Order until 1869-70 when the General Assembly of the State of Ohio assumed it and from that time has sustained the Home by legislative appropriations.

Charles L. Young,
Superintendent.

Orin A. Baker
Financial Officer.

This shows the inscription inside the Home's 1900 Annual Report. (Courtesy of Greene County Archives—Time Capsule Document.)

LOCATION AND DESCRIPTION OF FARM AND BUILDINGS.

The Home farm consists of 296 21-100 acres, is situated one mile south of east of Xenia, and commands a view of a portion of the town. The site is healthful and admirably adapted to its present purposes.

The farm lies between the Wilmington and Xenia turnpikes on the north, and the Burlington turnpike on the west, thus giving easy access to the surrounding country. The Dayton and Ironton branch of the C. H. & D. Railway runs within fifty feet of the premises on the north. The Pennsylvania Lines (Little Miami) railroad depot is within three-quarters of a mile of the Home buildings.

The land is at present fairly productive of all kinds of crops. With our present sewerage system, by which we are enabled to utilize the sewage, and the free use of the manures made on the premises, the land is improving.

The buildings consist of an administration building, with a large dining room attached, the two forming an Egyptian cross; twenty single cottages, and six double cottages—ten single cottages on the west side of the administration building, and ten single and six double cottages on the east side; two schoolhouses, chapel, hospital and four cottage hospitals, laundry, industrial buildings, pump house, engine rooms, electrical power house, mechanical building, gas house, greenhouses, slaughterhouse and all necessary farm buildings.

The administration and single cottage buildings are placed in a straight line running nearly due east and west, facing a few degrees east of north, making a front of nearly 1,500 feet. Five double cottages are placed in a circular line fronting west, at the east extremity of the front of the single cottages. The other double cottage is south of the east line of old cottages.

All the buildings are substantial brick structures, except the farm buildings, greenhouse, slaughterhouse, storehouse, and four hospital cottages.

The administration building has three stories, and is occuppied by the officers and teachers; the cottages are two stories high, and are arranged to accommodate about twenty-five children in the single cottages and sixty children in the double cottages. One of the schoolhouses is there stories high, and will accommodate nearly 700 children; the other schoolhouse has eleven schoolrooms (in two of which are conducted the schools of domestic economy. The chapel has a seating capacity of 1,200. The hospital is well arranged for the sick.

The building annexed to the administration building known as the domestic building is two stories in height, with a basement occupied by the kitchen and bakery; the first story is the children's dining room with a seating capacity of nearly 1,000; the second story contains sleeping apartments for certain of the employes, and the linen rooms.

The administration, domestic, hospital and industrial buildings, and the cottages, are heated by steam. Gas, manufactured from coal, and also electric lights, are furnished to all the buildings. Water is supplied to all the buildings through the general pipes under the system known as the Wagner system of the National Water Supply Company The water supplied comes from subterranean reservoirs, and is pumped into the water tower, in the rear of the administration building, from which it flows by its pressure into all parts of the institution, and is of an excellent quality.

This page, also from the 1900 Annual Report, describes the beautiful site of the Orphans' Home. (Courtesy of Greene County Archives—Time Capsule Document.)

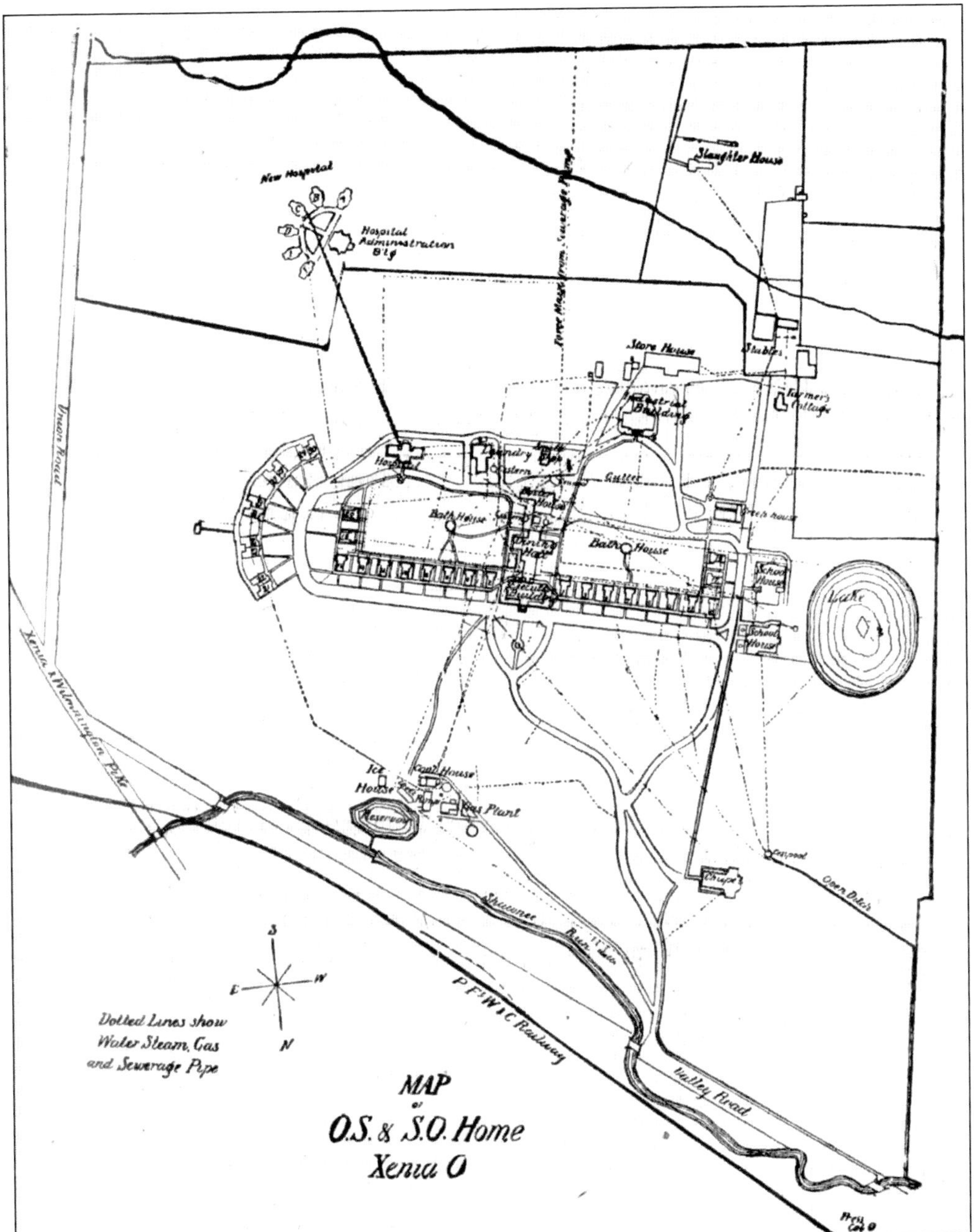

This map shows the layout of the OS&SO Home. (Courtesy of Greene County Archives—Time Capsule Document.)

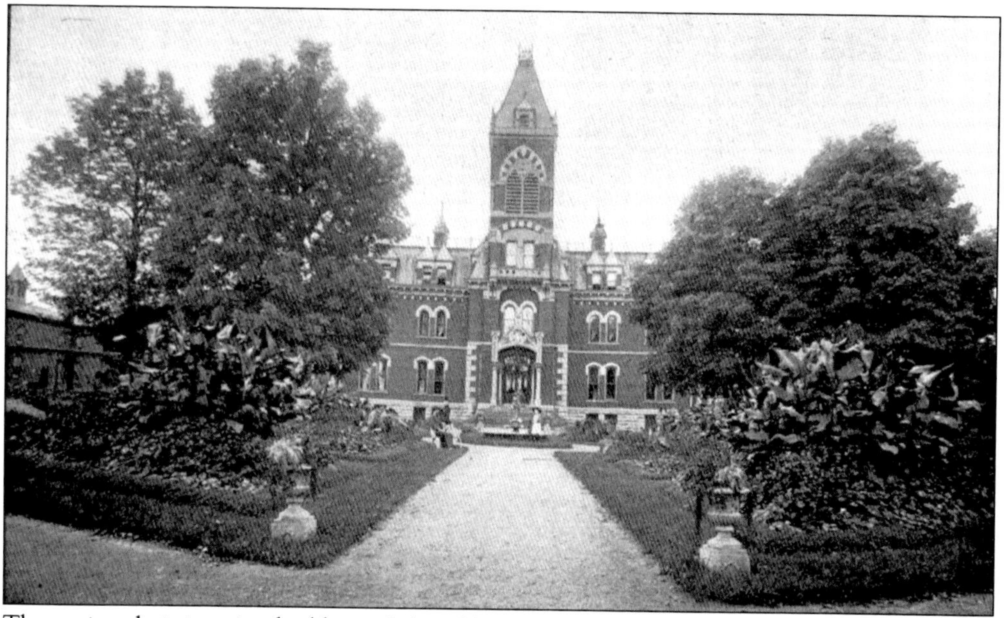

The main administrative building of the old orphanage is shown here. (Courtesy of Greene County Archives—Time Capsule Document.)

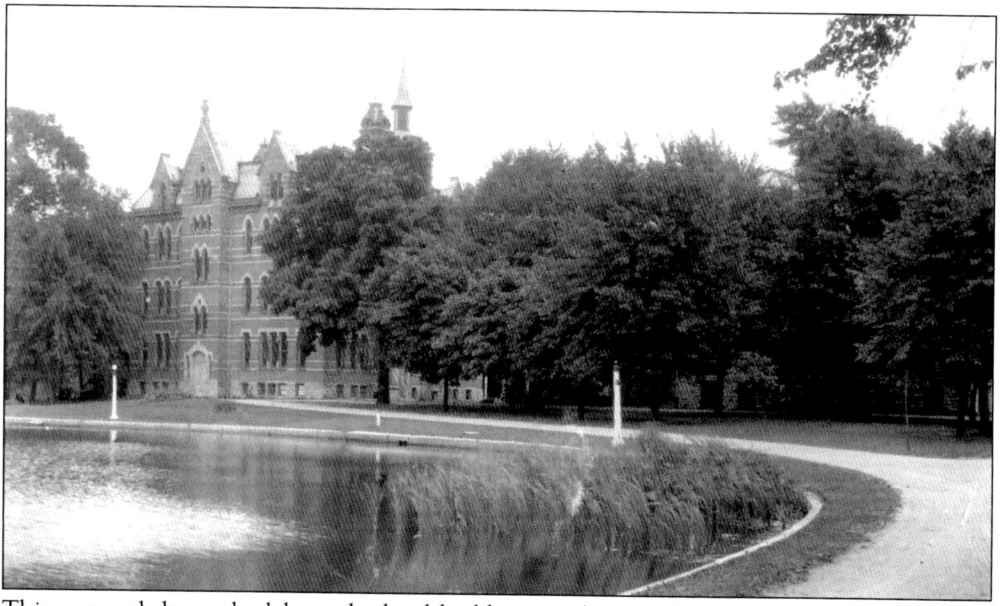

This postcard shows the lake and school buildings at the OS&SO Home. The lake was used for swimming and boating in the summer and for skating in the winter. (Courtesy of Greene County Room, Greene County Public Library.)

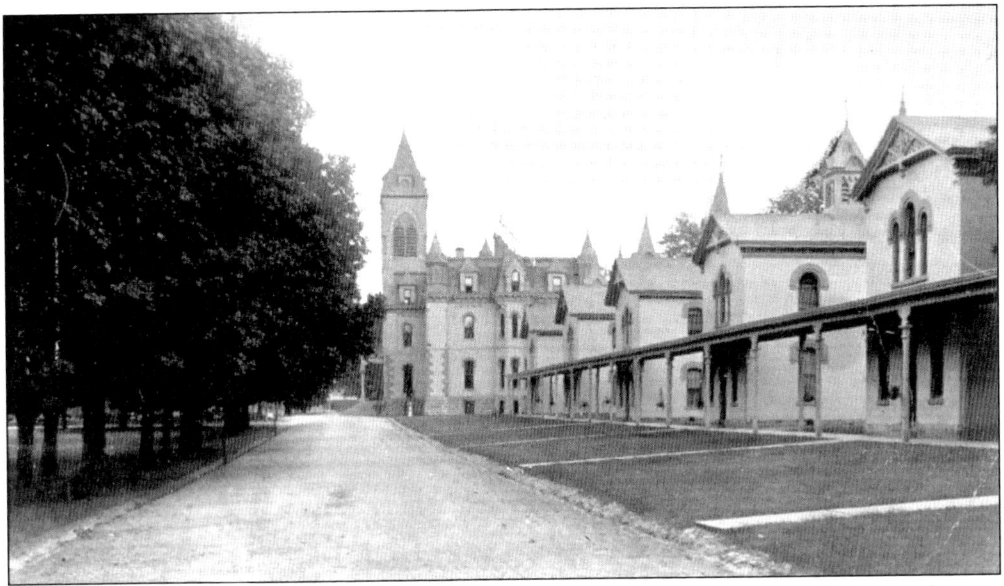

The children lived in cottages, some of which are shown here. (Courtesy of Greene County Room, Greene County Public Library.)

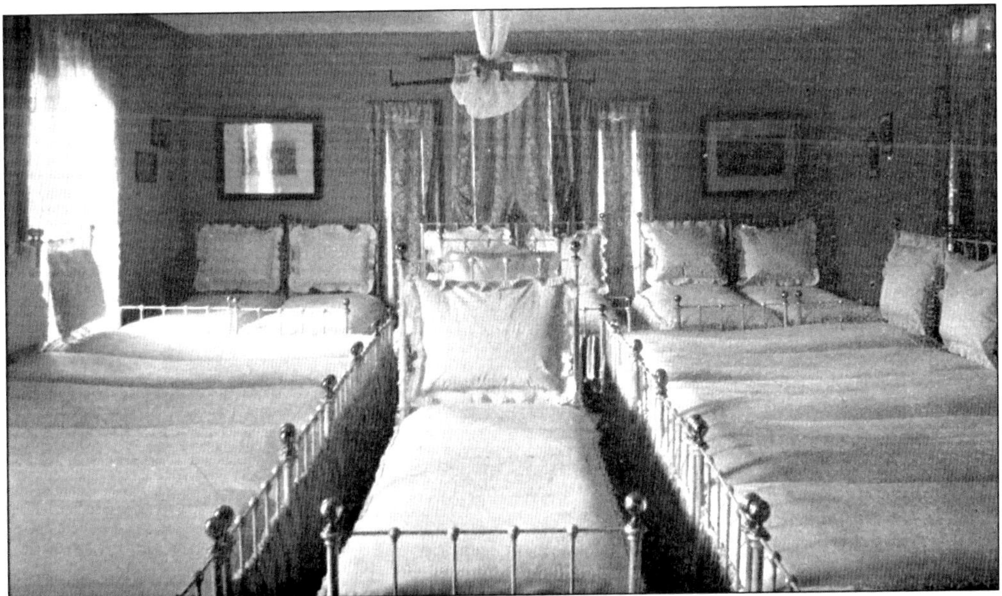

This interior shot shows a cottage dormitory room. (Courtesy of Greene County Archives—Time Capsule Document.)

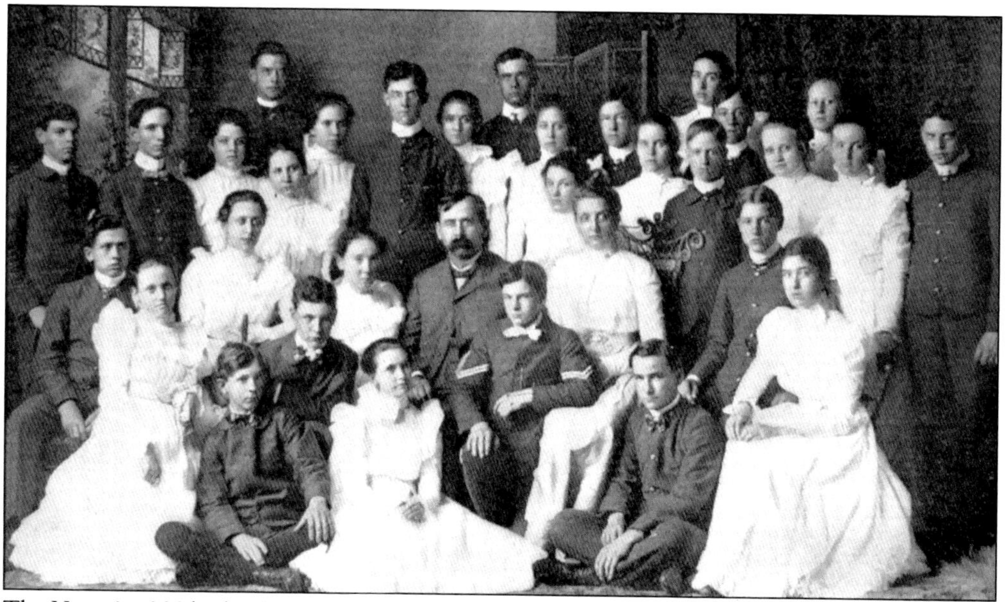

The Home's 1900 high school graduation class, from the annual report, shows Mr. T.A. Edwards, the superintendent of the schools in the center of the photograph, with teacher Miss Viola Sypherd next to him on the right. (Courtesy of Greene County Archives—Time Capsule Document, and names courtesy of the Association of Ex-Pupils, Ohio Soldiers' and Sailors' Orphans' Home.)

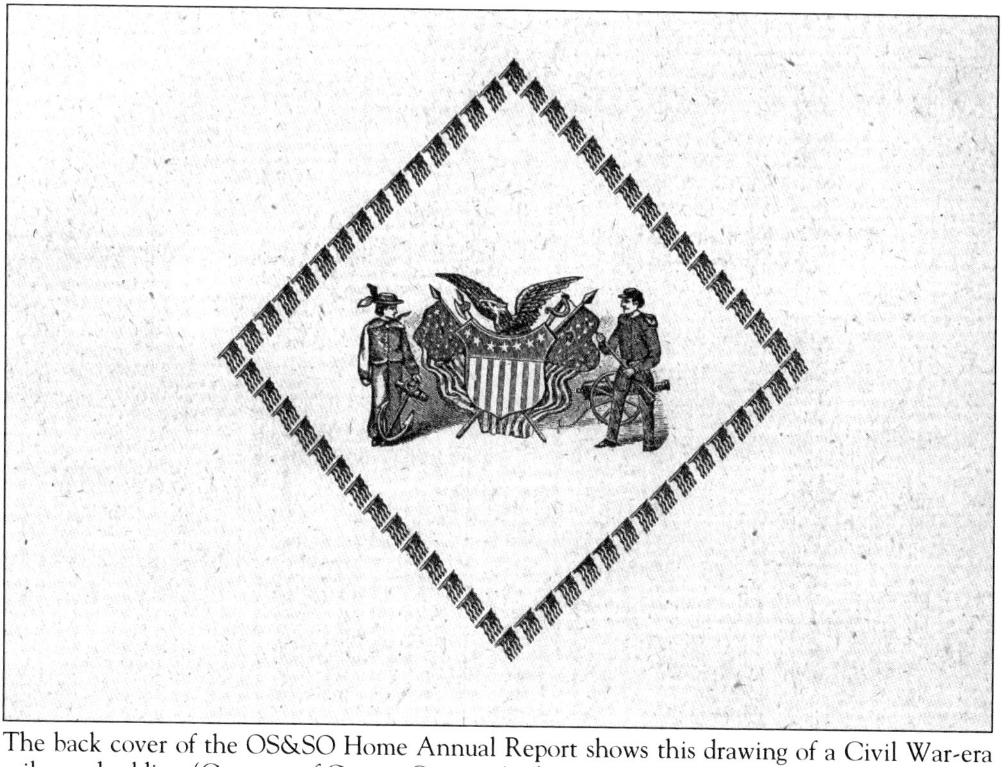

The back cover of the OS&SO Home Annual Report shows this drawing of a Civil War-era sailor and soldier. (Courtesy of Greene County Archives—Time Capsule Document.)

The 1899–1900 catalogue for Antioch College in Yellow Springs was deposited in the time capsule. The college was founded in 1852, and its first president was the great Unitarian educational innovator and reformer, Horace Mann. Antioch College was non-sectarian and co-educational, with strong humanistic values. (Courtesy of Greene County Archives—Time Capsule Document.)

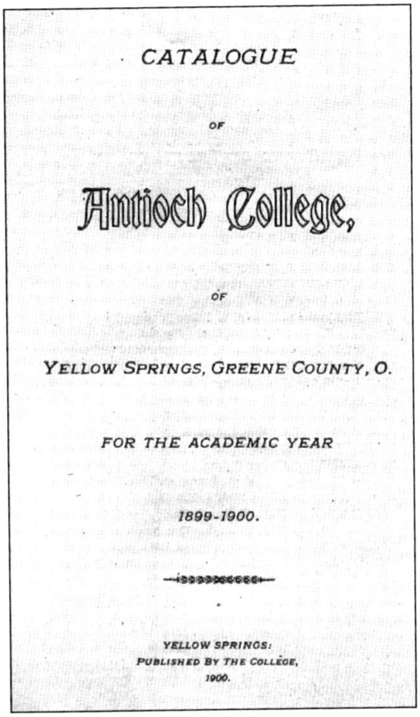

CATALOGUE

OF

Antioch College,

OF

YELLOW SPRINGS, GREENE COUNTY, O.

FOR THE ACADEMIC YEAR

1899-1900.

YELLOW SPRINGS:
PUBLISHED BY THE COLLEGE,
1900.

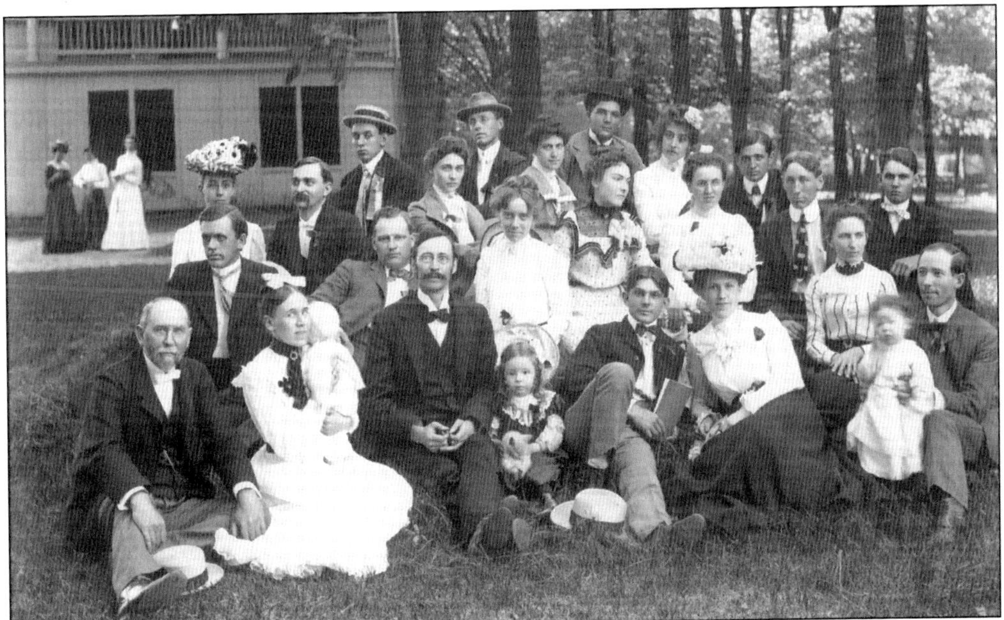

President of Antioch College, William Allen Bell, who served from 1899 to 1902, is shown seated in the bottom left of this photograph, taken on the lawn in front of the women's dormitory, North Hall, in June 1902. President Bell was the first Antioch graduate to become president of the college. Next to him in the photograph are Jessie Brown, instructor of music, and her husband, George S. Brown, professor of Latin language and literature, and musical director of the college, with their two children. Several of the students pictured are named in the 1899–1900 catalogue. (Courtesy of Antiochiana, Antioch College.)

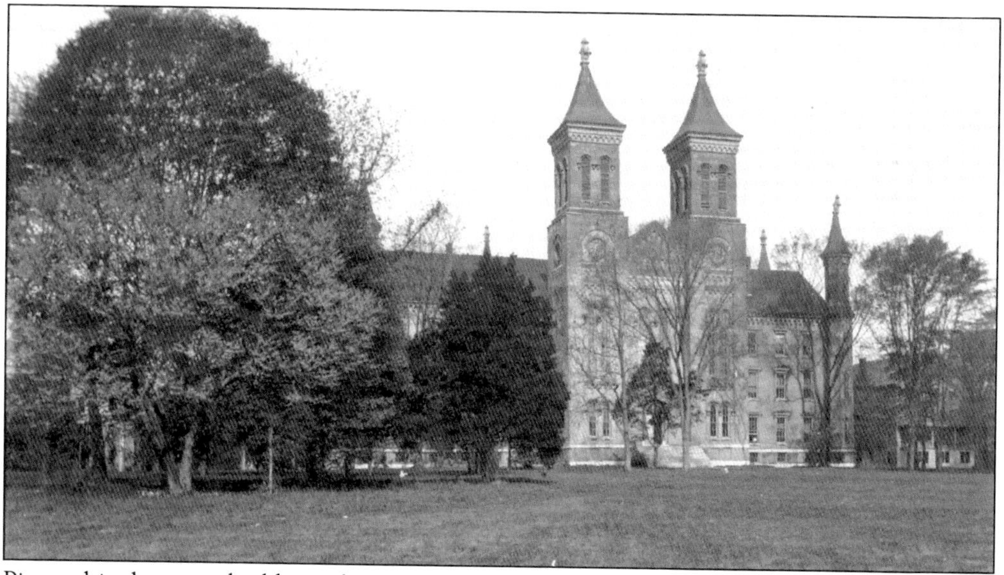

Pictured is the main building of Antioch College from the front. (Courtesy of Antiochiana, Antioch College.)

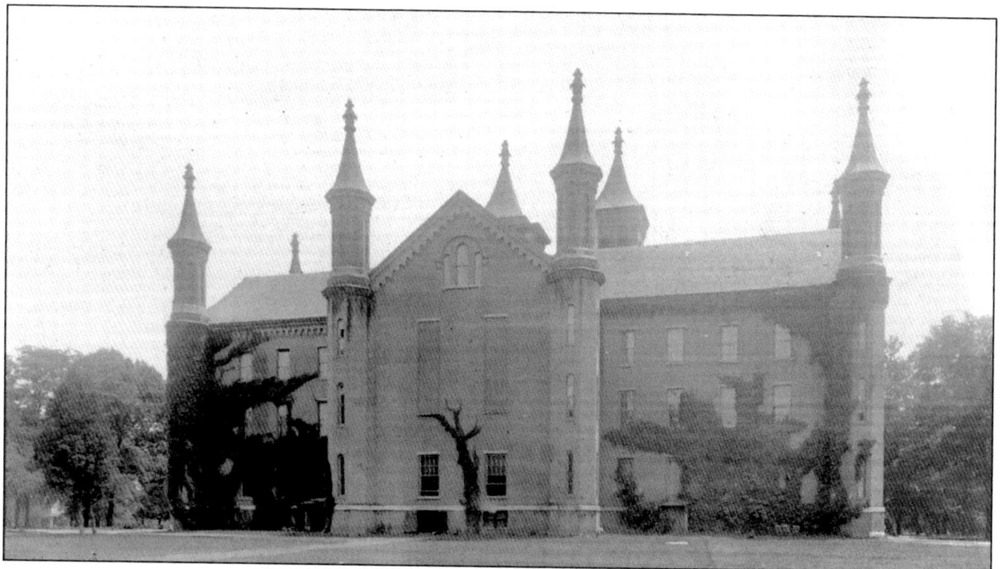

Pictured is the main building of Antioch College from the rear. (Courtesy of Greene County Room, Greene County Public Library.)

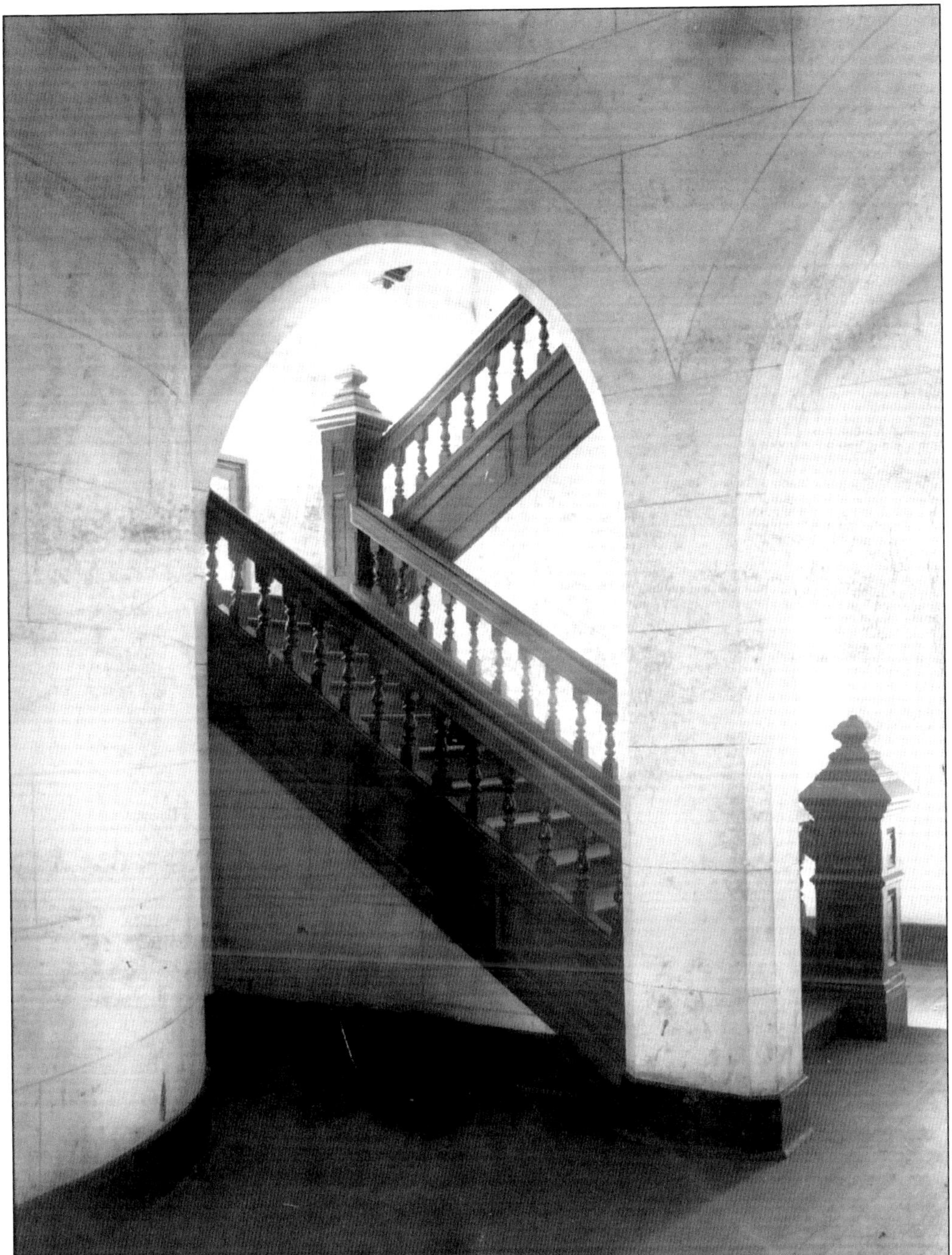

This shows the staircase in the main building. (Courtesy of Antiochiana, Antioch College.)

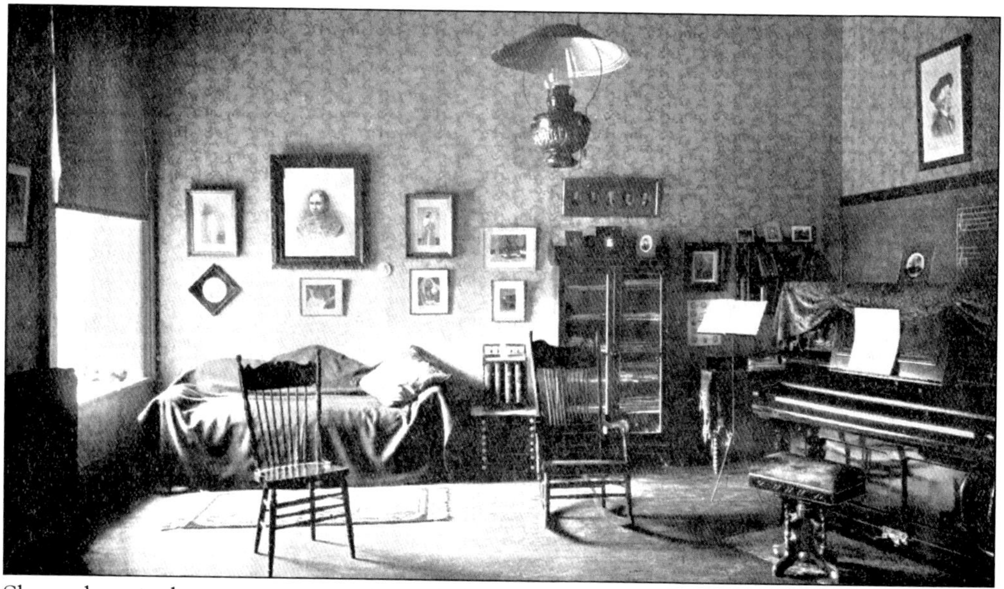

Shown here is the music room at Antioch College. (Courtesy of Greene County Archives—Time Capsule Document.)

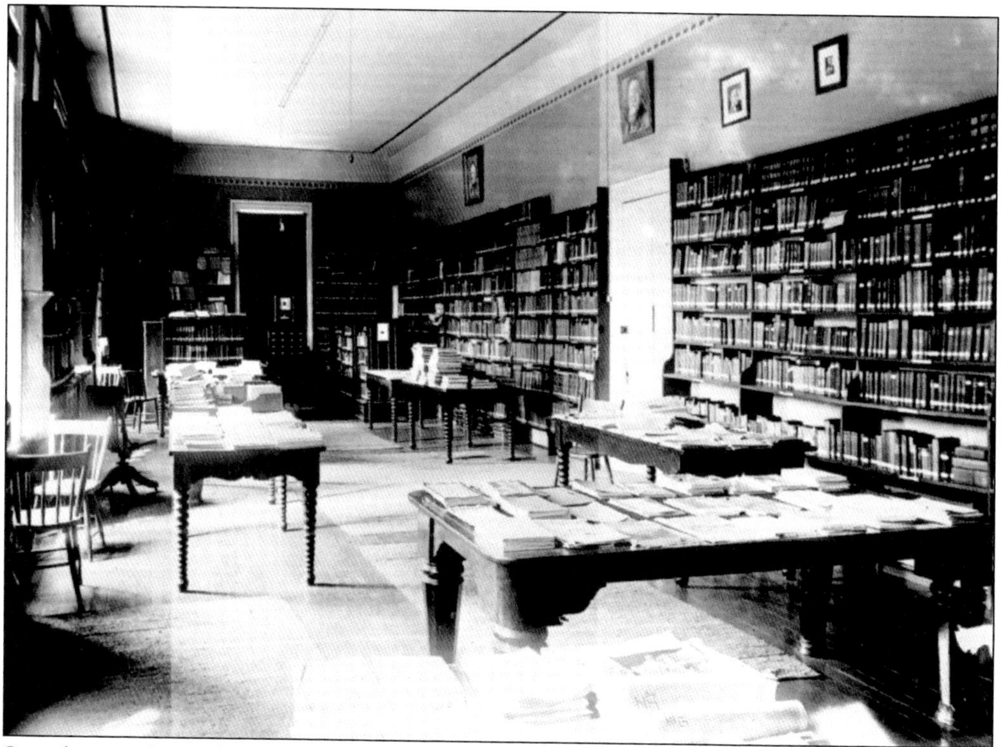

Seen here is Antioch's library *c.* 1900. Some of this furniture still exists in the Antiochiana room. (Courtesy of Antiochiana, Antioch College.)

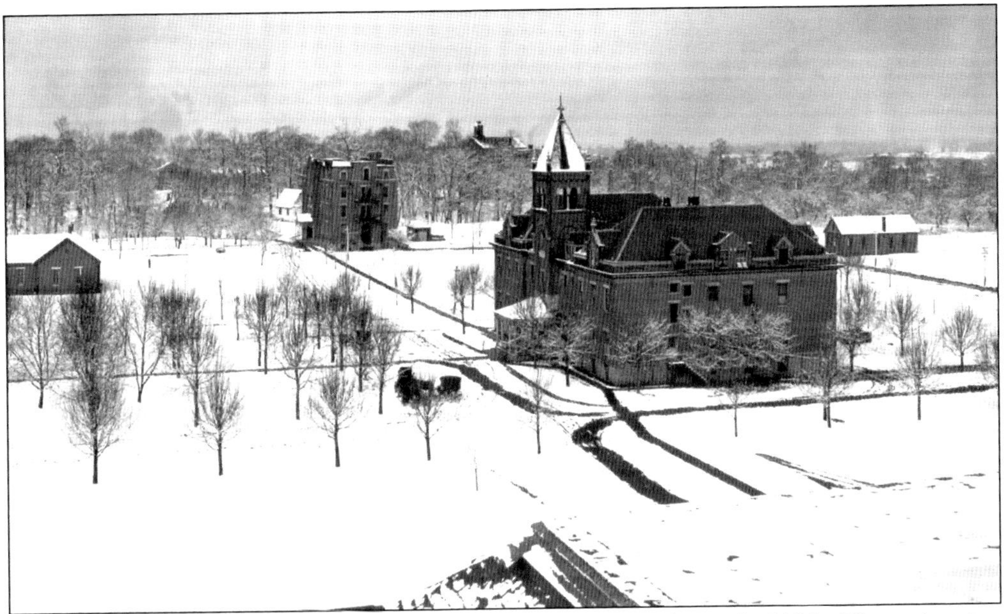

This winter scene shows Wilberforce University's campus in the early 1900s. The university, named for 18th century English abolitionist, William Wilberforce, was founded in 1856. It was the first institution of higher education in the country owned and operated by African Americans. The university's first students were mainly the children of southern planters, and the 1899–1900 catalogue declares, "that there shall never be any distinction among trustees, faculty, or students, on account of race or color." In this photograph, the Armory is shown on the left, and O'Neill Hall, which housed the classes of the Combined Normal Department, is in the middle rear of the picture. It was built in 1890. Arnett Hall, on the right, was under construction in 1901. (Courtesy of Central State University Archives.)

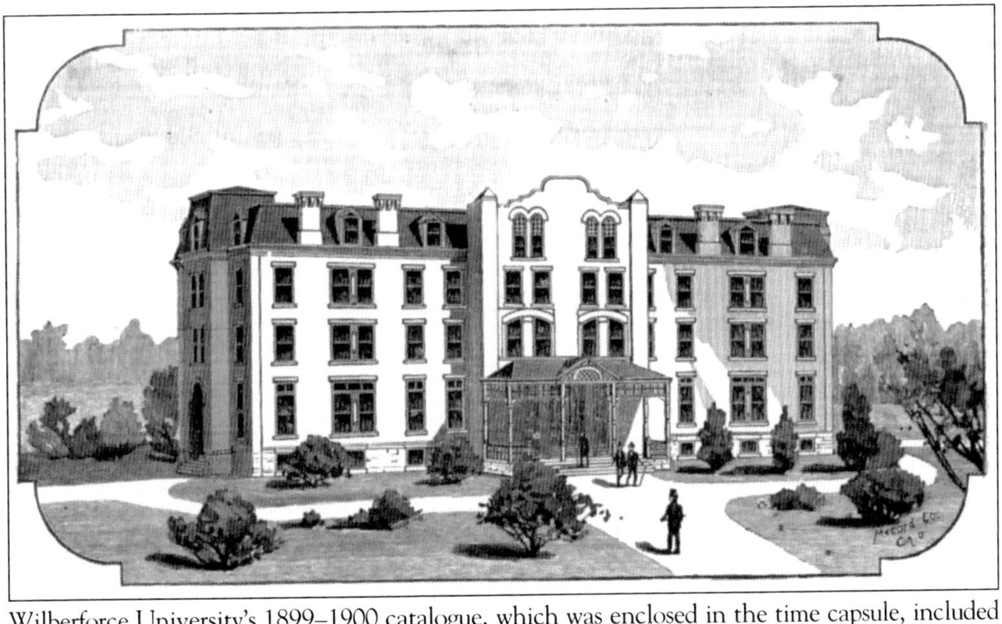

Wilberforce University's 1899–1900 catalogue, which was enclosed in the time capsule, included this picture of O'Neill Hall. (Courtesy of Greene County Archives—Time Capsule Document.)

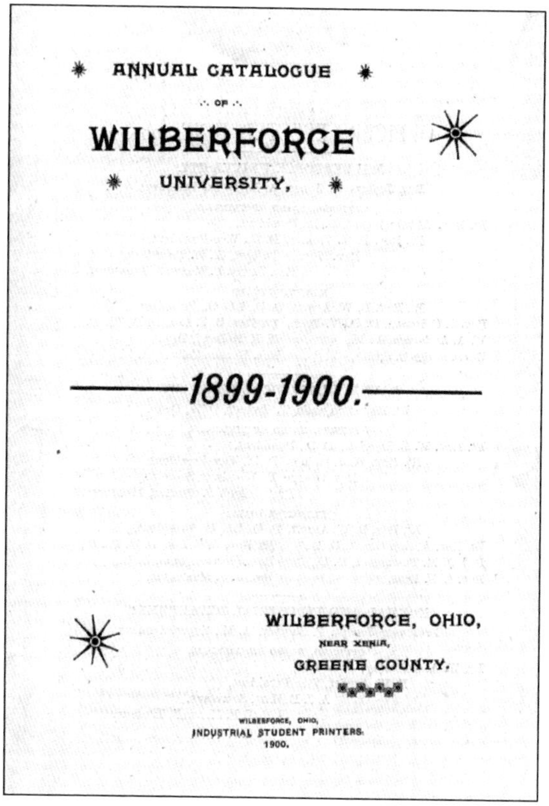
ANNUAL CATALOGUE

OF

WILBERFORCE

UNIVERSITY,

1899-1900.

WILBERFORCE, OHIO,

NEAR XENIA,

GREENE COUNTY.

WILBERFORCE, OHIO,

INDUSTRIAL STUDENT PRINTERS.

1900.

Here is the title page from the 1899–1900 catalogue for Wilberforce University. (Courtesy of Greene County Archives—Time Capsule Document.)

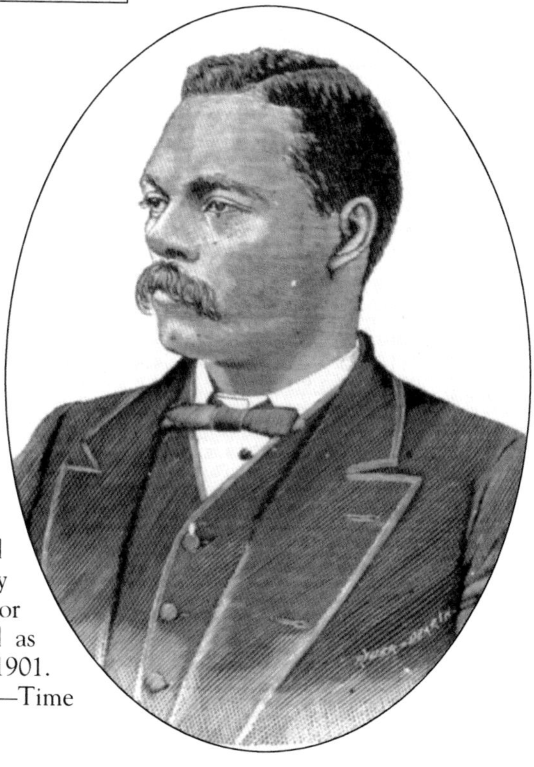

The Rev. Joshua H. Jones was elected president of Wilberforce University in June of 1900, succeeding Professor Samuel T. Mitchell, who had retired as president in 1900 and died in April of 1901. (Courtesy of Greene County Archives—Time Capsule Document.)

The Combined Normal and Industrial Department of Wilberforce University was founded in 1887 to provide vocational skills and teacher training. This annual report was enclosed in the time capsule. The Normal and Industrial Department, by then known as the State of Ohio's College of Education and Industrial Arts, separated from Wilberforce University in the 1940s to become Central State University. (Courtesy of Greene County Archives—Time Capsule Document.)

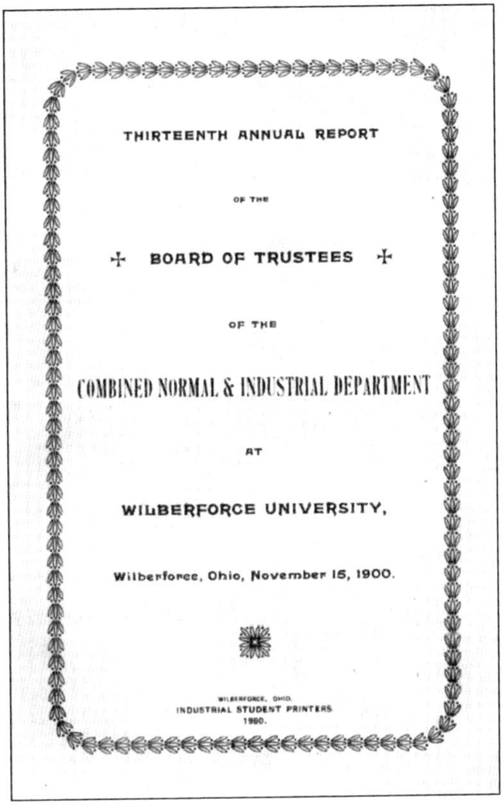
THIRTEENTH ANNUAL REPORT

OF THE

BOARD OF TRUSTEES

OF THE

COMBINED NORMAL & INDUSTRIAL DEPARTMENT

AT

WILBERFORCE UNIVERSITY,

Wilberforce, Ohio, November 15, 1900.

WILBERFORCE, OHIO.
INDUSTRIAL STUDENT PRINTERS
1900.

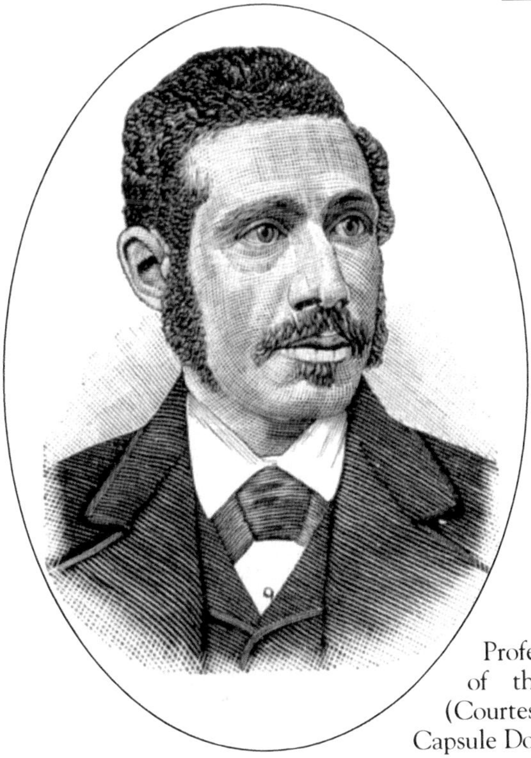

Professor Joseph Shorter served as superintendent of the Normal and Industrial Department. (Courtesy of Greene County Archives—Time Capsule Document.)

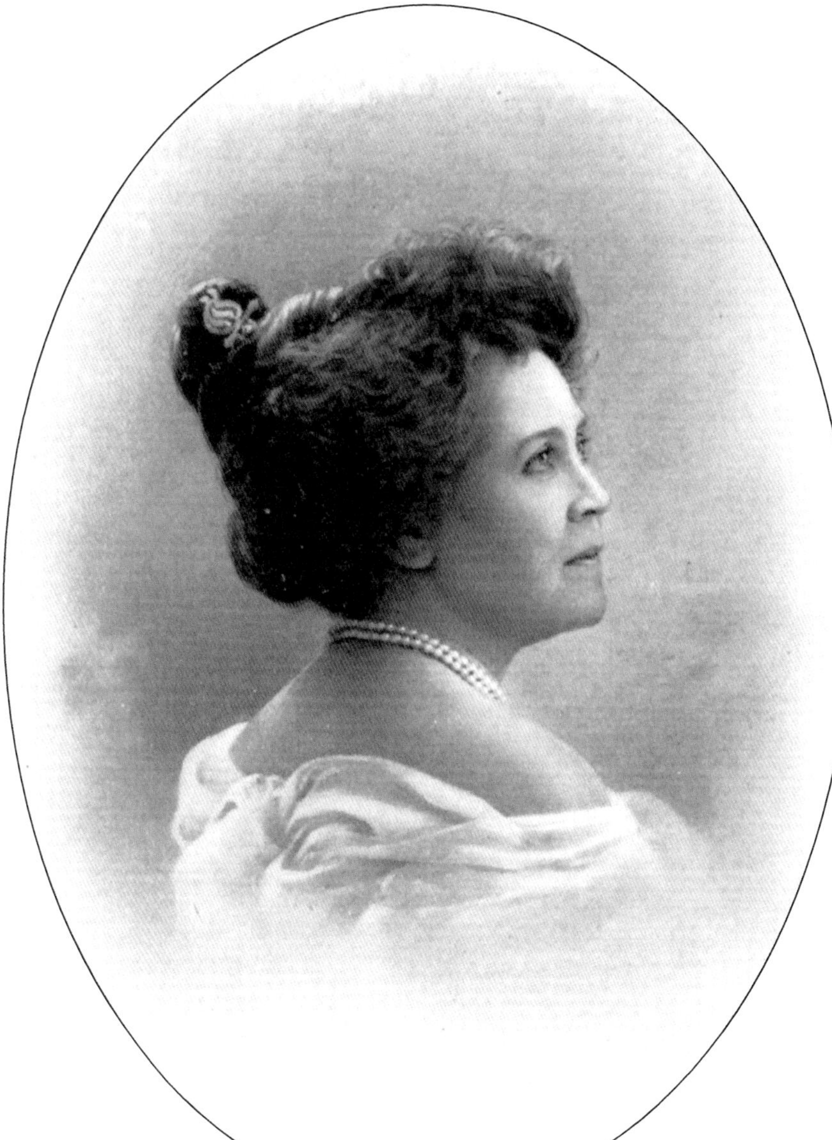

The catalogue lists one of Wilberforce University's most famous graduates, elocutionist Hallie Q. Brown. She was born in the 1840s, a daughter of former slaves, and taught elocution at Wilberforce University in the 1890s. A famous public speaker and civil rights advocate, she spent several years lecturing in Europe and met Queen Victoria in England. She later returned to Wilberforce to resume teaching there and become a member of the board of trustees. She lived until 1949. (Courtesy of Greene County Room, Greene County Public Library, Robinson's *History of Greene County, Ohio*, 1902.)

A graduate of the class of 1890, Frances A. Lee remained to teach at Wilberforce University. (Courtesy of Payne Theological Seminary.)

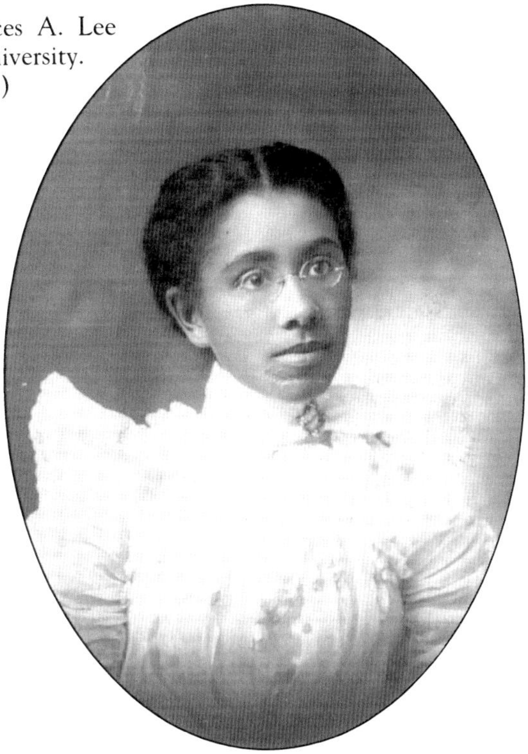

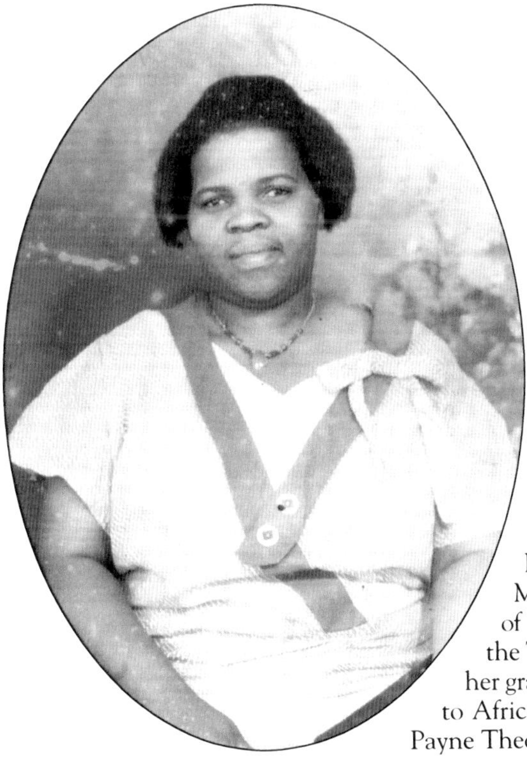

A student of the Normal and Industrial Department Sewing Course, Charlotte Manye, listed in the 1899–1900 catalogue of Wilberforce University, was a native of the Transvaal Republic, South Africa. After her graduation from Wilberforce, she returned to Africa to become a missionary. (Courtesy of Payne Theological Seminary.)

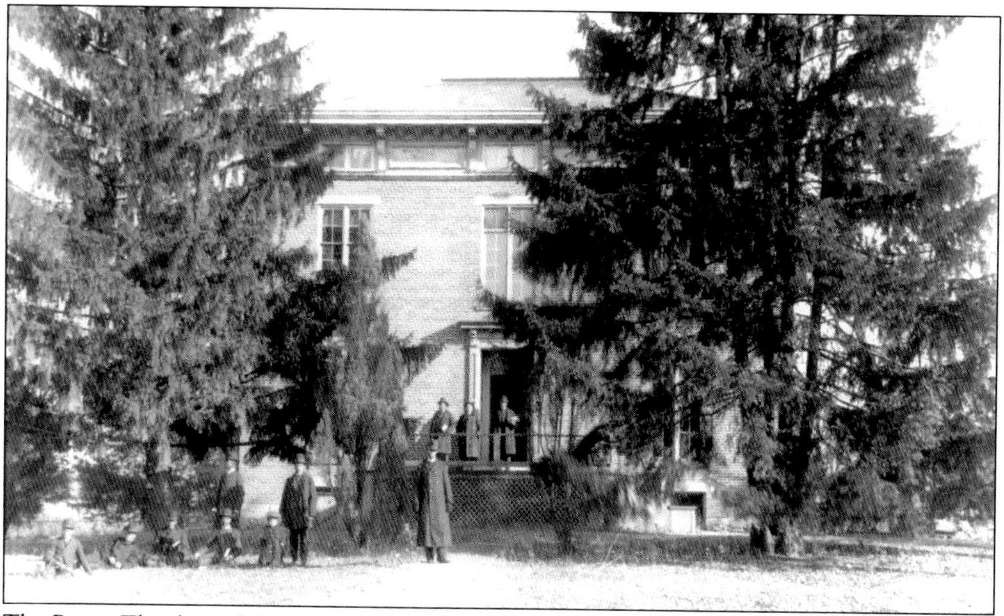

The Payne Theological Seminary at Wilberforce University was incorporated in 1894. Named for the African Methodist Episcopal bishop and prior president of the university, Daniel Payne, the seminary was housed in this building, Mitchell Hall. Mitchell Hall was purchased from the Rev. J.G. Mitchell and his wife. Dr. Mitchell had been one of the founders of Wilberforce University and a previous dean of the seminary. (Courtesy of Wilberforce University Library.)

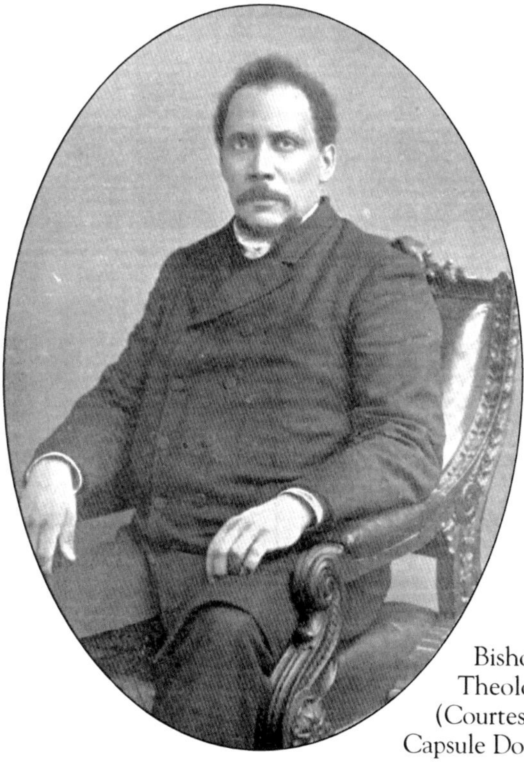

Bishop Benjamin Tanner became dean of Payne Theological Seminary after Dr. Mitchell's death. (Courtesy of Greene County Archives—Time Capsule Document.)

Four

ORGANIZATIONS

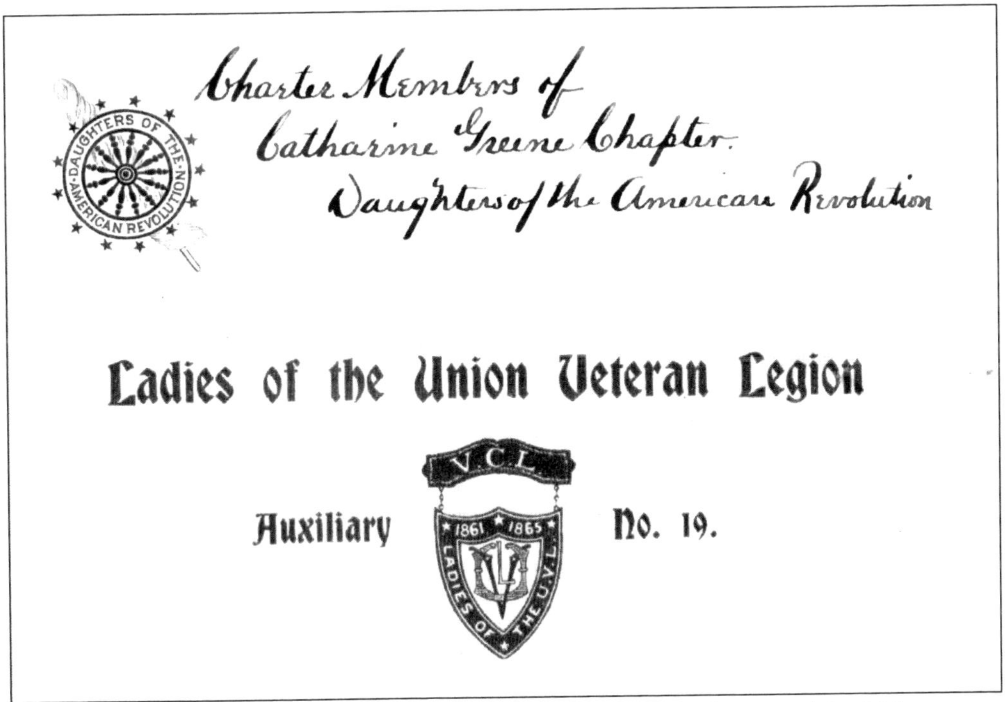

Charter Members of
Catharine Greene Chapter.
Daughters of the American Revolution

Ladies of the Union Veteran Legion

Auxiliary No. 19.

Fraternal and service organizations were prevalent in America at the turn of the 20th century. Most refused admittance to women, who formed their own ladies' auxiliary groups. The charter members of the Catherine Greene Chapter of the Daughters of the American Revolution, which was formed in 1894, and the elected officers and current members of the Ladies of the Union Veteran Legion are listed in these documents, which were included in the time capsule. (Courtesy of Greene County Archives—Time Capsule Document.)

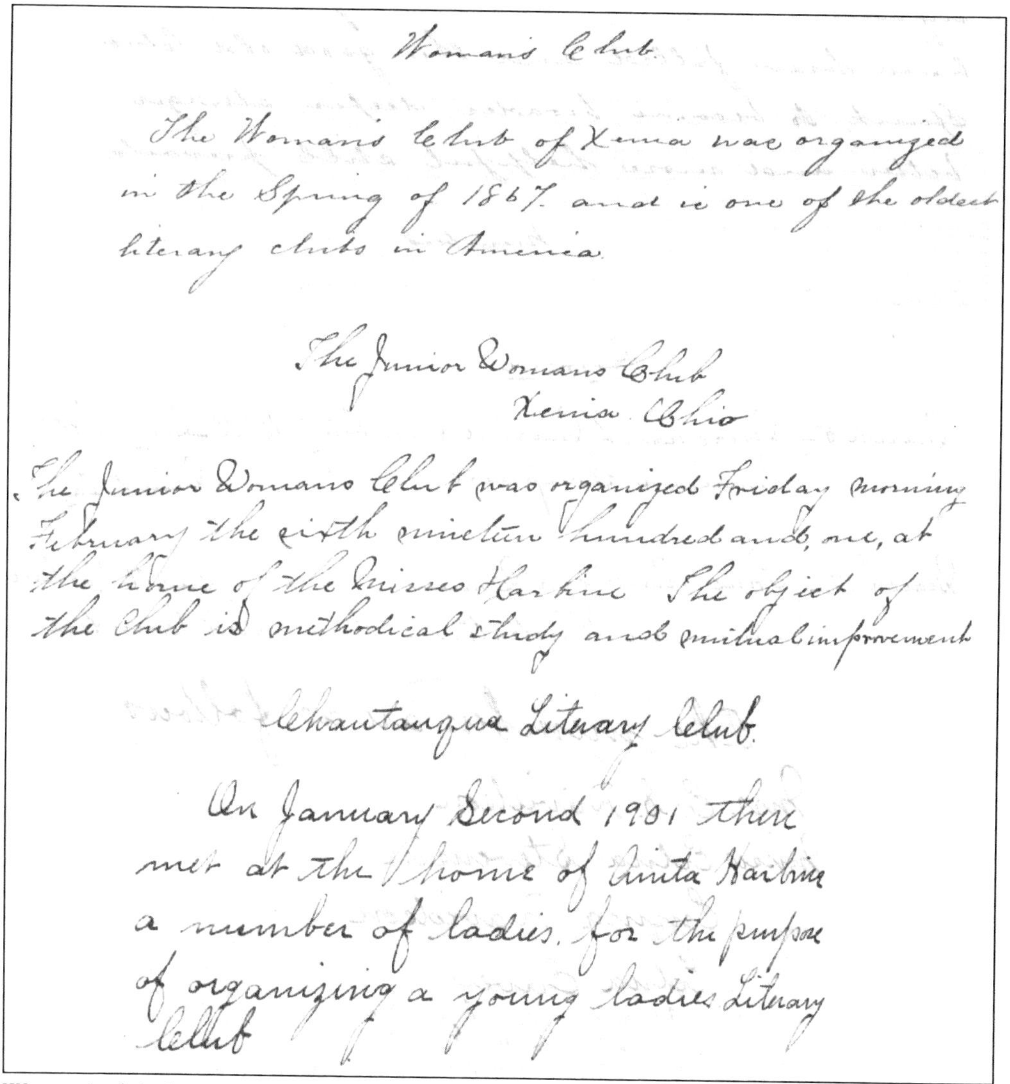
Womans Club

The Womans Club of Xenia was organized in the Spring of 1867 and is one of the oldest literary clubs in America.

The Junior Womans Club
Xenia Ohio

The Junior Womans Club was organized Friday morning February the sixth nineteen hundred and one, at the home of the Misses Harbine The object of the Club is methodical study and mutual improvement

Chautauqua Literary Club.

On January Second 1901 there met at the home of Anita Harbine a number of ladies, for the purpose of organizing a young ladies Literary Club

Women's clubs became increasingly popular at this time, as women with the free time to do so met for intellectual self-improvement. These three literary clubs submitted documents for the time capsule. The Women's Club was founded in 1867, and is said to be the first club founded exclusively for women in the United States. It still meets regularly in Xenia. The other two were organized later and held lively discussion groups on political issues and literature. (Courtesy of Greene County Archives—Time Capsule Document.)

Members Xenia Library Association.

		RETIRED MEMBERS:
*Miss Clara Allen,	Miss Clara Kinney,	*Miss Emma C. King,
Mrs. Louie M. Allison,	Miss Mary Little,	Mrs. Clara M. Littell,
*Miss Elizabeth Ewing,	*Miss Anna M. MacCracken,	*Miss Sallie McDowell,
Mrs. Elizabeth T. Flynn,	Mrs. Lestra K. MacMillen,	*Miss Jennie Morris,
*Miss Belle Gatch,	Miss Helen Moorehead,	*Mrs. Ella K. Nichols,
Mrs. Sarah Harbine,	Mrs. Flora Munger,	
*Miss Isadora F. King,	Miss Mary Munger,	
Mrs. Mary C. Kinney,	Mrs. Sarah Myers,	* Charter members.

Woman's Department.

THE HISTORY OF THE XENIA LIBRARY ASSOCIATION.

FIFTY years ago there existed in Xenia an organization known as "The Lyceum." This organization was the center of social and intellectual life, and to it is to be credited the beginning of Xenia's first library. Many years ago the Lyceum ceased to exist, but the books collected formed the nucleus of a library which later passed into the hands of the Y. M. C. A. Many valuable additions were made, but, after a precarious existence of several years, the library was virtually closed. Its re-opening was the outgrowth of the organization of a reading club of eight ladies, formed in 1878. Feeling the need of suitable books, this club resolved itself into "The Young Woman's Library Association," and made the following appeal to the Library Board:

"Recognizing the need of a public library in Xenia, 'The Young Woman's Library Association' has been organized. We have no room, no books, no money. We believe we have energy and perseverence. We hope to have success. Our object in coming to you is to ask the loan of your room, your furniture, your books, in consideration whereof we pledge ourselves to keep the library open at least once a week; to be responsible for the safe keeping of the books; to add new books to the library as we shall be able, such books to be the property of 'The Young Woman's Library Association.'" A favorable response was received, the inventory of possessions thus acquired being 1,100 volumes (in broken sets) with an average circulation of four volumes a week to the seven ticket holders.

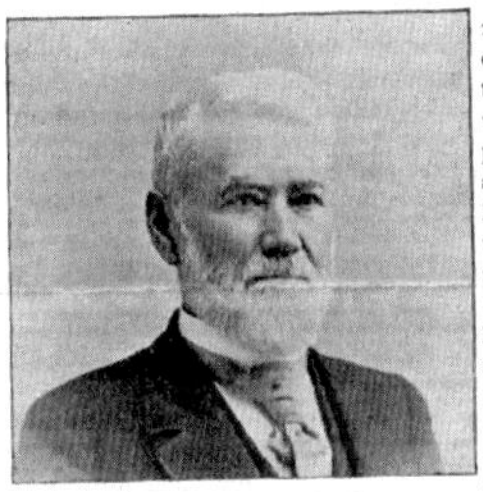

August 20th, 1878, "The Young Woman's Library Association" was formally organized by the election of officers and the adoption of a constitution. Three weeks later the library was opened to the public, the new association having found a generous friend in Mr. Eli Millen, who kindly continued the use of the library room free of rent. An empty treasury necessitated small beginnings, but, with the members of the Association acting as librarians, and the library open but one afternoon a week, the record at the close of the year was 117 new books, with an average circulation of 44 a week to 137 ticket holders. The income for the year was derived from the sale of tickets and proceeds of an entertainment given in City Hall, December 5th, entitled "An Evening With Dickens." Exclusive of $19.20 expended in fitting up the room, the entire outlay for the year was $7.30. $158.49 had been invested in new books, and the Association entered upon its second year with a balance in the treasury. Who shall say that the interests of the Library were not well conserved?

In November, 1881, the Association became an incorporated body and the name was changed to the "Xenia Library Association." It being the purpose of the Association not to call upon the citizens for financial aid until it could be fully demonstrated that the library had become a successful and well-established institution, the policy of rigid economy was continued for seven years, the members of the Association continuing to give their services as librarians, and the income being derived from sale of tickets and proceeds of entertainments given by the ladies, supplemented by several timely gifts from Mr. Millen and other citizens.

But in 1885 it was found that, in order to meet the growing demand for books, the library must be kept open a part of each day, a librarian must be employed, and additional funds must be secured. Then, at last, the Assciation felt itself justified, after seven years of growing prosperity, in making an appeal to the public for financial aid. A subscription was made, and the citizens of Xenia have continued to manifest their confidence and appreciation by making a similar subscription each succeeding year. In the year 1885, the Association was fortunate also in securing as librarian, Miss Etta McElwain, whose faithfulness and efficiency from that day to this have contributed much to the success of the library.

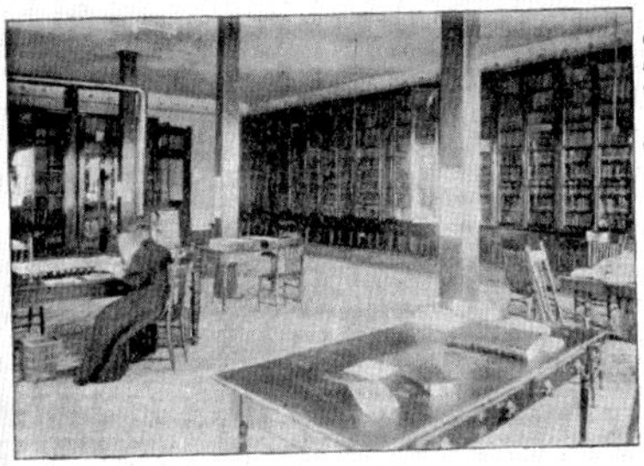

After ten years of very gradual, steady growth, the library was found to have outgrown its old quarters, 3,741 new books having been added; and, so, 1889, it was moved into the very pleasant large room still occupied, and for which the association has not failed to express its gratitude to Mr. Millen, from year to year. During the same year the reference department, which had grown to valuable proportions, was opened to the public.

In 1892 the work of cataloguing the library according to the Dewey system was done. This was also the work of a woman now at the head of the Department of Library Instruction at the Atheneum, Chicago, who paid the Xenia Association the compliment of pronouncing ours the best selected small library of which she had any knowledge. In January, 1865, a new departure was taken, and many of the citizens have found out only since the introduction of the Magazine department how delightful a reading room the library is. That the Association has "made haste slowly" is evidenced by the fact that important steps in advance have been taken only at intervals of three and four years. All the expenses incurred in these advanced movements have been met from special funds—largely from proceeds of entertainments given by the Association. All the running expenses are met from sale of tickets. All the contributions of citizens go to the purchase of books. October 1st, 1895, the Library Association entered on its nineteenth year, up to which time 5,559 books had been added to the library and 123,826 volumes had been given out. This is a result of which the founders and members of the Association feel justly proud—a result which cannot but give satisfaction to those who gave aid and encouragement to the Association in the beginning, and to all who have contributed to its success—a result which renders certain also the permanency of a library in our city.

CLARA ALLEN.

OFFICERS.—Miss Belle Gatch, President; Miss Clara Kinney, Vice President; Mrs. Flora B. Munger, Secretary and Treasurer.

Several of the same women whose names show up on the lists of club members were also members of the Library Association in Xenia. Until 1900, the library was supported by subscriptions, but then it became free to the public, supported by a city tax. Until the new Carnegie Library building was ready for use in 1906, the library was located on the second floor of the Millen Building, on the corner of Market and Greene Streets. The librarian was Miss Etta McElwain. The owner of the building, Eli Millen, provided the room and furniture free of charge. (Courtesy of Greene County Archives—Time Capsule Document.)

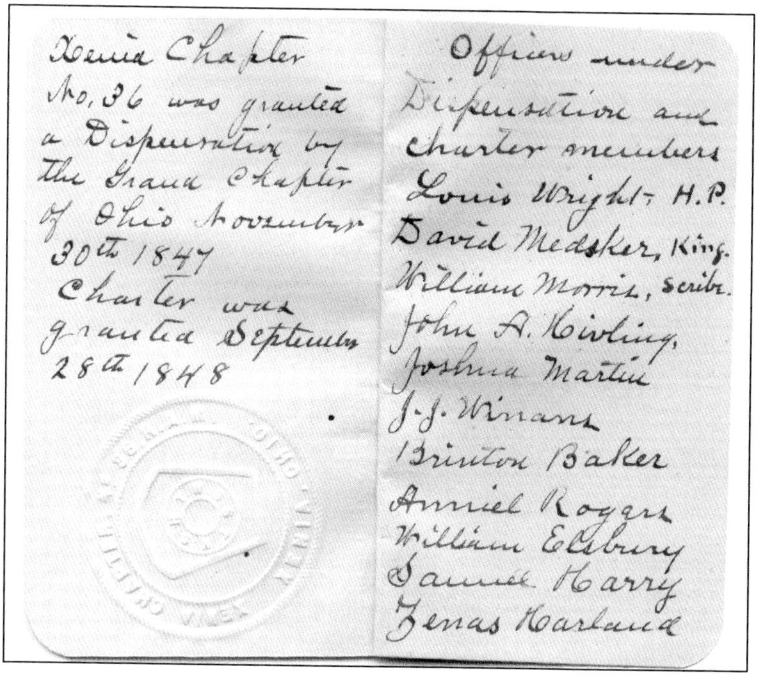

Xenia Chapter No. 36 was granted a Dispensation by the Grand Chapter of Ohio November 30th 1847
Charter was granted September 28th 1848

Officers under Dispensation and charter members
Louis Wright H.P.
David Medsker, King.
William Morris, scribe.
John A. Hivling,
Joshua Martin
J.J. Winans
Brinton Baker
Anniel Rogers
William Elsbury
Samuel Harry
Zenas Harland

Millions of white, middle-class men in the United States belonged to secret fraternal societies, such as the Freemasons, which had originated in London in the 1700s, when the trade guilds of working stonemasons began to accept honorary members. The men of Greene County were no exception, and many of them belonged to more than one organization. Several Masonic directories were included in the time capsule. (Courtesy of Greene County Archives—Time Capsule Documents.)

...MEMBERS...

Arthur, Frank	*McGuire, Frank
Blaine, S. L.	Mock, J. W.
Becker, O. D.	Moon, Wm.
*Christopher, J. B.	Martin, Joseph
Clemans, F. M.	*McMillen, W. F.
*Clark, Chas.	McCreight, M. T.
Christy, R. W.	Pierce, S. H.
Dobbins, Jas.	*Paxson, W. A.
Davis, C. A.	Pettit, W. M.
Ensign, H. N.	Stover, S. S.
Ensign, Theo. W.	Sanders, J. H.
Frank, J. P.	Sanders, Moses
*Flannery, M. J.	Shigley, Frank.
Galvin, W. S.	Smith, Chas. F.
Gross, A. T.	Shifflette, W. K.
Ginn, J. L.	Taylor, Jesse
Harness, Gideon	Taylor, Daniel
Harness, Marion	Thuma, C. E.
Haughey, W. J.	Wilson, Jacob
Layman, Josiah	*Walker, L. C.
*Laird, H. K.	*Zeiner, J. G.

*Past Masters.

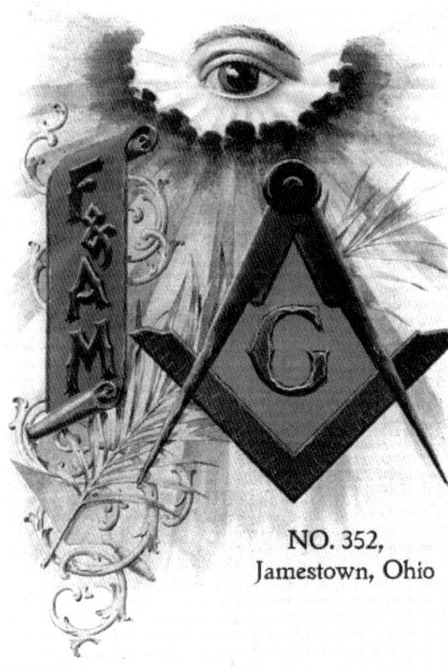

NO. 352,
Jamestown, Ohio

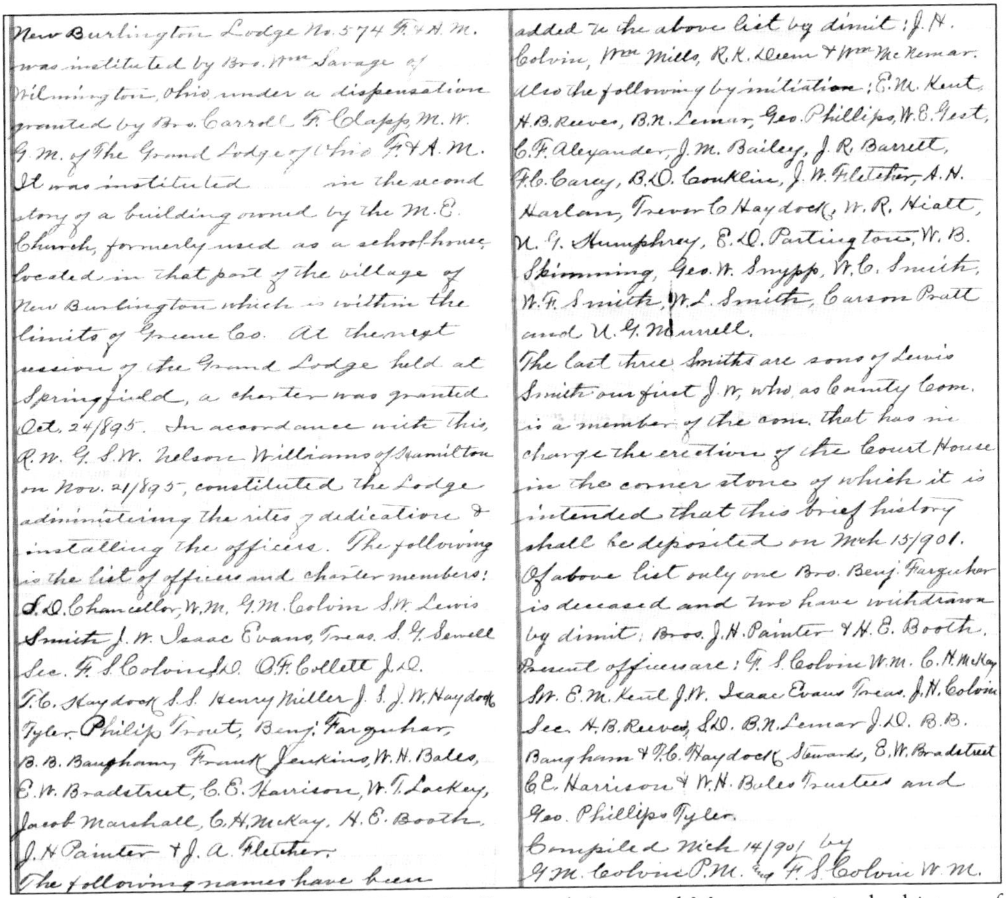

New Burlington Lodge No. 574 F.&A.M. was instituted by Bro. Wm Savage of Wilmington, Ohio, under a dispensation granted by Bro. Carroll F. Clapp, M.W. G.M. of The Grand Lodge of Ohio F.&A.M. It was instituted   in the second story of a building owned by the M.E. Church, formerly used as a schoolhouse, located in that part of the village of New Burlington which is within the limits of Greene Co. At the next session of the Grand Lodge held at Springfield, a charter was granted Oct. 24/895. In accordance with this, R.W. G.S.W. Nelson Williams of Hamilton on Nov. 21/895, constituted the Lodge administering the rites of dedication & installing the officers. The following is the list of officers and charter members: S.D. Chancellor, W.M. G.M. Colvin S.W. Lewis Smith J.W. Isaac Evans, Treas. S.G. Sewell Sec. F.S. Colvin S.D. O.F. Collett J.D. T.C. Haydock S.S. Henry Miller J.S. J.W. Haydock Tyler. Philip Trout, Benj. Farquhar, B.B. Baugham, Frank Jenkins, W.H. Bales, E.W. Bradstreet, C.E. Harrison, W.T. Lackey, Jacob Marshall, C.H. McKay, H.E. Booth, J.H. Painter & J.A. Fletcher.

The following names have been added to the above list by dimit: J.H. Colvin, Wm Mills, R.K. Deem & Wm McKemar. Also the following by initiation: E.M. Kent, H.B. Reeves, B.N. Lemar, Geo. Phillips, W.E. Gest, C.F. Alexander, J.M. Bailey, J.R. Barrett, F.C. Carey, B.D. Conklin, J.W. Fletcher, A.H. Harlan, Trevor C. Haydock, W.R. Hiatt, U.G. Humphrey, E.D. Partington, W.B. Skimming, Geo. W. Snypp, W.C. Smith, W.F. Smith, W.L. Smith, Carson Pratt and U.G. Murrell.

The last three Smiths are sons of Lewis Smith our first J.W., who as County Com. is a member of the com. that has in charge the erection of the Court House in the corner stone of which it is intended that this brief history shall be deposited on Mch 15/901.

Of above list only one Bro. Benj. Farquhar is deceased and two have withdrawn by dimit: Bros. J.H. Painter & H.E. Booth.

Present officers are: F.S. Colvin W.M. C.H. McKay S.W. E.M. Kent J.W. Isaac Evans Treas. J.H. Colvin Sec. H.B. Reeves S.D. B.N. Lemar J.D. B.B. Baugham & T.C. Haydock Stewards, E.W. Bradstreet C.E. Harrison & W.H. Bales Trustees and Geo. Phillips Tyler.

Compiled Mch 14/901 by
G.M. Colvin P.M. & F.S. Colvin W.M.

The New Burlington Lodge No. 574 of the Free and Accepted Masons sent in the history of their lodge. Their junior warden was Lewis Smith, a Greene County commissioner and member of the Courthouse Building Commission. (Courtesy of Greene County Archives—Time Capsule Document.)

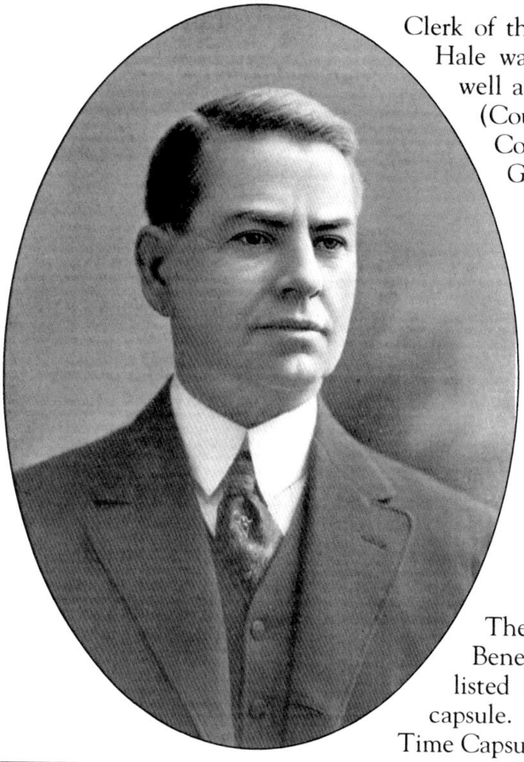

Clerk of the Common Pleas Court and educator Silas Hale was a charter member of the Xenia Elks, as well as a member of the Masons and Oddfellows. (Courtesy of Greene County Room, Greene County Public Library, Broadstone's *History of Greene County, Ohio*, 1918.)

The charter members of the Xenia Lodge of the Benevolent and Protective Order of Elks (BPOE) listed their names on a document for the time capsule. (Courtesy of Greene County Archives—Time Capsule Document.)

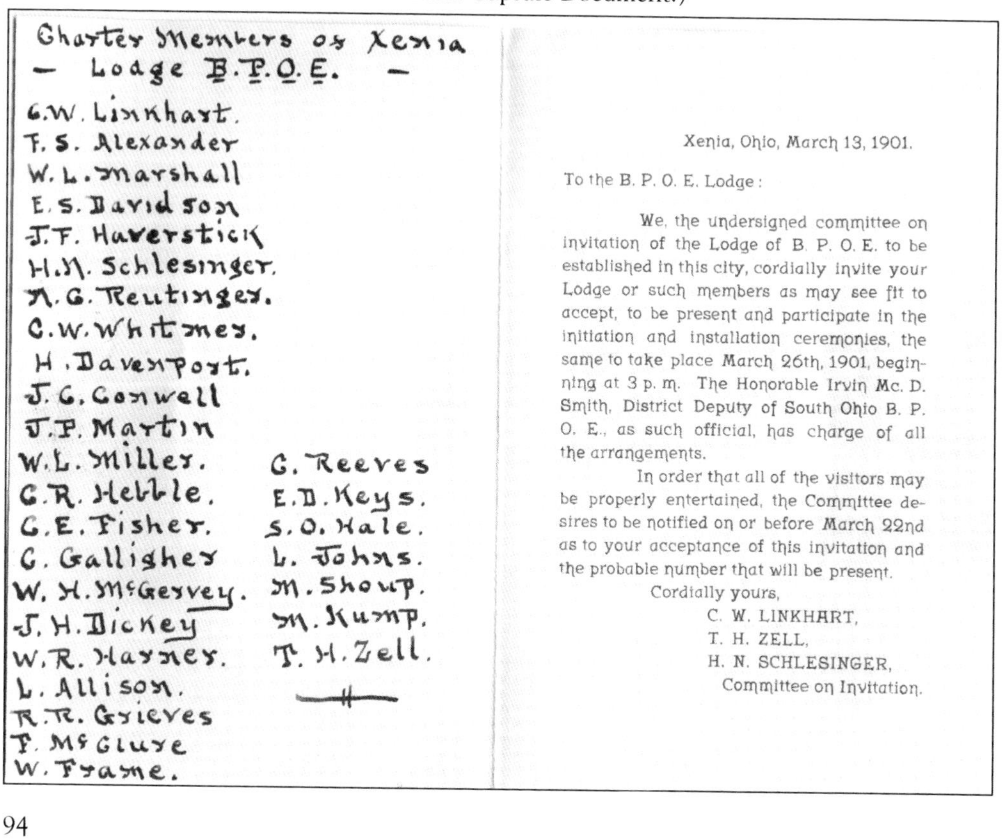

Charter Members of Xenia
— Lodge B.P.O.E. —

C.W. Linkhart.
F.S. Alexander
W.L. Marshall
E.S. Davidson
J.F. Haverstick
H.N. Schlesinger.
A.G. Reutinger.
C.W. Whitmer.
H. Davenport.
J.G. Conwell
J.P. Martin
W.L. Miller.
C.R. Hebble.
C.E. Fisher.
C. Galligher
W.H. McGervey.
J.H. Dickey
W.R. Harner.
L. Allison.
R.R. Grieves
F. McClure
W. Frame.

G. Reeves
E.D. Keys.
S.O. Hale.
L. Johns.
M. Shoup.
M. Kump.
T.H. Zell.

Xenia, Ohio, March 13, 1901.

To the B. P. O. E. Lodge:

We, the undersigned committee on invitation of the Lodge of B. P. O. E. to be established in this city, cordially invite your Lodge or such members as may see fit to accept, to be present and participate in the initiation and installation ceremonies, the same to take place March 26th, 1901, beginning at 3 p. m. The Honorable Irvin Mc. D. Smith, District Deputy of South Ohio B. P. O. E., as such official, has charge of all the arrangements.

In order that all of the visitors may be properly entertained, the Committee desires to be notified on or before March 22nd as to your acceptance of this invitation and the probable number that will be present.

Cordially yours,
C. W. LINKHART,
T. H. ZELL,
H. N. SCHLESINGER,
Committee on Invitation.

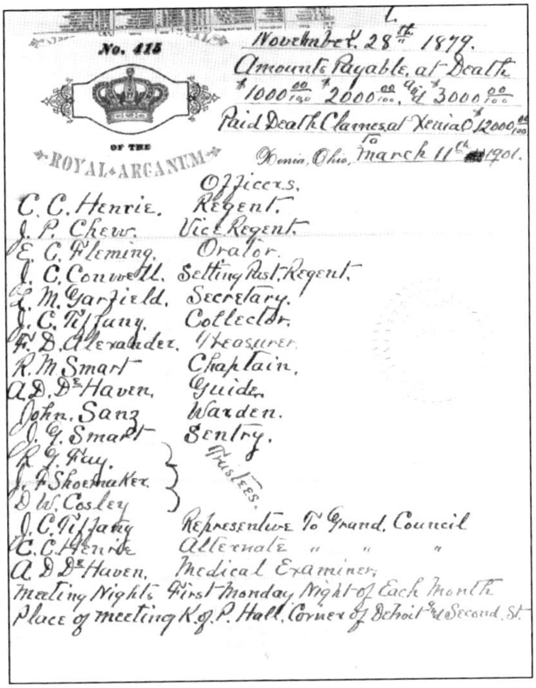

No. 415
November 28th 1879.
Amounts Payable at Death
$1000.00 $2000.00 and $3000.00
Paid Death Claims at Xenia O. $12000.00
to
OF THE
ROYAL ARCANUM
Xenia, Ohio, March 11th 1901.

Officers.
C. C. Henrie. Regent.
J. P. Chew. Vice Regent.
E. C. Fleming. Orator.
J. C. Conwell. Setting Past Regent.
L. M. Garfield. Secretary.
J. C. Tiffany. Collector.
F. D. Alexander. Treasurer.
R. M. Smart Chaplain.
A. D. DeHaven. Guide.
John. Sanz Warden.
J. G. Smart Sentry.
R. G. Hay.
J. F. Shoemaker } Trustees.
D. W. Cosley
J. C. Tiffany Representive To Grand Council
C. C. Henrie Alternate " " "
A. D. DeHaven. Medical Examiner.
Meeting Nights First Monday Night of Each Month
Place of meeting K. of P. Hall, Corner of Detroit and Second St.

The Royal Arcanum was a fraternal order founded in 1877 with the idea of providing life insurance protection for members, before commercial insurance was readily available for ordinary people. This is a list of members of the Shawnee Council No. 415 of the Royal Arcanum in Xenia. (Courtesy of Greene County Archives—Time Capsule Document.)

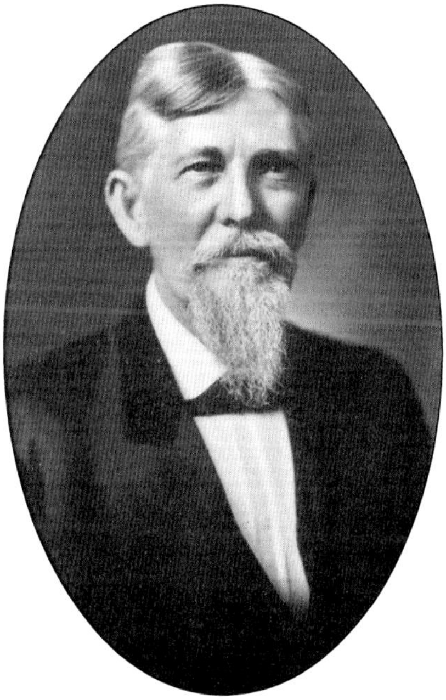

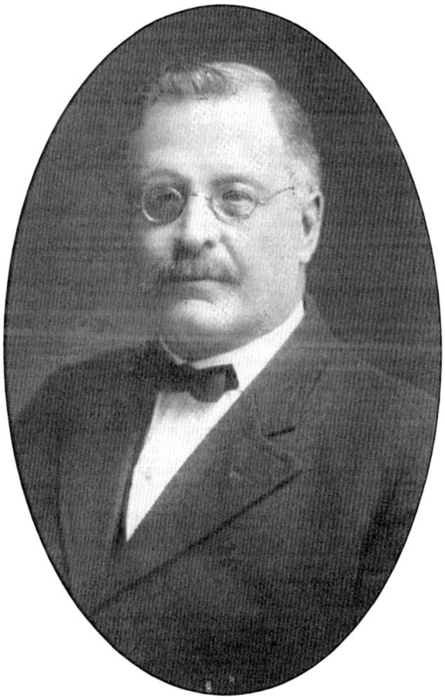

James P. Chew, seen on the left, was the vice-regent of the Xenia lodge of the Royal Arcanum. He was also the senior member of the Chew Publishing Company and owner of the *Xenia Gazette*. On the right is Lyman Garfield, secretary of the Xenia lodge. He was the superintendent of the Miami Powder Company in Goes. He was also a Mason and a member of the First Methodist Episcopal Church. (Courtesy of Greene County Room, Greene County Public Library, Broadstone's *History of Greene County, Ohio*, 1918.)

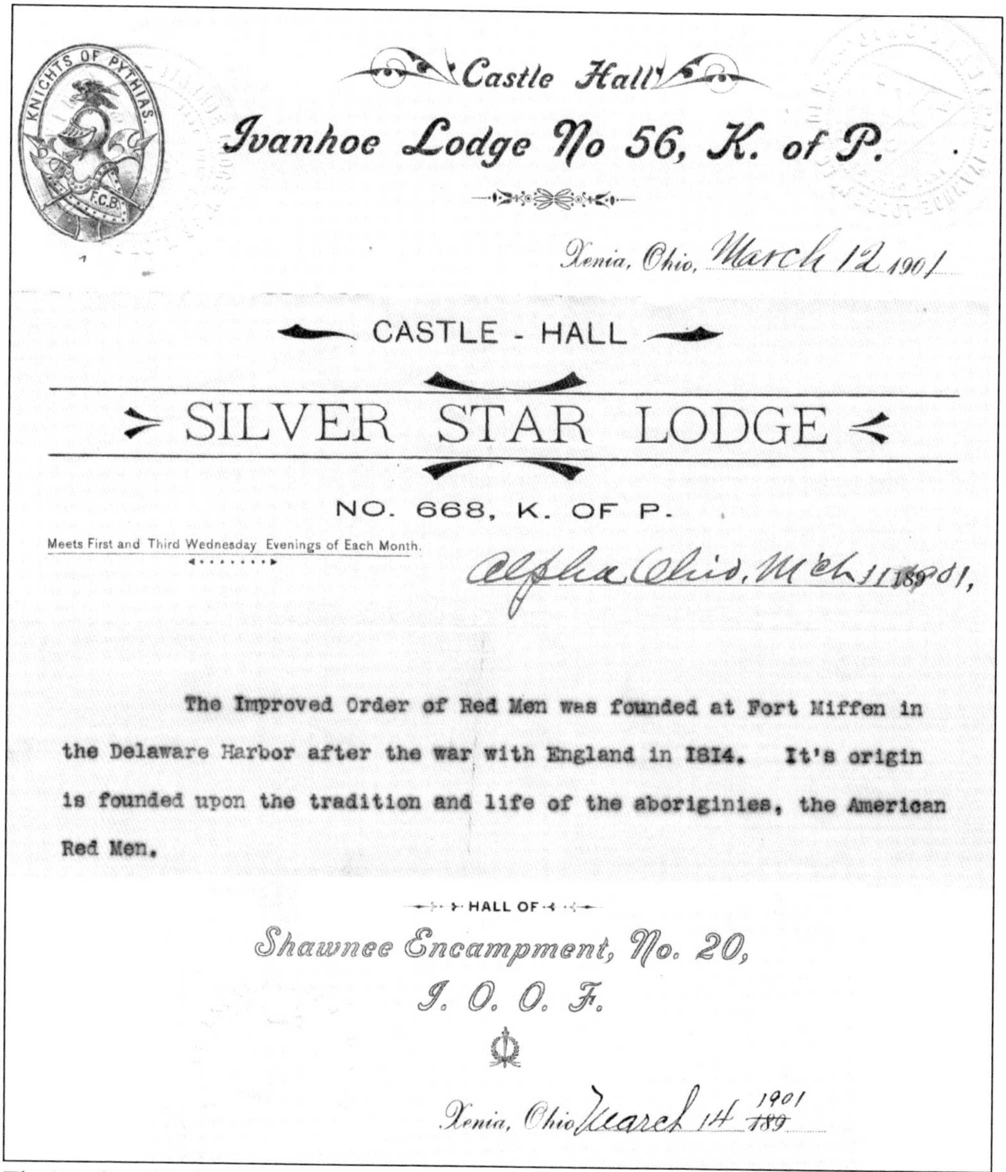

Castle Hall

Ivanhoe Lodge No 56, K. of P.

Xenia, Ohio, March 12 1901

CASTLE - HALL

SILVER STAR LODGE

NO. 668, K. OF P.

Meets First and Third Wednesday Evenings of Each Month.

Alpha Ohio, Mch 11 1901,

The Improved Order of Red Men was founded at Fort Miffen in the Delaware Harbor after the war with England in 1814. It's origin is founded upon the tradition and life of the aboriginies, the American Red Men.

HALL OF

Shawnee Encampment, No. 20,

I. O. O. F.

Xenia, Ohio March 14 1901

The Knights of Pythias was another fraternal organization that drew the men of Greene County. Founded in 1864, it stressed understanding and cooperation among men of goodwill. Ivanhoe Lodge No. 56 and the Silver Star Lodge No. 668, from Alpha, listed their officers for the time capsule. The Improved Order of Red Men developed out of a society founded in 1765 in the United States as the Sons of Liberty. The name was changed after the American Revolution to the Order of Red Men. Although Native Americans were not allowed to join, this patriotic society patterned itself after the democratic customs of the Iroquois. The Wahoo Tribe and the Red Jacket Tribe met weekly in Xenia. The Order of Oddfellows originated in England in the late 18th century as a mutual benefit society providing insurance facilities for members. The Independent Order of Oddfellows (IOOF) became established in the United States in the early years of the 19th century. Shawnee Encampment No. 20 of Xenia was chartered in 1846, and in 1901 was meeting twice a month at their lodge room on Detroit Street. (Courtesy of Greene County Archives—Time Capsule Document.)

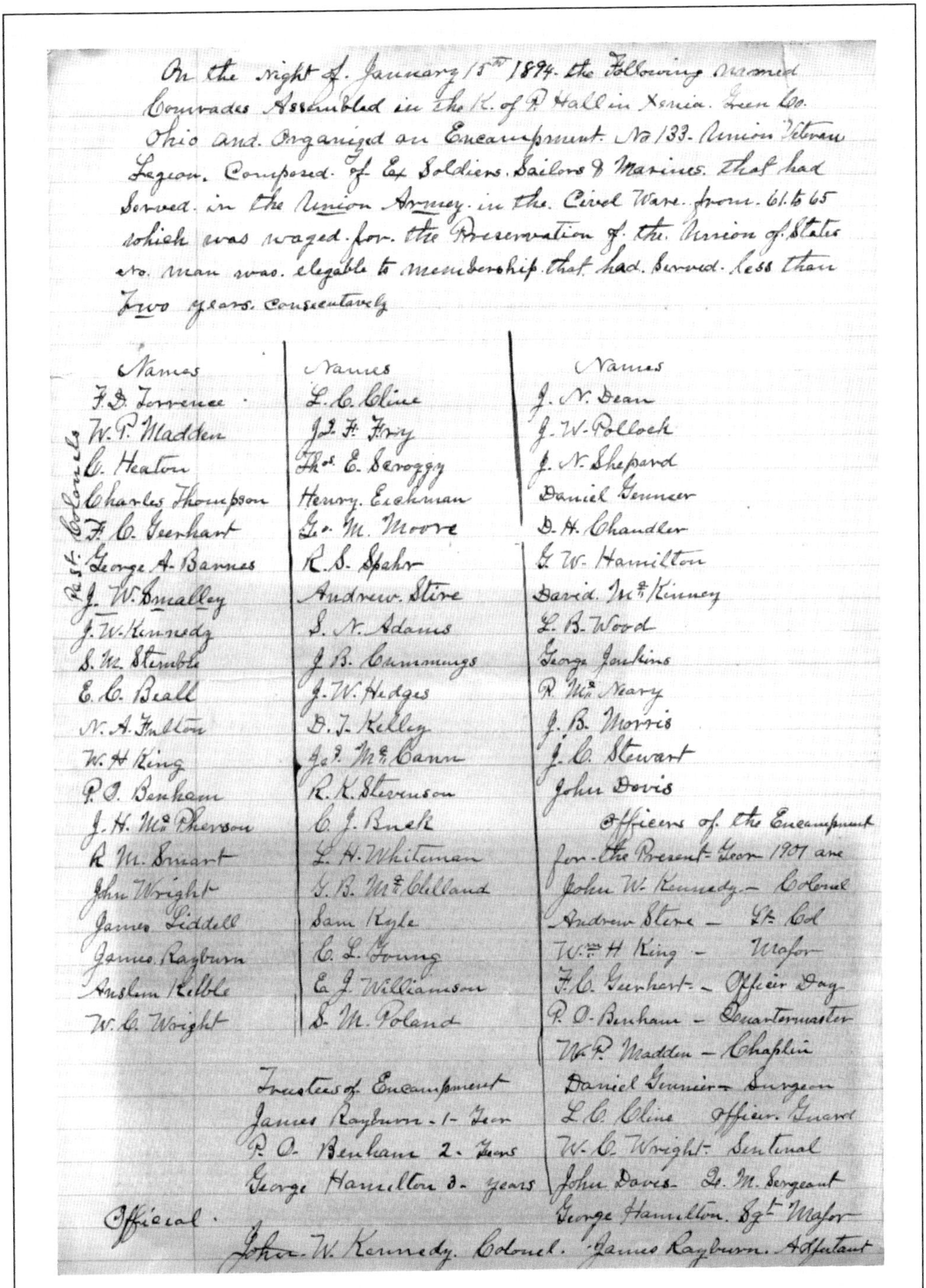

On the night of January 15th 1894 the following named Comrades Assembled in the K. of P. Hall in Xenia. Green Co. Ohio and Organized an Encampment No 133 Union Veteran Legion. Composed of Ex Soldiers. Sailors & Marines. that had Served in the Union Army. in the Civil Ware. from 61 to 65 which was waged for the Preservation of the Union of States no man was elegable to membership that had served less than two years consecutavely

Names	Names	Names
F. D. Torrence	L. C. Cline	J. N. Dean
W. P. Madden	Jas F. Fry	J. W. Pollock
C. Heaton	Thos E. Scroggy	J. N. Shepard
Charles Thompson	Henry. Eickman	Daniel Gennier
F. C. Geerhart	Geo. M. Moore	D. H. Chandler
George A. Barnes	R. S. Spahr	G. W. Hamilton
J. W. Smalley	Andrew. Stire	David. McKinney
J. W. Kennedy	S. N. Adams	L. B. Wood
S. M. Stimble	J. B. Cummings	George Jenkins
E. C. Beall	J. W. Hedges	R. McNeary
N. A. Fulton	D. T. Kelley	J. B. Morris
W. H. King	Jas McCann	J. C. Stewart
P. O. Benham	R. K. Stevenson	John Davis
J. H. McPherson	C. J. Buck	
R. M. Smart	L. H. Whiteman	
John Wright	G. B. McClelland	
James Liddell	Sam Kyle	
James. Rayburn	C. L. Young	
Anslem Kibble	E. J. Williamson	
W. C. Wright	S. M. Poland	

Past Colonels

Officers of the Encampment for the Present Year 1901 are
John W. Kennedy – Colonel
Andrew Stire – Lt. Col
Wm H King – Major
F. C. Geerhart – Officer Day
P. O. Benham – Quartermaster
W. P. Madden – Chaplin
Daniel Gunnier – Surgeon
L. C. Cline – Officer. Guard
W. C. Wright – Sentinal
John Davis – Q. M. Sergeant
George Hamilton. Sgt Major

Trustees of Encampment
James Rayburn. 1 Year
P. O. Benham 2. Years
George Hamilton 3. years

Official.
John W. Kennedy. Colonel. James Rayburn. Adjutant

Encampment No. 133 of the Union Veteran Legion was founded in 1894 and was made up of ex-soldiers, sailors, and marines who had served in the Union Army for at least two consecutive years. It was this group which Judge Joe Dean had hoped would be allowed to lay the cornerstone of the courthouse in 1901. (Courtesy of Greene County Archives—Time Capsule Document.)

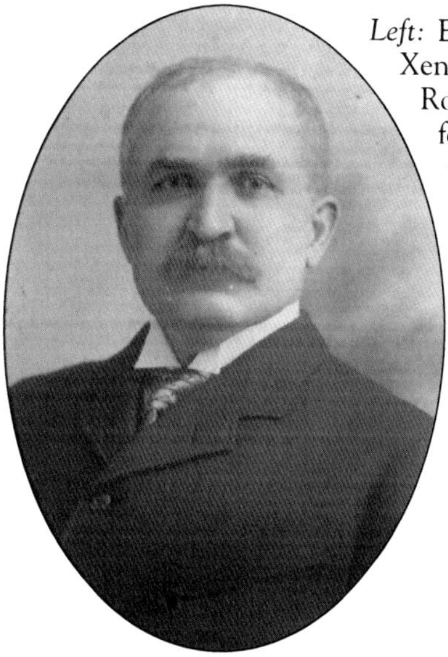

Left: Eber Reynolds, a dentist in Xenia, was a member of the Xenia Chapter of the Free and Accepted Masons as well as the Royal Arch Masons. He was responsible for collecting items for the time capsule, and he wrote the inscription on the front page of the bible donated by the Royal Arch Masons for the time capsule.

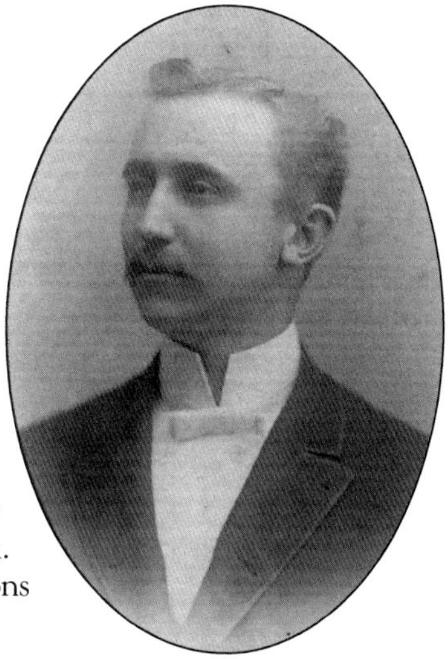

Right: Dr. W.A. Galloway was from a prominent Greene County family and a member of the Greene County Medical Association. (Courtesy of Xenia Lodge No. 49 of the Free and Accepted Masons and of Greene County Historical Society.)

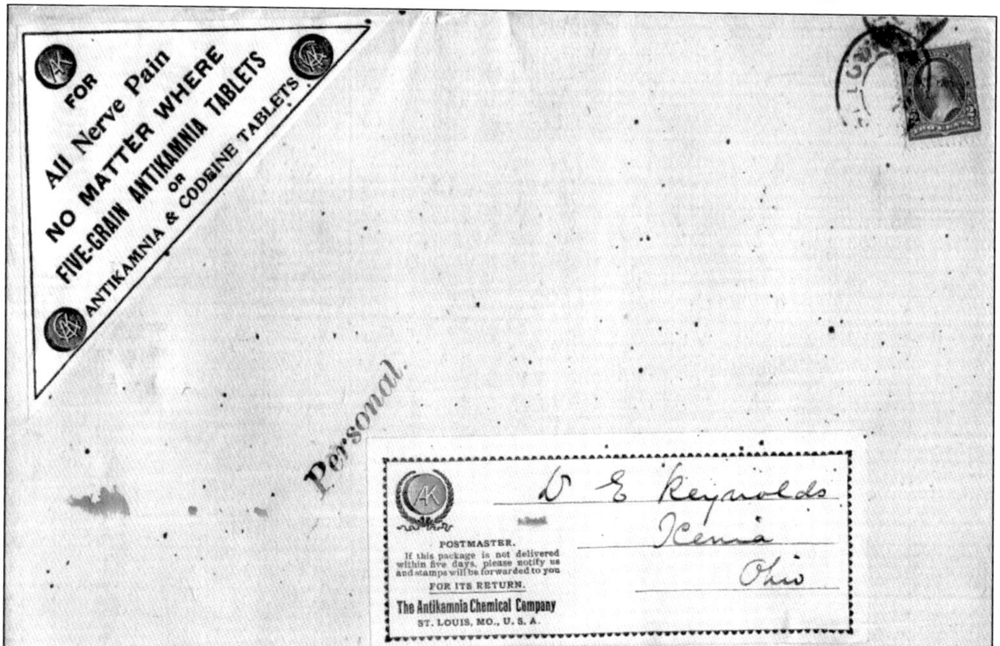

Dr. Eber Reynolds received this interesting looking envelope containing items for the time capsule from Dr. W.A. Galloway. It included material from the Nathaniel Greene Chapter of the Sons of the American Revolution. The National Society of the Sons of the American Revolution was organized in 1889 as a fraternal and civic society of descendants of men who supported American independence. (Courtesy of Greene County Archives—Time Capsule Document.)

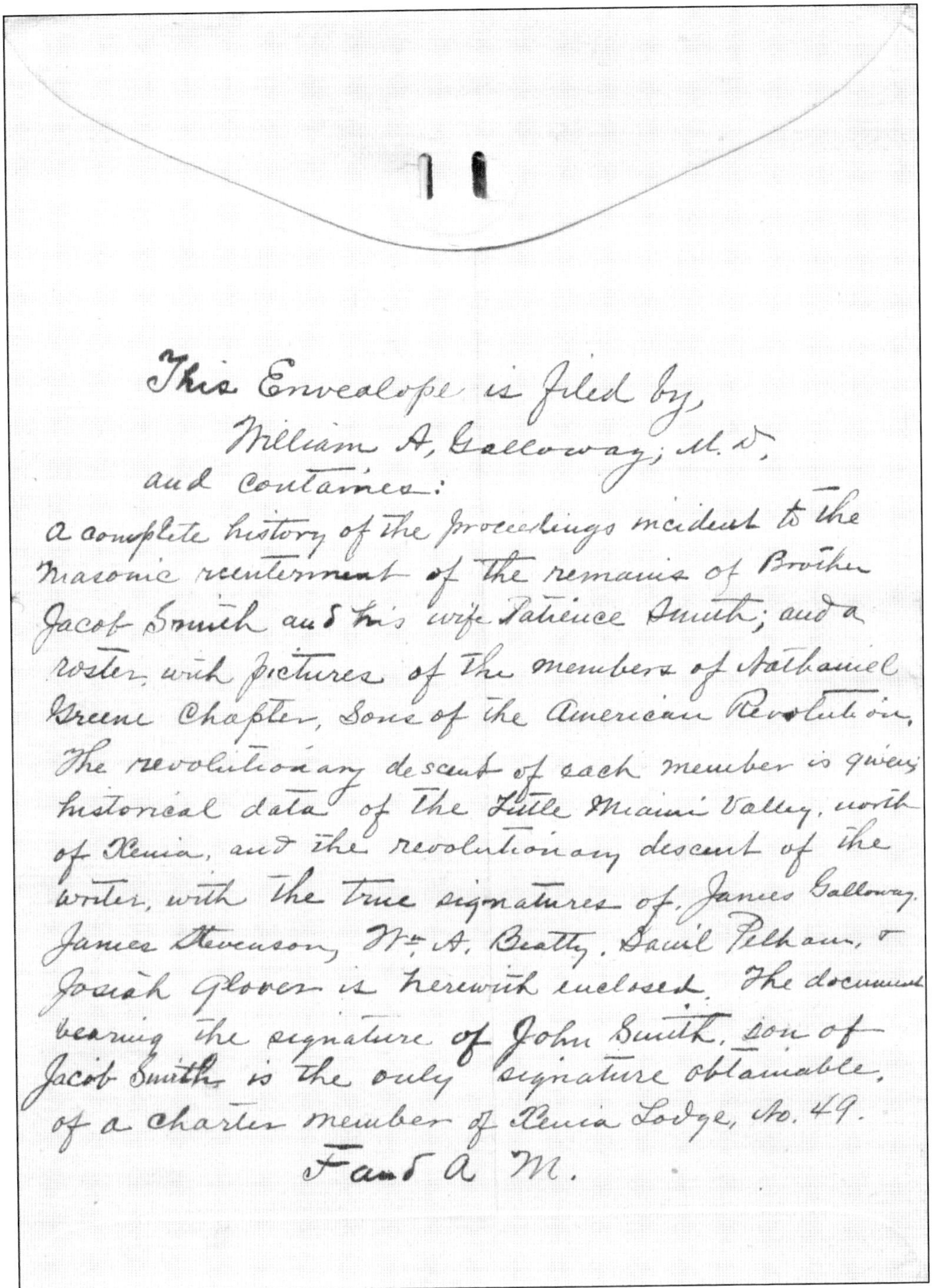

This Envealope is filed by,
William A, Galloway, M.D.
and containes:
a complete history of the proceedings incident to the masonic reinterment of the remains of Brother Jacob Smith and his wife Patience Smith; and a roster with pictures of the members of Nathaniel Greene Chapter, Sons of the American Revolution. The revolutionary descent of each member is given; historical data of the Little Miami Valley, north of Xenia, and the revolutionary descent of the writer, with the true signatures of, James Galloway, James Stevenson, Wm. A. Beatty, Saml Pelham, & Josiah Glover is herewith enclosed. The document bearing the signature of John Smith, son of Jacob Smith is the only signature obtainable of a charter member of Xenia Lodge, No. 49.
F and A M.

On the back of the envelope, Dr. Galloway describes the contents. Included were the revolutionary descents of his family and of other members of the Nathaniel Greene Chapter, photographs of members, and the charming story of his grandmother, Rebecca Galloway, and her friendship, as a young girl, with the famous local Shawnee Indian Chief, Tecumseh. (Courtesy of Greene County Archives—Time Capsule Document.)

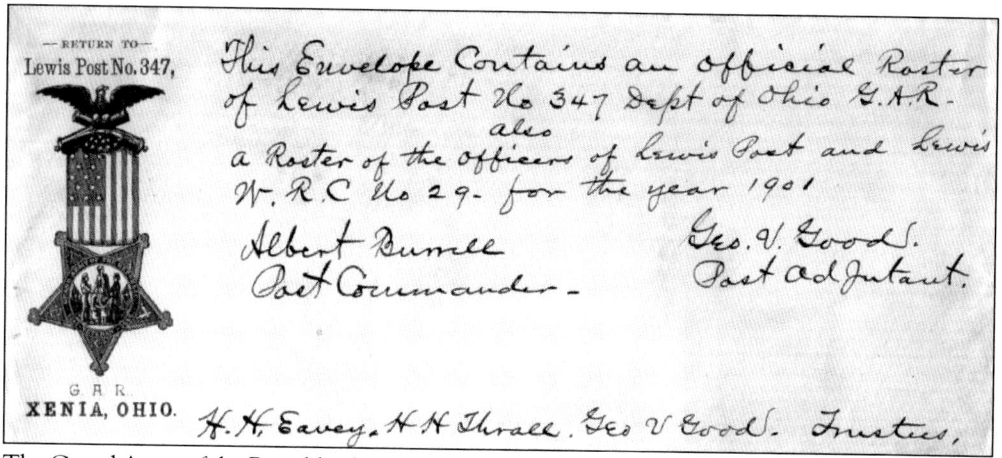

— RETURN TO —
Lewis Post No. 347,

G. A. R.
XENIA, OHIO.

This Envelope Contains an official Roster of Lewis Post No 347 Dept of Ohio G.A.R. also a Roster of the officers of Lewis Post and Lewis W. R. C No 29- for the year 1901

Albert Burrell
Post Commander-

Geo. V. Good.
Post Adjutant.

H. H. Eavey. H H Thrall. Geo V Good. Trustees,

The Grand Army of the Republic (GAR) was founded in 1866 for honorably discharged veterans of the Civil War. Each community level organization was called a post, run by an elected Post Commander. The GAR founded soldiers' homes, and in Xenia, it had been responsible for the beginnings of the Ohio Soldiers' and Sailors' Orphans' Home. The Lewis Post No. 347 of the GAR submitted a roster of members for the time capsule. (Courtesy of Greene County Archives—Time Capsule Document.)

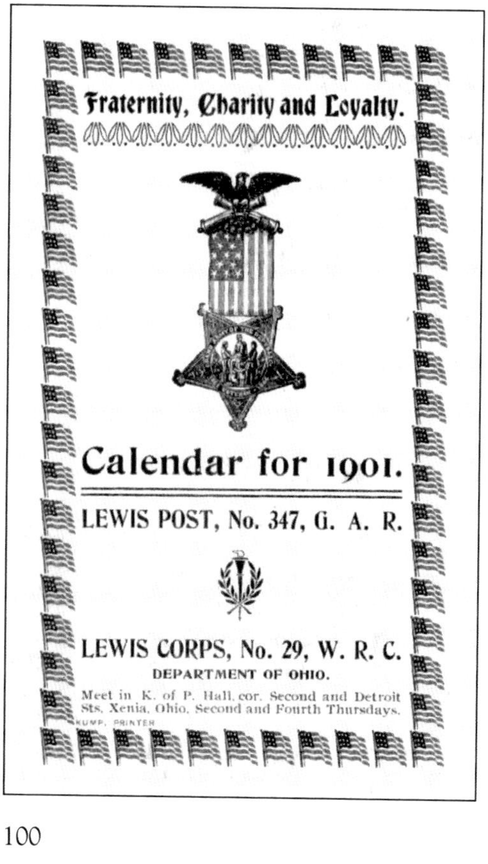

Fraternity, Charity and Loyalty.

Calendar for 1901.

LEWIS POST, No. 347, G. A. R.

LEWIS CORPS, No. 29, W. R. C.
DEPARTMENT OF OHIO.

Meet in K. of P. Hall, cor. Second and Detroit Sts. Xenia, Ohio, Second and Fourth Thursdays.
KUMP, PRINTER

The calendar of the Lewis Post No. 347 of the GAR for the year 1901 is shown here. (Courtesy of Greene County Archives—Time Capsule Document.)

This letter, addressed to Eber Reynolds, accompanied items from Jamestown for the time capsule. Included were a Grand Army of the Republic button and a Sons of Veterans badge. The Sons of Veterans of the United States of America (later the Sons of Union Veterans of the Civil War) was endorsed by the Grand Army of the Republic as its heir. (Courtesy of Greene County Archives—Time Capsule Document.)

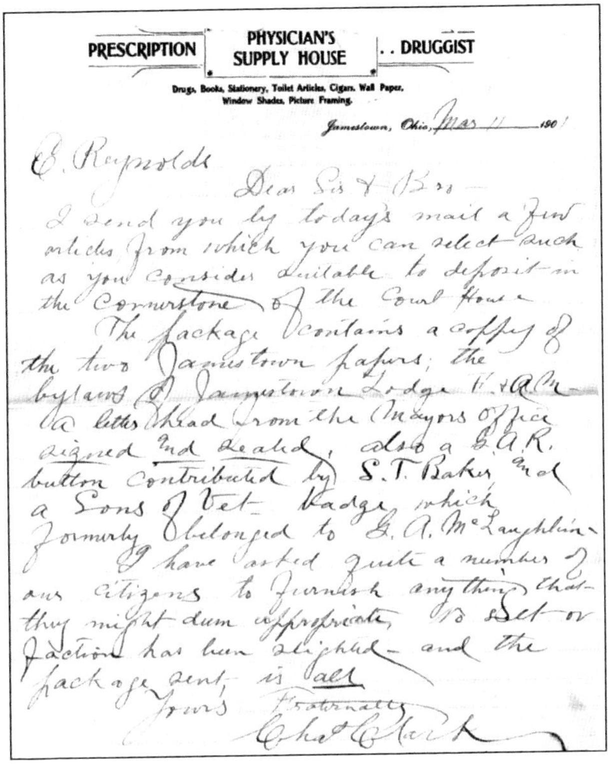

PRESCRIPTION | PHYSICIAN'S SUPPLY HOUSE | .. DRUGGIST

Drugs, Books, Stationery, Toilet Articles, Cigars, Wall Paper, Window Shades, Picture Framing.

Jamestown, Ohio, Mar 11 1901

E. Reynolds

Dear Sir & Bro —

I send you by today's mail a few articles from which you can select such as you consider suitable to deposit in the Cornerstone of the Court House.

The package contains a copy of the two Jamestown papers; the bylaws of Jamestown Lodge F. & A. M. a letter head from the Mayors office signed and sealed; also a G.A.R. button contributed by S.T. Baker and a Sons of Vet. badge which formerly belonged to G. A. McLaughlin.

I have asked quite a number of our citizens to furnish anything that they might deem appropriate. No sect or faction has been slighted — and the package sent is all.

Yours Fraternally

Chas Clark

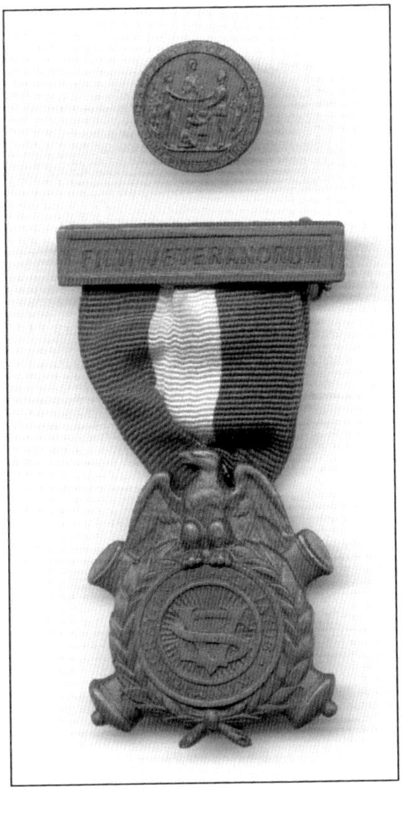

The GAR button and the Sons of Veterans badge are shown here. The badge had belonged to G.A. McLaughlin, and S.T. Baker contributed the button. (Courtesy of Greene County Archives—Time Capsule Document.)

Jr. O. U. A. M., Xenia Council, No. 67, meets every Wednesday evening at 7:30 in winter and 8 in summer, at 36½ West Main. A. E. Grimshaw, Secretary.

COLORED LODGES.

Wilberforce Lodge, No. 21, F. & A. M., meets 1st Thursday evening of each month in Masonic hall, over 17 East Main street. Wm. Rogers, Secretary.

Lincoln Chapter, No. 2, R. A. M., meets 2d Thursday evening of each month, over 17 East Main street.

Xenia Commandery, No. 8, K. T., meets 3d Thursday evening of each month, over 17 East Main street. C. E. Nichols, Secretary.

Grand United Order of Odd Fellows, Townsend Lodge, No. 1823, meets 2d and 4th Tuesday evenings of each month.

Damon Lodge, No. 29, K. of P., meets every 1st and 3d Tuesday evening, at corner of Main and Whiteman streets. John Lewis, Secretary.

Daniel's Post, No. 500, G. A. R., meets 1st and 3d Tuesday evenings, over 17 East Main street.

Eastern Star, No. 7, U. B. F., meets 1st and 3d Monday evening, at the corner of Fair and Main streets. Que E. Winn, Secretary.

Daniel's Corps, No. 228, W. R. C., meets on Friday afternoon preceding the meeting of Daniel's Post, No. 500. G. A. R., at 17 East Main street.

C. U. A. meets 1st Tuesday of each month, at 629 East Church street.

Bell of Ohio DT. Tabernacle, No. 511, meets 1st and 3d Thursdays, at M. M. hall, East Main street. Hattie Jackson, Secretary.

Mt. Olive Lodge, No. 25, Good Samaria, meets 1st Thursday and last Friday, at M. M. hall, East Main street. Sallie Jackson, Secretary.

BANKS.

The Citizen's National Bank, s w cor Detroit and Main. Incorporated 1882, capital $100,000.00, surplus $40,000.00. Henry H. Eavey, pres.; Jacob H. Harbine, vice pres.; Frank E. McGervey, cashier; Marshall L. Wolf, teller.

The African-American citizens of Greene County also formed branches of many of the fraternal organizations and held regular meetings, as this page from the Xenia and Greene County Directory for 1898–99 indicates. (Courtesy of Greene County Archives—Time Capsule Document.)

Five

BUSINESSES

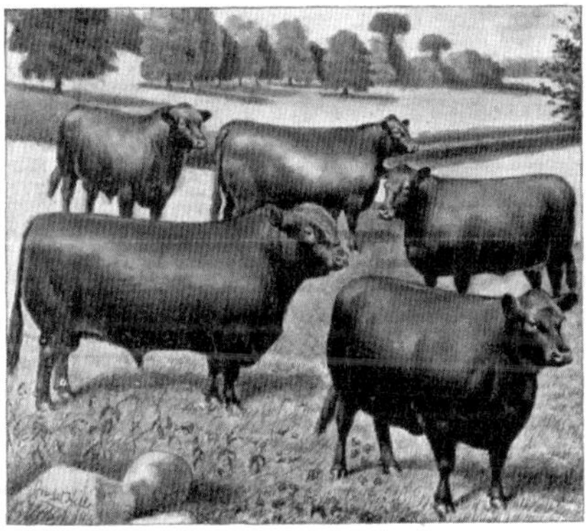

Group of ✤ ✤

Aberdeen-Angus Cattle

At Meadow Brook Farm.

The Property of

D. Bradfute & Son.

Cedarville O. ✤ ✤

LIST OF PURE-BRED POLLED

Aberdeen-Angus Cattle

AT MEADOW BROOK STOCK FARM.

THE PROPERTY OF

D. BRADFUTE & SON,

CEDARVILLE, GREEN COUNTY, OHIO.

CEDARVILLE is on the P. C. C. & ST. L. R. R. (Little Miami Division) 47 miles Southwest of Columbus, and 72 miles Northeast of Cincinnati, O. The farm is four miles West of Cedarville and six miles north of Xenia, or only two miles East of Goe's Station, a regular stopping place between Xenia and Springfield. Good roads.

TELEPHONE at the farm, Cedarville Independent Telephone Co., and U. S. Long Distance.

INSPECTION SOLICITED. Visitors always welcome, except on Sabbath, and will be met at trains if word is sent of their coming. Extended Pedigrees and further particulars furnished on application.

THE MEADOW BROOK HERD OF ABERDEEN-ANGUS CATTLE has been carefully selected and bred, and comes before the public resting on its merits. The group of cattle sent out from this herd to the Ohio State Fair during the last ten consecutive years has won more prizes than all competitors combined. The same thing can be said of Indiana and Michigan for the past five years. In 1895, 1896, 1898 and 1899 they won Grand Sweepstakes over all beef breeds at the Ohio State Fair, making them the champion herd of beef cattle in Ohio. In 1898 and 1899 they won nearly 200 prizes, of which 40 were championships, at such state fairs as Ohio, Indiana, Kentucky, Wisconsin, Illinois, and St. Louis fair. *Lady of Meadow Brook* was the champion beef cow of America for 1899. We breed our show cattle, we bred their dams and most of their grand dams. We do not have to buy our prize winners as many do. Thirty head of the cattle listed have won prizes at prominent state fairs. The great prize winning

Bulls, ZAIRE 5th, 13067, and GAY ERIC, 19528,

are in service in this herd. No herd in America can show two bulls of PROVEN MERIT equal to these.

He's a Star 31370 and Black Prince of Estill 33626 complete the quartette of remarkable bulls at Meadow Brook.

THE YOUNG BULLS on hand are a lot of unusual excellence. They are the low down blocky kind that please. Our prices are low considering the quality.

PERSONS WISHING TO BUY Aberdeen-Angus Cattle of either sex, for show or breeding purposes, will do well to see this herd before purchasing. Again we invite you to come and see them.

Yours very truly,

Sept. 1st, 1900. **D. BRADFUTE & SON.**

D. Bradfute and Sons was a prominent family-owned cattle breeding business for several generations. Oscar Bradfute introduced the Aberdeen Angus breed to the stock farm. (Courtesy of Greene County Archives—Time Capsule Document.)

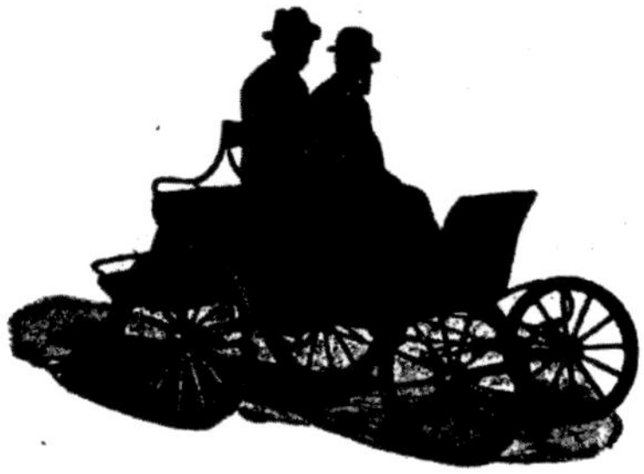

This is a picture of the first automobile that ever appeared on the streets of Xenia. And it is a matter in which we can take local pride for this automobile is a home product, as it was constructed in Xenia by a Xenia man—Mr. Jacob Baldner. The automobile is operated by gasoline and possesses good speed and qualities that make it reliable for long trips. Since it was constructed Mr. Baldner has built another automobile of greater speed and the inventor and his automobile are a familiar sight on the streets. In the picture the occupants of the vehicle are Mr. Baldner, the inventor and Mr. Joseph B. Fleming.

This picture of Xenia's first automobile, with its inventor, Jacob Baldner, and Joseph Fleming seated in it, was published in the *Xenia Semi-Weekly Gazette* of March 15, 1901. (Courtesy of Greene County Archives—Time Capsule Document.)

Below: On the left is Lou, son of Fred Baldner, brother and partner of Jacob Baldner, and on the right, George, son of Jacob, in a Baldner car. (Courtesy of Greene County Room, Greene County Public Library.)

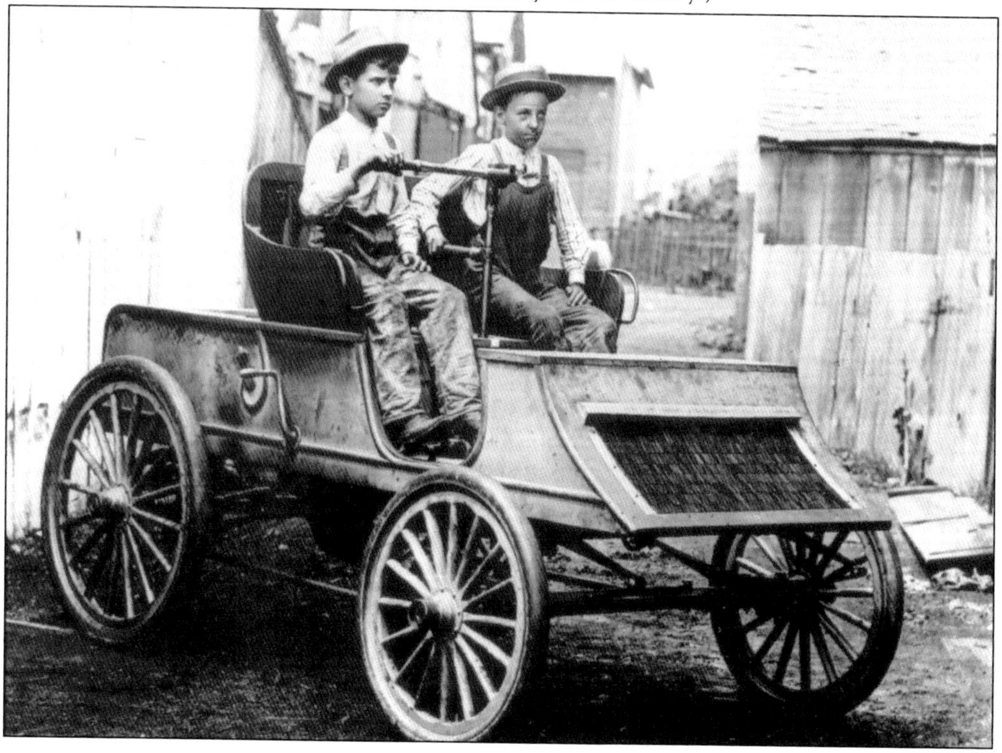

The time capsule contained many interesting donations from local businessmen. This was one of several calendars that were included. J.P. Bocklett specialized in plumbing, gas, and steam fitting. He owned his business for more than 60 years. (Courtesy of Greene County Archives—Time Capsule Document.)

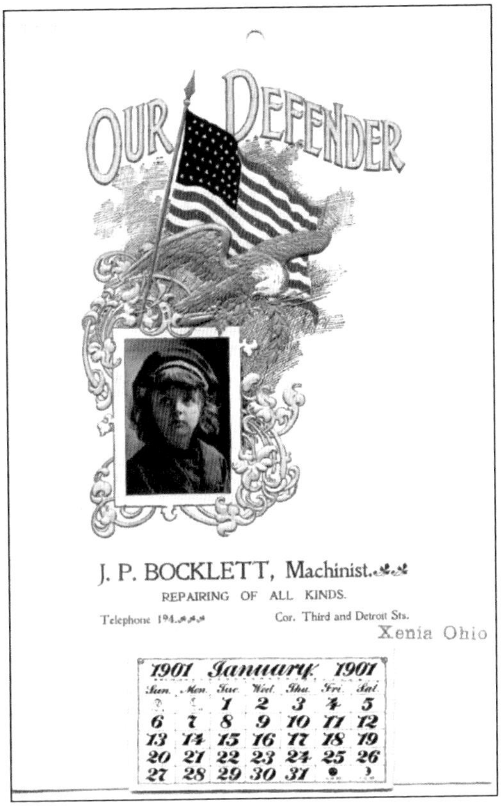

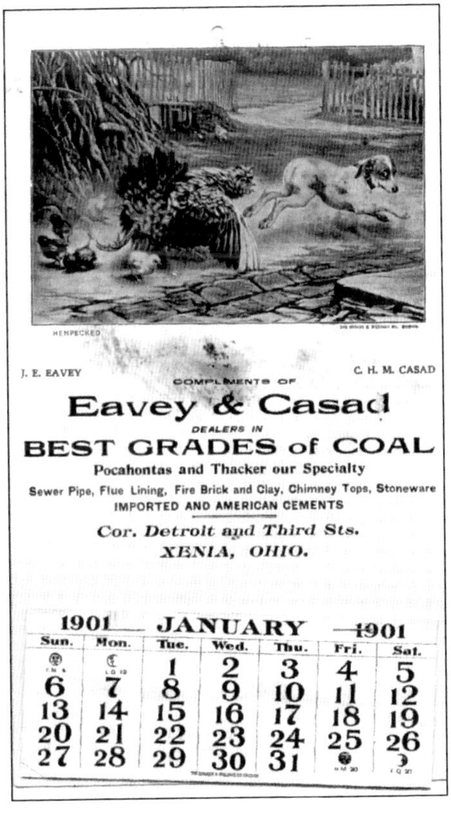

Here is another calendar from the time capsule. Messrs. Joseph Eavey and Charles H.M. Casad were partners in this coal business for a few years. (Courtesy of Greene County Archives—Time Capsule Document.)

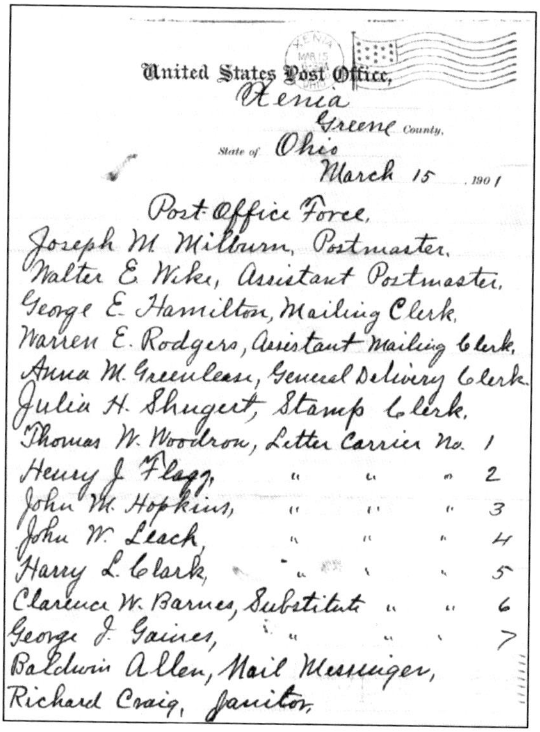

United States Post Office,
Xenia
Greene County,
State of Ohio
March 15 , 1901

Post Office Force,
Joseph M. Milburn, Postmaster.
Walter E. Wike, Assistant Postmaster.
George E. Hamilton, Mailing Clerk.
Warren E. Rodgers, Assistant Mailing Clerk.
Anna M. Greenlease, General Delivery Clerk.
Julia H. Shugert, Stamp Clerk.
Thomas W. Woodrow, Letter Carrier No. 1
Henry J. Flagg, " " " 2
John M. Hopkins, " " " 3
John W. Leach, " " " 4
Harry L. Clark, " " " 5
Clarence W. Barnes, Substitute " " 6
George J. Gaines, " " " 7
Baldwin Allen, Mail Messenger,
Richard Craig, Janitor,

The Xenia Post Office sent in a document postmarked the day that the cornerstone was laid, listing the names of all employed there. (Courtesy of Greene County Archives—Time Capsule Document.)

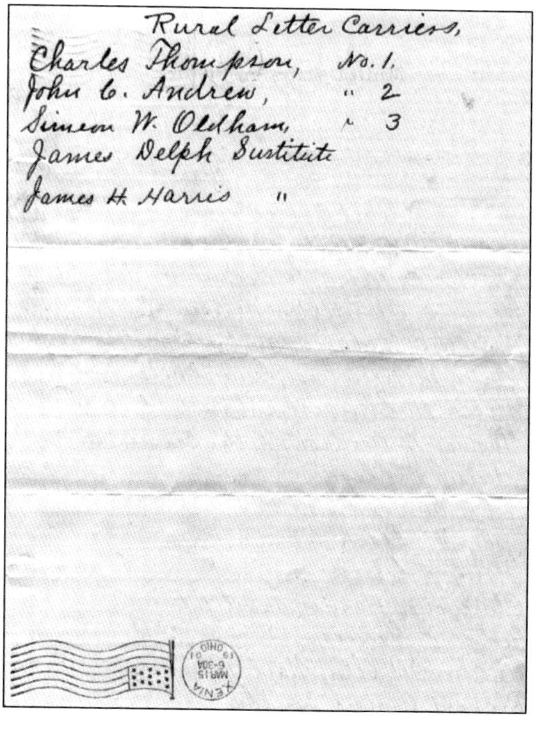

Rural Letter Carriers,
Charles Thompson, No. 1.
John C. Andrew, " 2
Simeon W. Oldham, " 3
James Delph Sustitute
James H. Harris "

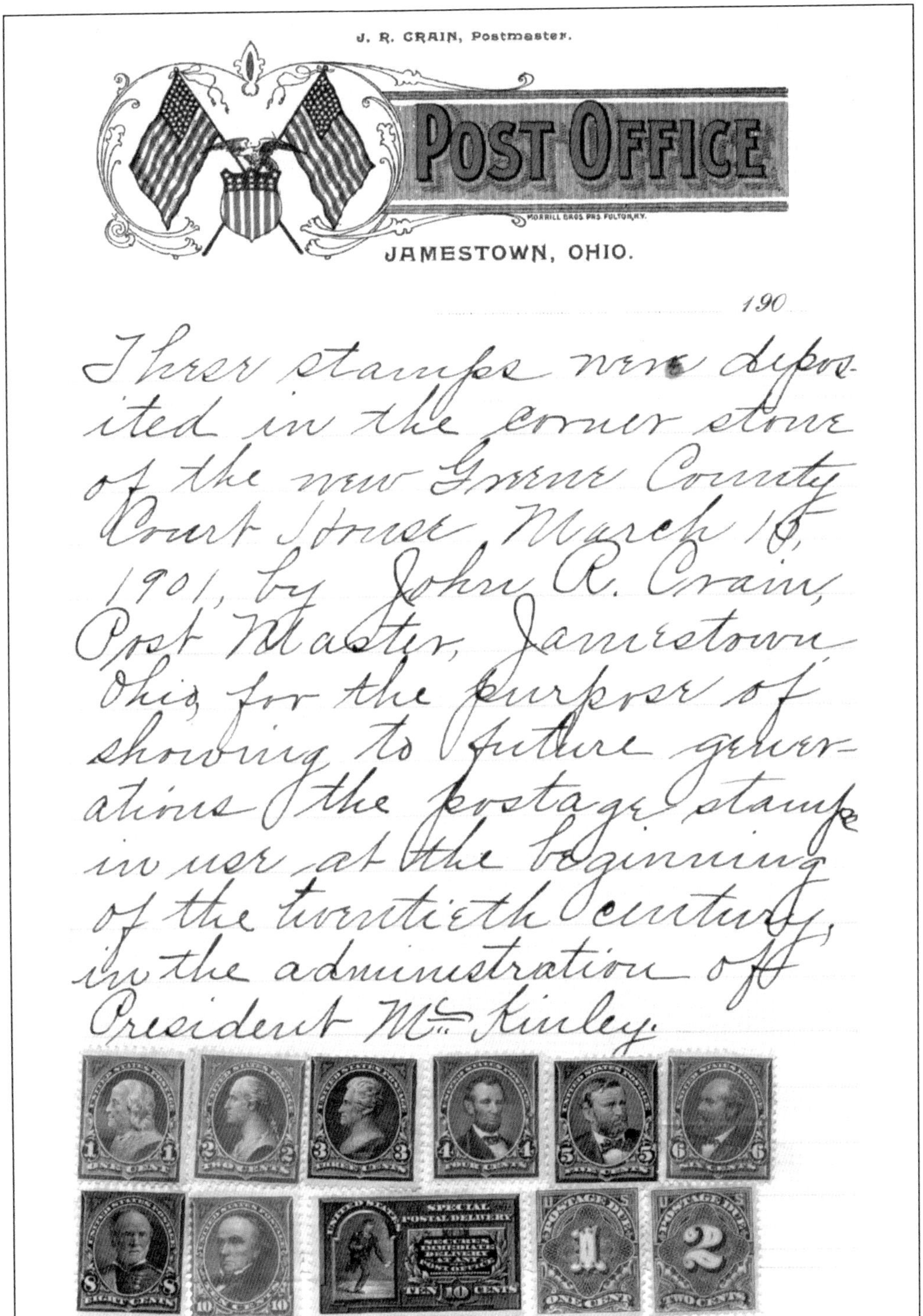
J. R. CRAIN, Postmaster.

POST OFFICE

MORRILL BROS. PRS. FULTON, N.Y.

JAMESTOWN, OHIO.

190

These stamps were deposited in the corner stone of the new Greene County Court House March 16, 1901, by John R. Crain, Post Master, Jamestown Ohio, for the purpose of showing to future generations the postage stamps in use at the beginning of the twentieth century, in the administration of President McKinley.

Jamestown Post Office sent these beautiful stamps for inclusion in the time capsule to show future generations the stamps in use during the administration of President McKinley. (Courtesy of Greene County Archives—Time Capsule Document.)

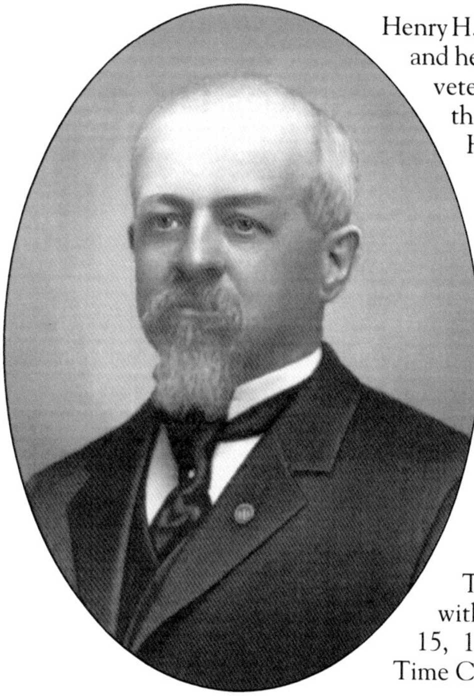

Henry H. Eavey was president of the Citizen's National Bank and head of Eavey's wholesale grocery firm. A Civil War veteran, Mr. Eavey was a member of the Grand Army of the Republic and of the Free and Accepted Masons. He was the man who had charge of the time capsule, read the list of items enclosed in it, and placed it under the cornerstone of the courthouse during the Masons' cornerstone laying ceremonies. (Courtesy of Greene County Room, Greene County Public Library, Broadstone's *History of Greene County, Ohio*, 1918.)

The Citizens National Bank book was inscribed with the names of those employed there on March 15, 1901. (Courtesy of Greene County Archives—Time Capsule Document.)

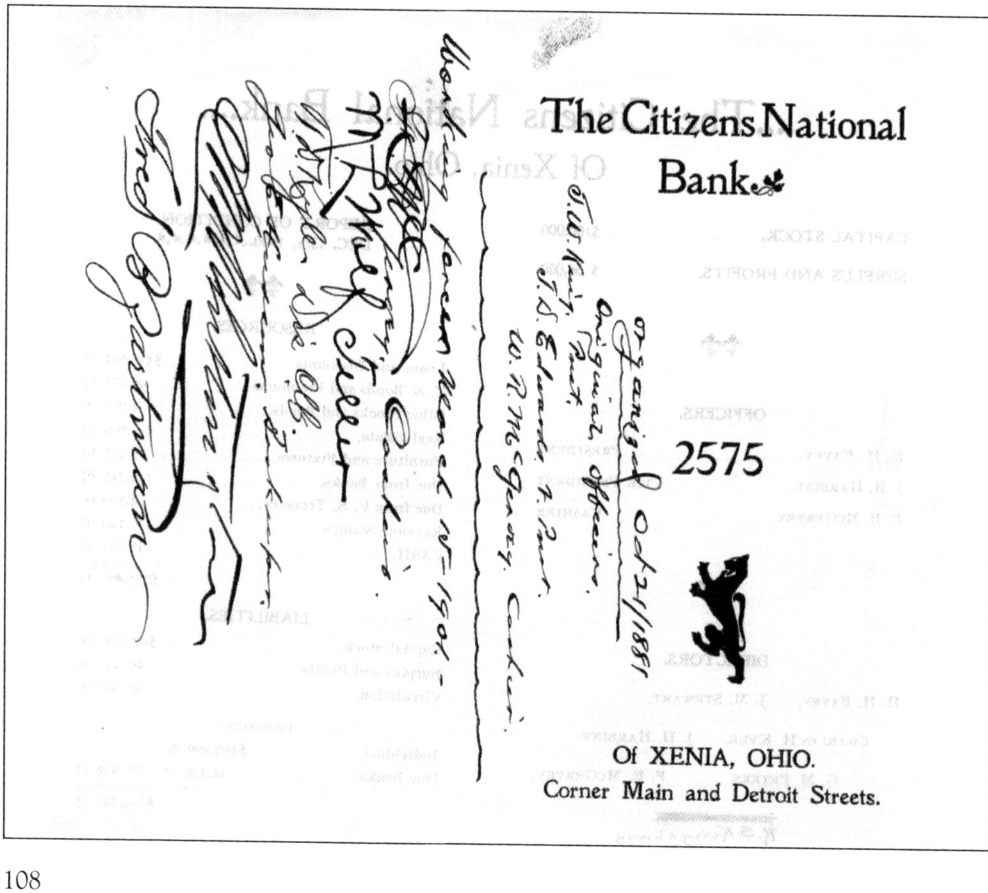

The Citizens National Bank

2575

Of XENIA, OHIO.

Corner Main and Detroit Streets.

F.D. Torrence served as the director of the Home Building and Savings Company for about 20 years. He was a Civil War veteran, ran a successful lumber business in Xenia, and was active in the United Presbyterian Church. (Courtesy of Greene County Room, Greene County Public Library, Broadstone's *History of Greene County, Ohio*, 1918.)

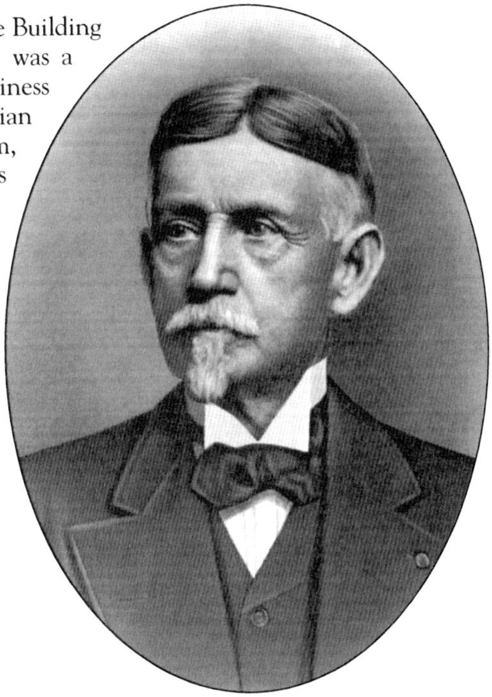

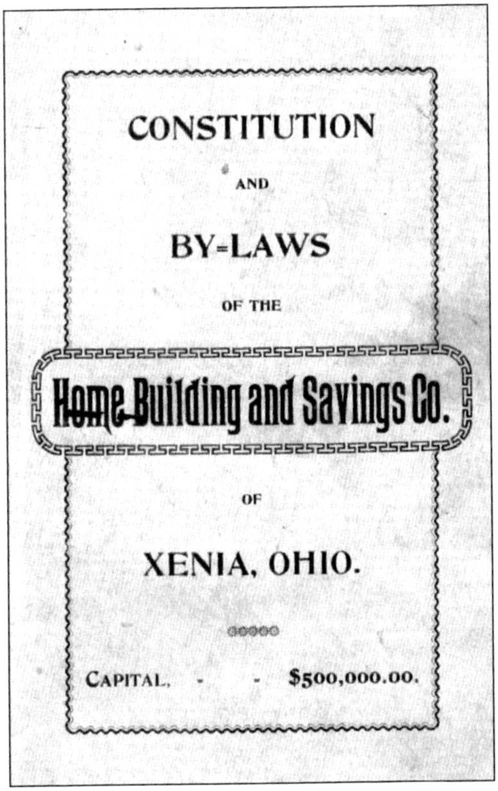

CONSTITUTION

AND

BY-LAWS

OF THE

Home Building and Savings Co.

OF

XENIA, OHIO.

CAPITAL, - - $500,000.00.

The Home Building and Savings Company was located on Detroit Street in Xenia. (Courtesy of Greene County Archives—Time Capsule Document.)

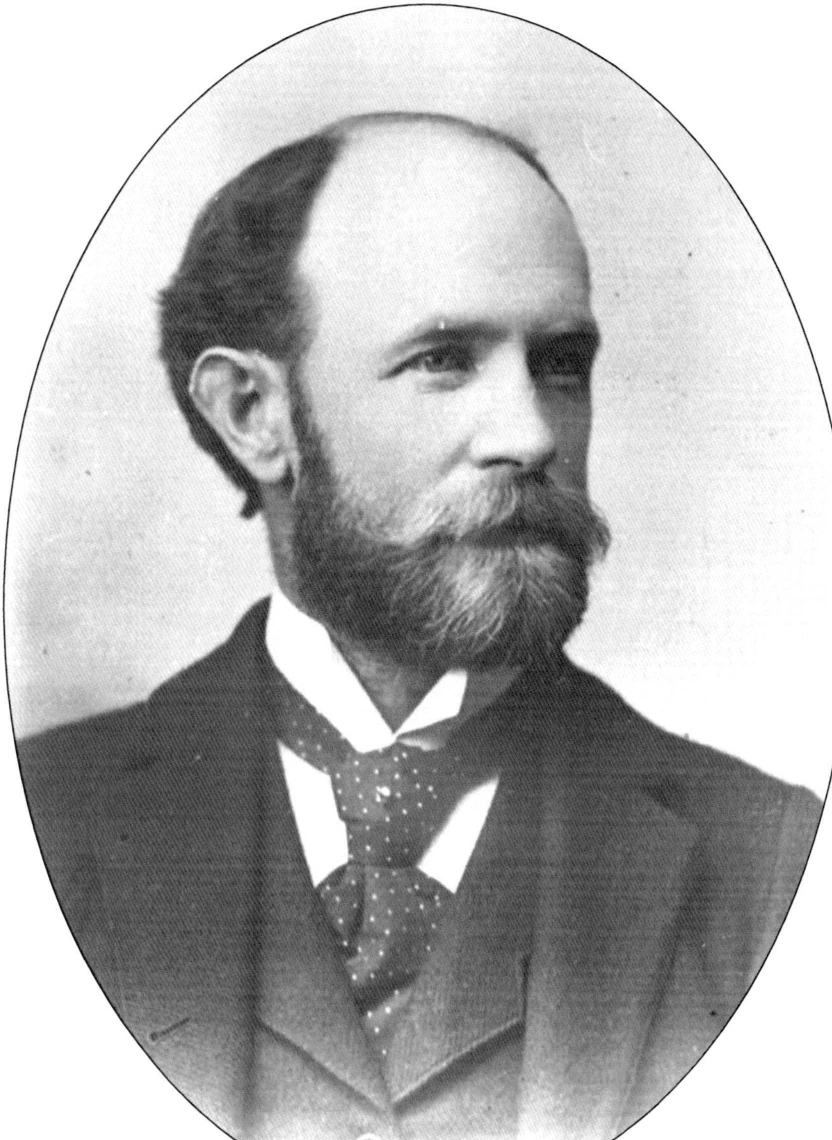

Dr. Asa C. Messenger, shown here, was the resident physician at the Ohio Soldiers' and Sailors' Orphans' Home (from 1892 to 1903) and the president of the Greene County Medical Society. He was a Mason, a member of the Oddfellows, and a member of the Sons of Veterans. (Courtesy of Greene County Room, Greene County Public Library.)

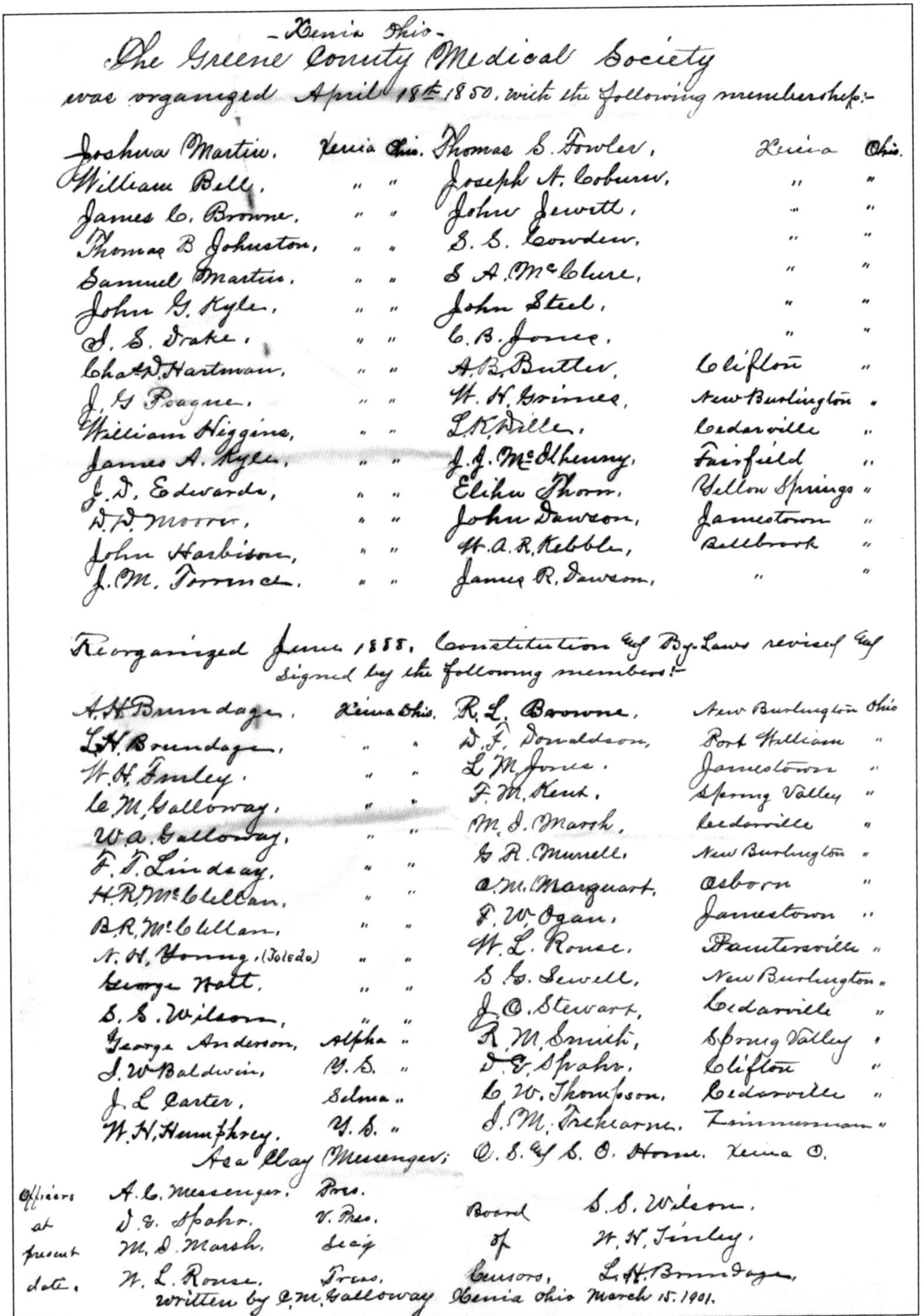

-Xenia Ohio-

The Greene County Medical Society

was organized April 18th 1850. with the following membership:-

Joshua Martin.	Xenia	Ohio.	Thomas S. Fowler.	Xenia	Ohio.
William Bell.	"	"	Joseph N. Coburn.	"	"
James C. Browne.	"	"	John Jewett.	"	"
Thomas B Johnston.	"	"	S. S. Cowden.	"	"
Samuel Martin.	"	"	S A. McClure.	"	"
John G. Kyle.	"	"	John Steel.	"	"
S. S. Drake.	"	"	C. B. Jones.	"	"
Chas D. Hartman.	"	"	A. B. Butler.	Clifton	"
J. G Poague.	"	"	W. H. Grimes.	New Burlington	"
William Higgins.	"	"	L K Dille.	Cedarville	"
James A. Kyle.	"	"	J. J. McElhenny.	Fairfield	"
J. D. Edwards.	"	"	Elihu Thorn.	Yellow Springs	"
D. D. Moore.	"	"	John Dawson.	Jamestown	"
John Harbison.	"	"	W. A. R. Kebble.	Bellbrook	"
J. M. Torrence.	"	"	James R. Dawson.	"	"

Reorganized June 1888. Constitution & By-Laws revised & signed by the following members:-

A. H. Brundage.	Xenia	Ohio.	R. L. Browne.	New Burlington	Ohio
L. H. Brundage.	"	"	D. F. Donaldson.	Port William	"
W. H. Finley.	"	"	L. M. Jones.	Jamestown	"
C. M. Galloway.	"	"	F. M. Kent.	Spring Valley	"
W. A. Galloway.	"	"	M. D. Marsh.	Cedarville	"
F. T. Lindsay.	"	"	G. R. Murrell.	New Burlington	"
H. R. McClellan.	"	"	O. M. Marquart.	Osborn	"
B. R. McClellan.	"	"	F. W. Ogan.	Jamestown	"
N. H. Young. (Toledo)	"	"	W. L. Rouse.	Paintersville	"
George Watt.	"	"	S. G. Sewell.	New Burlington	"
S. S. Wilson.	"	"	J. O. Stewart.	Cedarville	"
George Anderson.	Alpha	"	R. M. Smith.	Spring Valley	"
S. W. Baldwin.	Y. S.	"	D. E. Spahr.	Clifton	"
J. L. Carter.	Selma	"	C. W. Thompson.	Cedarville	"
W. H. Humphrey.	Y. S.	"	J. M. Trehearne.	Zimmerman	"
Asa Clay Messenger.			O. S. & S. O. Home.	Xenia O.	

Officers at present date.				
A. C. Messenger.	Pres.		Board	S. S. Wilson.
D. E. Spahr.	V. Pres.		of	W. H. Finley.
M. D. Marsh.	Sec'y		Censors.	L. H. Brundage.
W. L. Rouse.	Treas.			

written by C. M. Galloway Xenia Ohio March 15. 1901.

Pictured is the Greene County Medical Society roster listing the names of prominent members. (Courtesy of Greene County Archives—Time Capsule Document.)

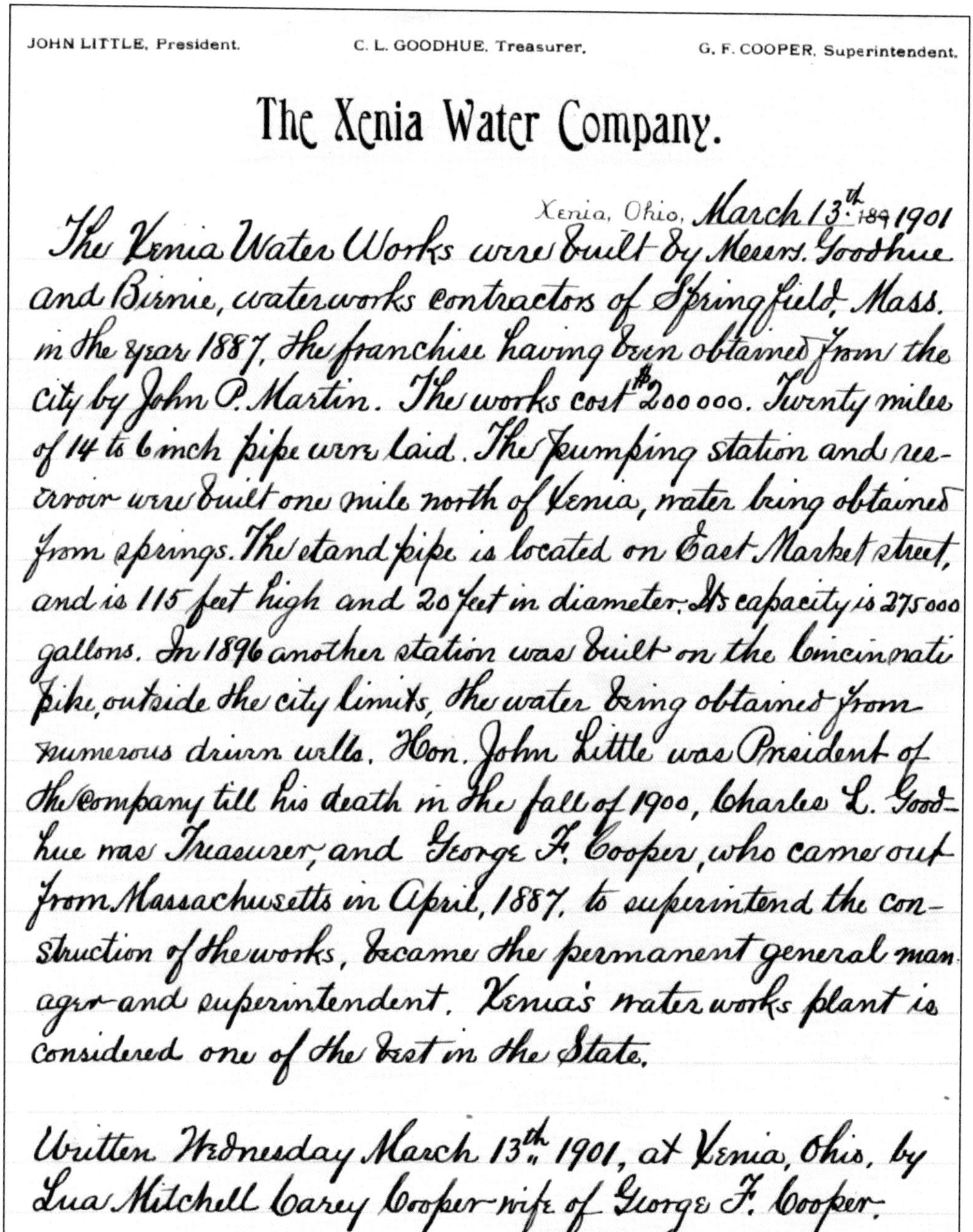
JOHN LITTLE, President. C. L. GOODHUE, Treasurer. G. F. COOPER, Superintendent.

The Xenia Water Company.

Xenia, Ohio, March 13th 1901

The Xenia Water Works were built by Messrs. Goodhue and Birnie, waterworks contractors of Springfield, Mass. in the year 1887, the franchise having been obtained from the city by John P. Martin. The works cost $200000. Twenty miles of 14 to 6 inch pipe were laid. The pumping station and reservoir were built one mile north of Xenia, water being obtained from springs. The stand pipe is located on East Market street, and is 115 feet high and 20 feet in diameter. Its capacity is 275000 gallons. In 1896 another station was built on the Cincinnati pike, outside the city limits, the water being obtained from numerous driven wells. Hon. John Little was President of the Company till his death in the fall of 1900, Charles L. Goodhue was Treasurer, and George F. Cooper, who came out from Massachusetts in April, 1887, to superintend the construction of the works, became the permanent general manager and superintendent. Xenia's water works plant is considered one of the best in the State.

Written Wednesday March 13th 1901, at Xenia, Ohio, by Lua Mitchell Carey Cooper wife of George F. Cooper.

Lua Mitchell Carey Cooper, wife of the superintendent of the Xenia Water Company, George F. Cooper, wrote this document in her beautiful handwriting. (Courtesy of Greene County Archives—Time Capsule Document.)

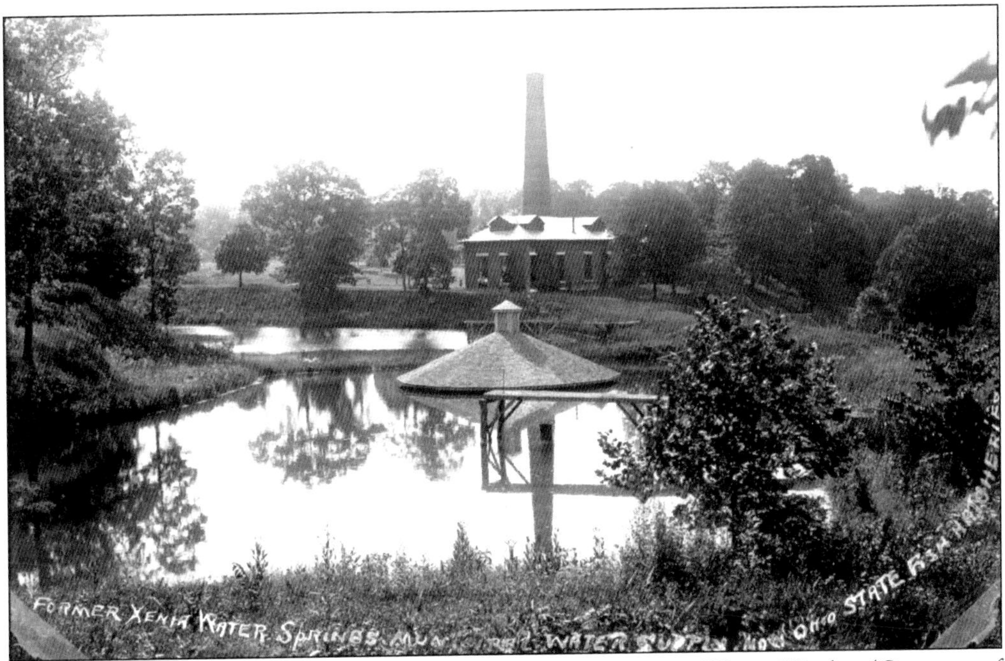

Pictured is the Springfield Pike pumping station of the Xenia Water Works. (Courtesy of Greene County Room, Greene County Public Library.)

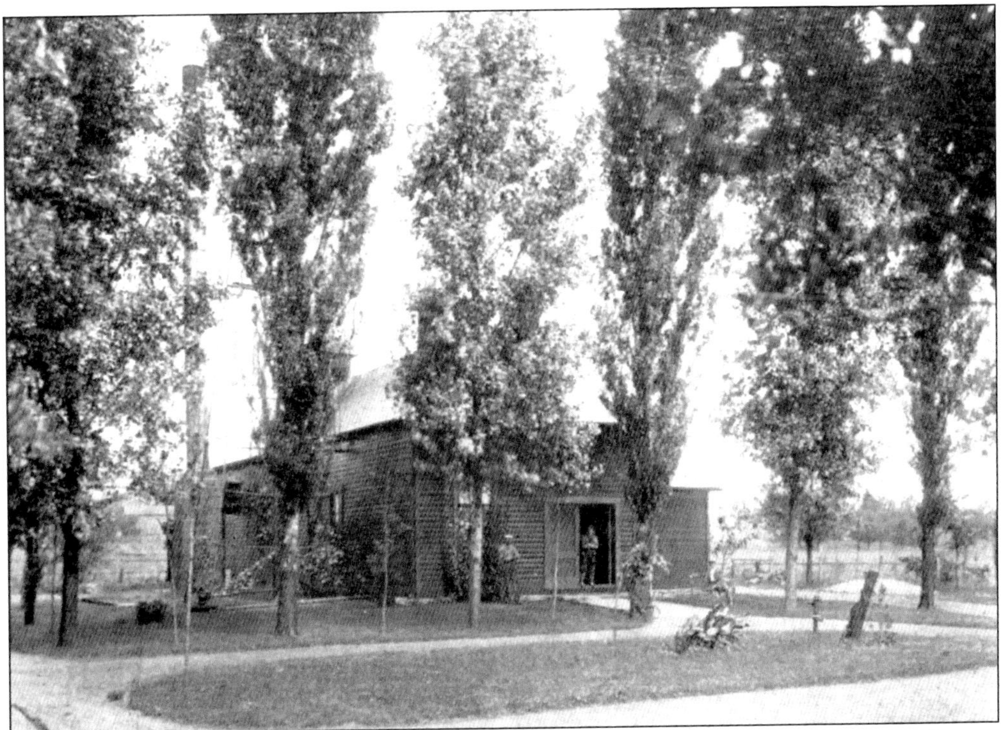

Here is the Cincinnati Pike pumping station of the Xenia Water Works. (Courtesy of Greene County Room, Greene County Public Library, *Greene County 1803–1908*, Home Coming Association, 1908.)

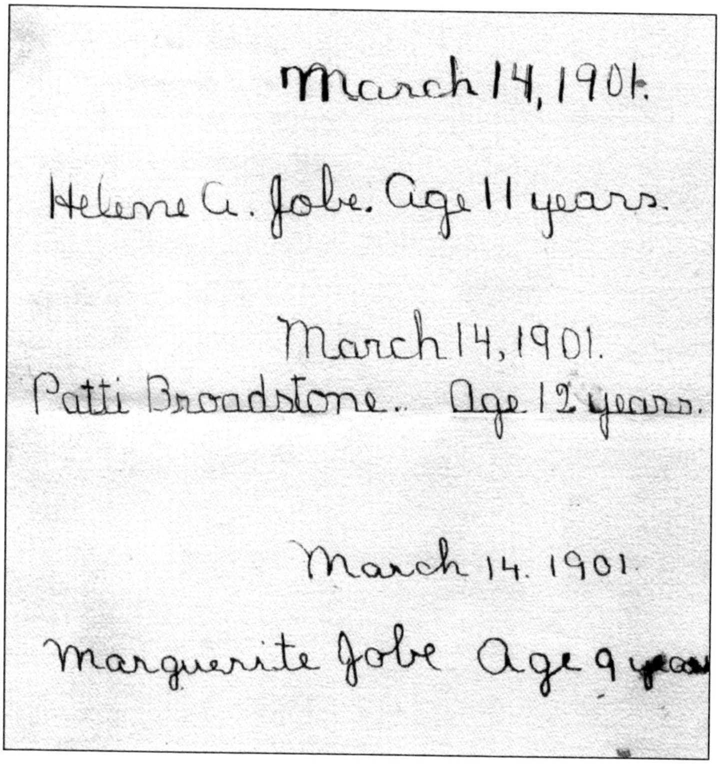

March 14, 1901.
Helene A. Jobe. Age 11 years.

March 14, 1901.
Patti Broadstone.. Age 12 years.

March 14. 1901.
Marguerite Jobe Age 9 years

These little girls wrote their names and ages on a scrap of paper enclosed in the time capsule. Helen and Margaret Jobe used the French version of their names, writing "Helene" and "Marguerite." The three girls' fathers were prominent businessmen in Xenia. (Courtesy of Greene County Archives—Time Capsule Document.)

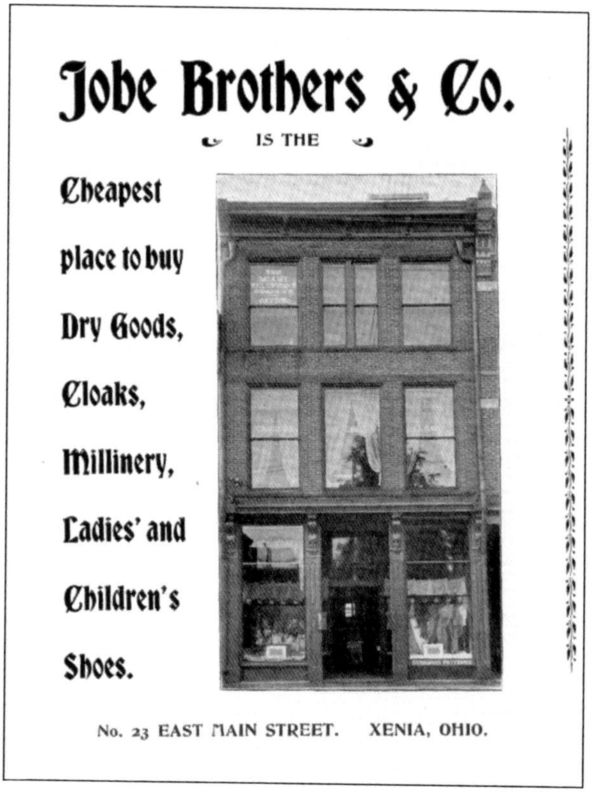

Charles L. Jobe, the father of Helen and Margaret, with his brother, J. Riley Jobe, owned Jobe Brothers and Company. The advertisement shown here was published in the St. Brigid's souvenir booklet. (Courtesy of Greene County Archives—Time Capsule Document.)

Lawyer and father of Patti (and two other older daughters, Louise and Jean), M.A. Broadstone served as county recorder. He was a Mason, a member of the Knights of Pythias, and of the Oddfellows. He owned the funeral business of Thomas M. Moore. (Courtesy of Greene County Room, Greene County Public Library, Robinson's *History of Greene County, Ohio*, 1902.)

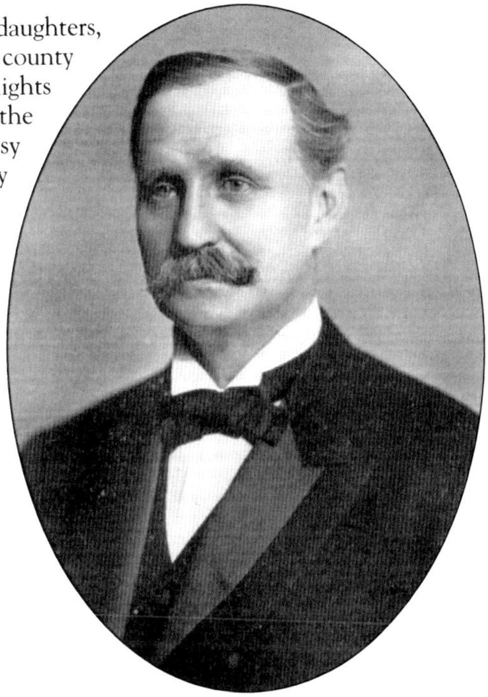

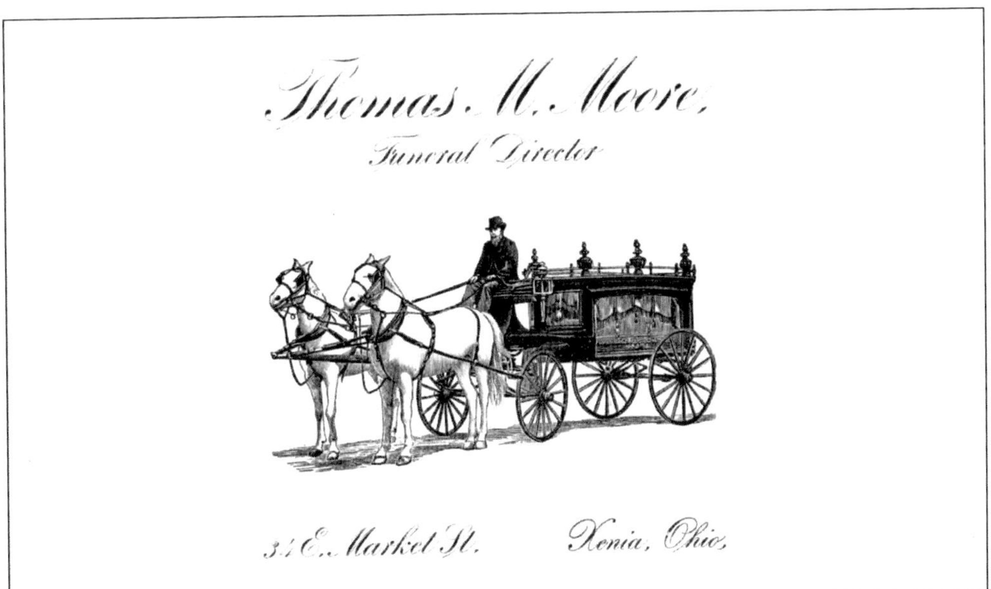

This is the advertisement for Thomas M. Moore, funeral director, published in the St. Brigid's souvenir booklet. (Courtesy of Greene County Archives—Time Capsule Document.)

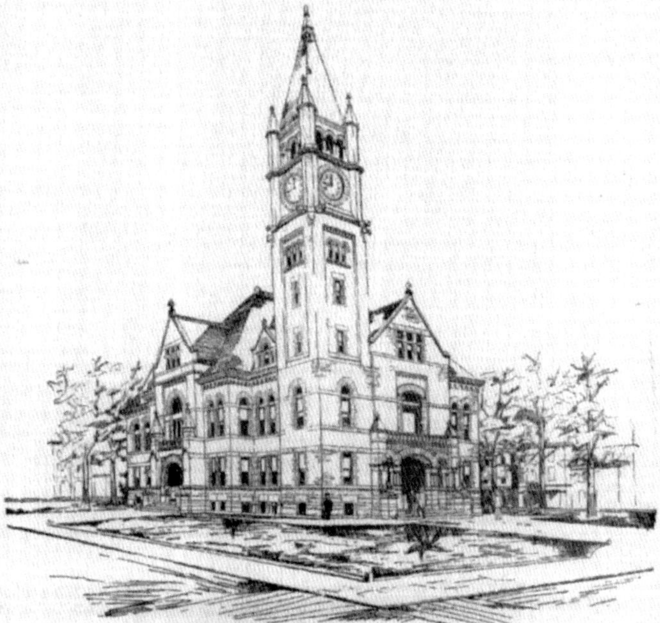

SOUVENIR

Corner Stone Laying of the New Greene County Court House, Xenia, Ohio, March 15, 1901.

COMPLIMENTS OF

..The Xenia Business Men's Association..

MEMBERSHIP

Adair, R. D., Furniture.
Arnold, R., House Furnishings.
Ambuhl & Co., Meat.
Brady & Steinfels, Clothiers.
Broadstone, M. A., Undertaker.
Babb, C. L., Hardware.
Binder, H. L. Coal.
Breen, Mrs. C., Groceries.
Brundage, Dr. A. H.
Baldner & Fletcher, Plumbers.
Conwell, J. C., Hardware.
Cooley, W. D.
Chambliss, Wm., Groceries.
Currie & Co., Merchant Tailors.
Chandler, C. W., Insurance.
Chatfield, A. J.
Dodds & Son., Monuments.
Davidson, E. S., Drugs.
Davis, Herbert, Feed Store.
Drees, F. B., Hardware.
Dines, Isaac, Carriage Mfg.
Eavey & Casad, Coal.
Edwards, C. L., Coal.
Evans, Chas. R., Livery.
Ervin Bros., Flour.
Eavey & Co., Wholesale Grocers.
Frazer, C. S., Shoes.
Fleming, E. C., Drugs.
Fisher, Geo., Dry Goods.
Farrell, T. J., Groceries.
Fifer, Matt, Livery.
Faul, Andy, Barber.
Fetz Bros., Groceries.
Finley, Dr. W. H
Grice & Son, Restaurant.
Galloway, Dr. W. A.
Grottendick, H., Bakery.
Galligher, Harry, Laundry.
Grieve, R. R., Insurance.
Hutchinson & Gibney, Dry Goods.
Henrie, C. C., Tinner.
Hiller, A. J., Cheap Store.
Hannon, W. H., Grocer.
Haverstick, J. F., Mgr. Tel. Co.
Jobe Bros. & Co., Dry Goods.
Johnston, J. A., Shoes.
Jones & Co., J. E., Dry Goods.
Kingsbury, R. S., Clothing.
Kany, Jacob, Merchant Tailor.
Kelble, Robert, Merchant Tailor.
Kyle & Tate, Jewelers.
Kelso Bros., Coal.
Kump, Matt, Job Printer.
Lazier, W. D., Drugs.
Lupton & Drake.
Lupton, M. D., Planing Mill.
Labron, Dr. W. A., Veterinary.
Madden, Dr. W. P.
Marshall, Geo. H., Meat.
Maddux & Co., Coal.
Moore, R. W., Groceries.
Marshall, W. L., Livery.
Mason, T. O., Groceries.
Madden, Dr. P. R., Oculist.
McClain, G. G., Furniture.
McDowell & Torrence, Lumber.
McGervey & LeSourd, Insurance.
McCormick, J. O.
North, J. A., Plumber.
Norckauer, J. F., Groceries.
Orr, W. F. Attorney.
Owens, T. C., Contractor.
Owens, H. W., Architect.
Parrett, L. A., Laundry.
Poland & Son, Groceries.
Ralls, Geo., Meat.
Robb, Jordon, Groceries.
Spahr, O. A., Dry Goods.
Smart, R. M., Grain.
Sanger, F. W., Meat.
Schmidt, H. E., Groceries.
Schell, Fred J. H., Jewelry.
Smith & Son, J. W., Pork Packers.
Sutton, F., Dairy.
Steinmetz, Joe, Cigars.
Schlesinger, H. N., Attorney for Association.
Thompson, G. A., Clothing.
Tiffany, A. P., Optician.
Thornhill, Chas. N., Coal.
Thomas, A. E., Bee Hive Store.
Trebein, The F. C. Co., Grain.
Trader, C. W. & Son., Groceries.
Vanderpool, Jno., Jewelry.
West, R. C., Book Store.
White, Geo. L., Wall Paper.
Wright & Carruthers, Coal.
Wolsey, Dr. Ida.
Zell, Frank, Cigars.

MATT KUMP, Printer, Room 23, Allen Building, Xenia, Ohio.

The Xenia Business Men's Association had their names printed on this specially designed silk souvenir commemorating the laying of the cornerstone. (Courtesy of Greene County Archives—Time Capsule Document.)

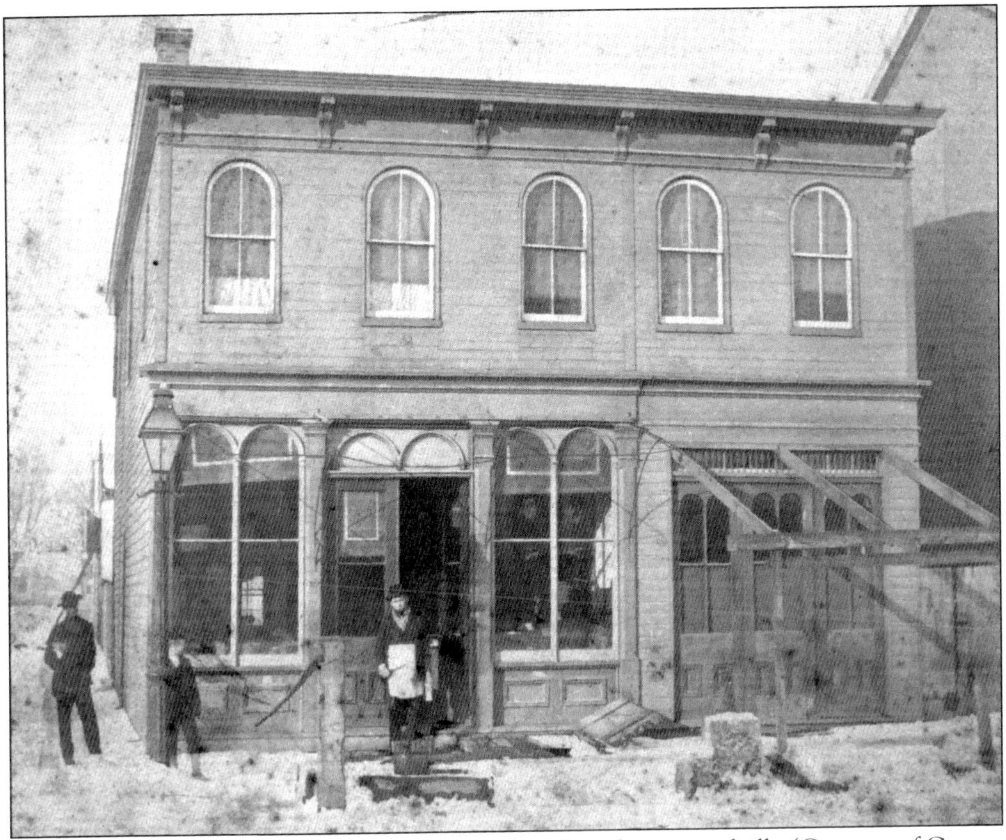

Amhuhl and Company, the meat business, was listed on the piece of silk. (Courtesy of Greene County Room, Greene County Public Library.)

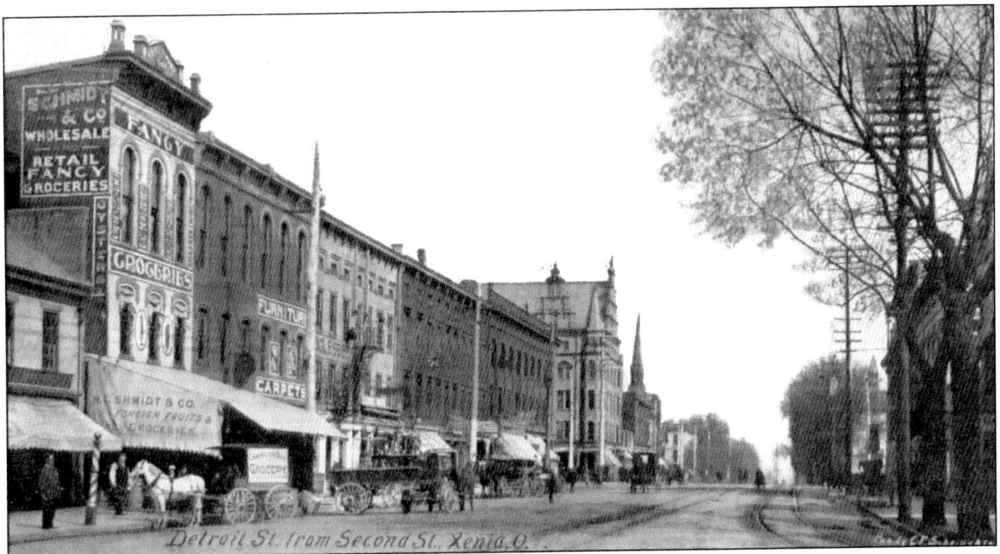

H.E. Schmidt and Company, the grocery company, was listed on the piece of silk. This postcard of Detroit Street in Xenia shows the store on the left-hand side of the street. (Courtesy of Greene County Room, Greene County Public Library.)

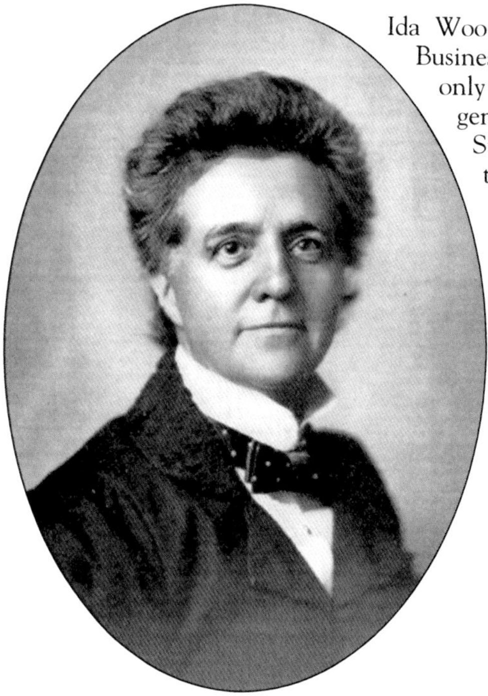

Ida Woolsey, M.D., was also a member of the Xenia Business Men's Association. She was Greene County's only woman physician in 1901, having set up a general practice in her home at 118 West Main Street in Xenia in 1892. She specialized in the treatment of women and children. (Courtesy of Greene County Room, Greene County Public Library, Robinson's *History of Greene County, Ohio*, 1902.)

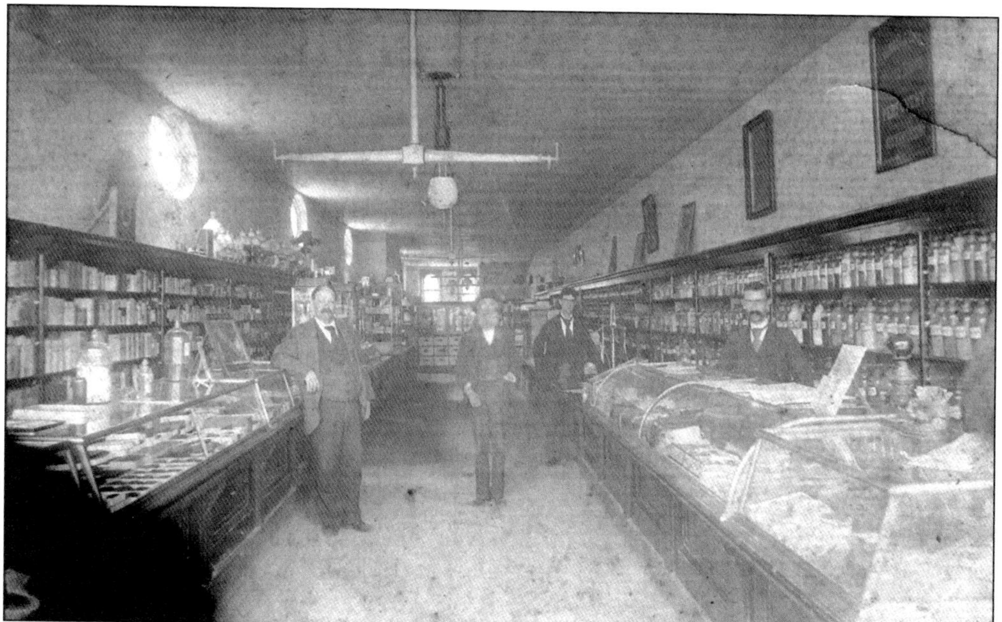

E.C. Fleming's Drugstore was listed on the piece of silk. This photograph shows the interior of the store. (Courtesy of Greene County Historical Society.)

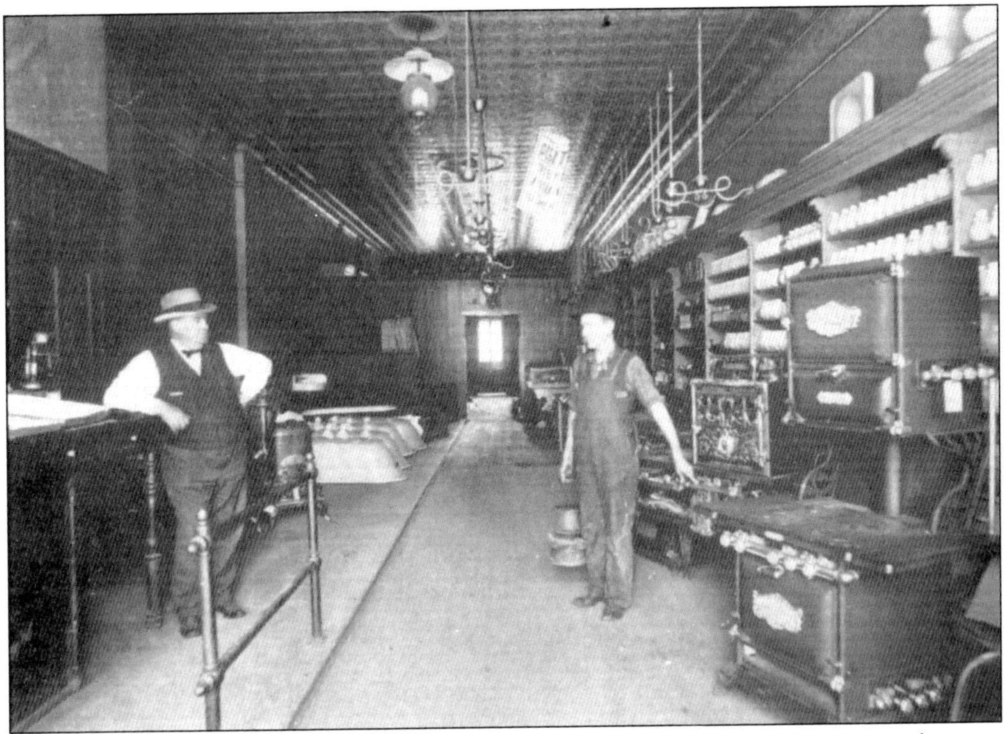

Here is an interior shot of John A. North's plumbing establishment. John A. North was a member of the Xenia Business Men's Association. (Courtesy of Greene County Room, Greene County Public Library, *Greene County 1803–1908*, Home Coming Association, 1908.)

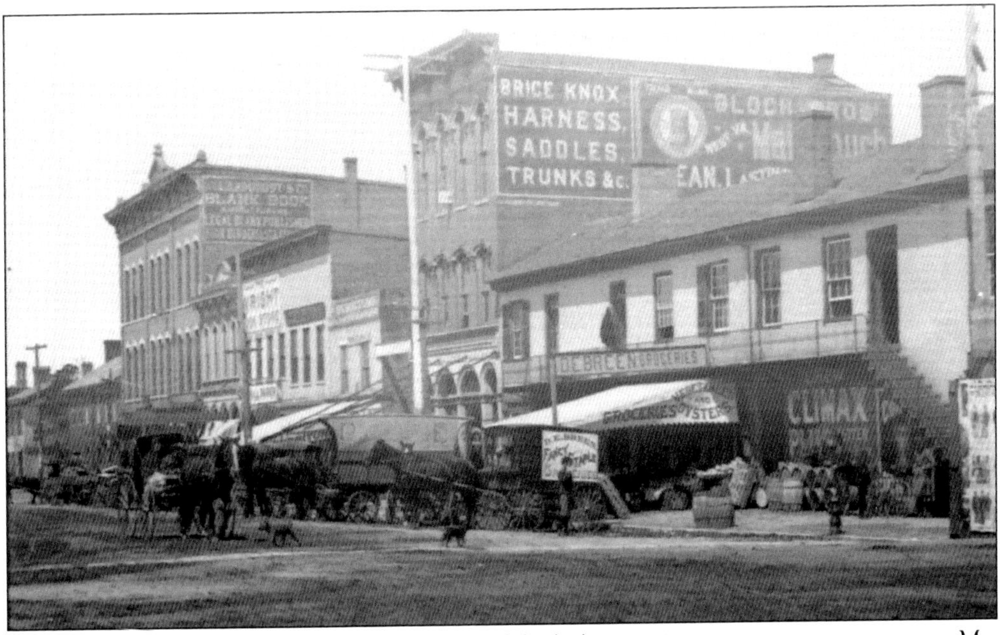

Another woman member of the Xenia Business Men's Association was grocery store owner, Mrs Catherine Breen, widow of D.E. Breen. Her grocery store at 238 West Second Street in Xenia is shown here. (Courtesy of Greene County Room, Greene County Public Library.)

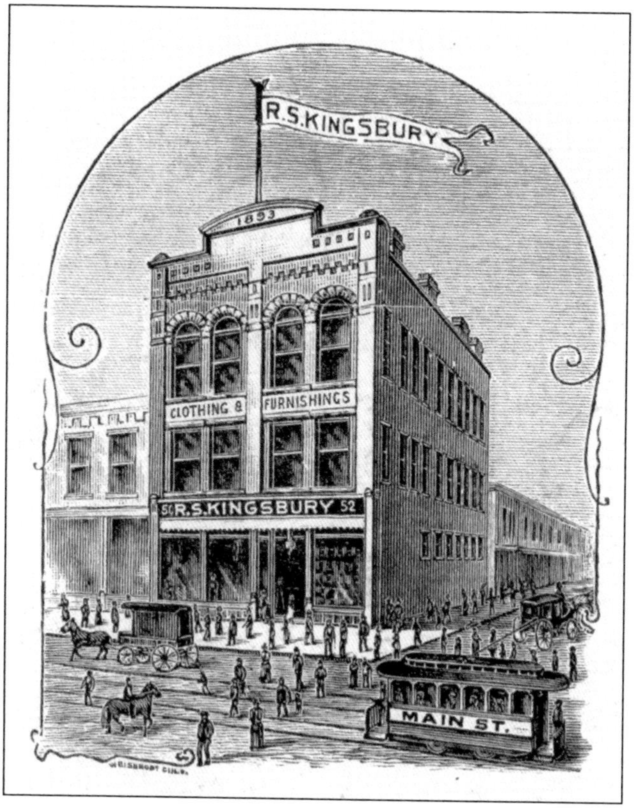

The R.S. Kingsbury Clothing Store was listed on the piece of silk. This advertisement for R.S. Kingsbury was published in the *Xenia Semi-Weekly Gazette* of March 15, 1901. (Courtesy of Greene County Archives—Time Capsule Document.)

Hutchison and Gibney's dry goods store was listed on the piece of silk. (Courtesy of Greene County Room, Greene County Public Library, *Greene County 1803–1908*, Home Coming Association, 1908.)

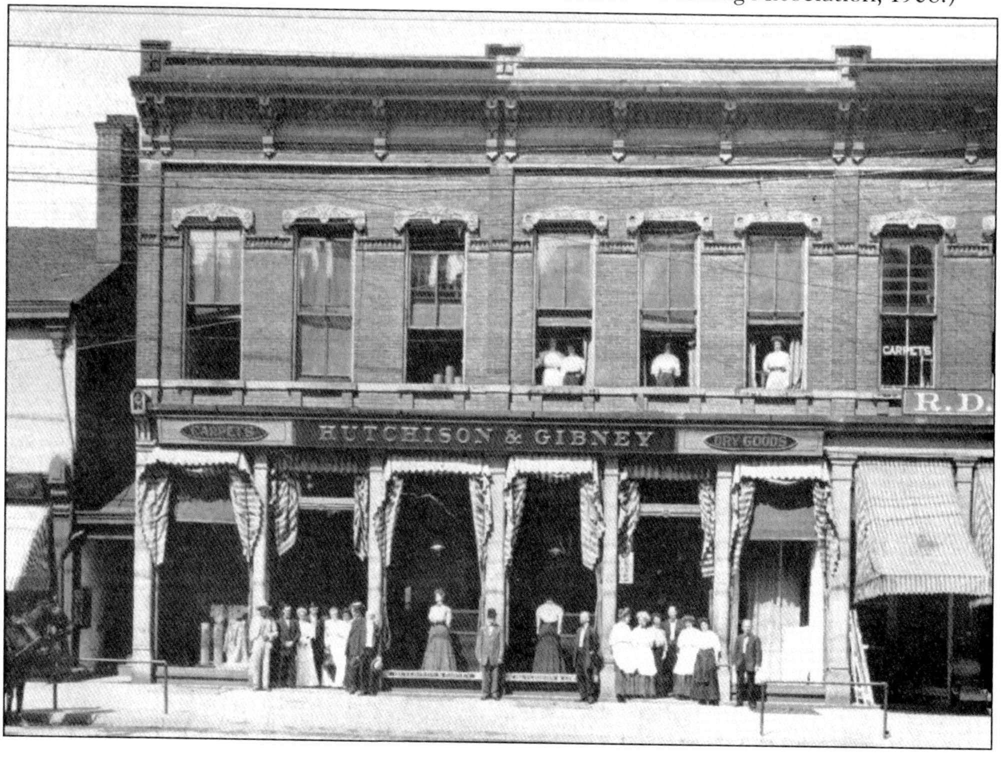

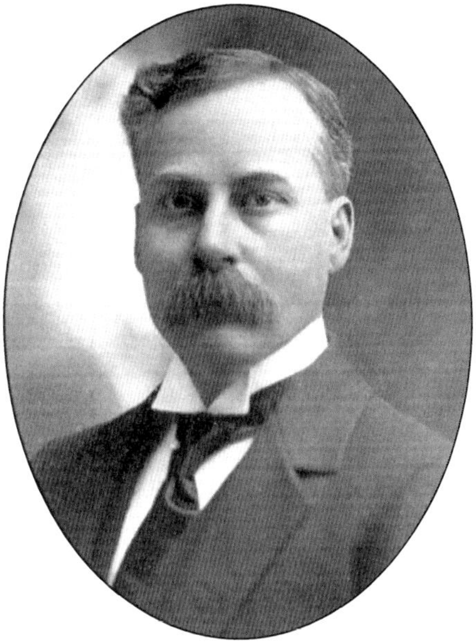

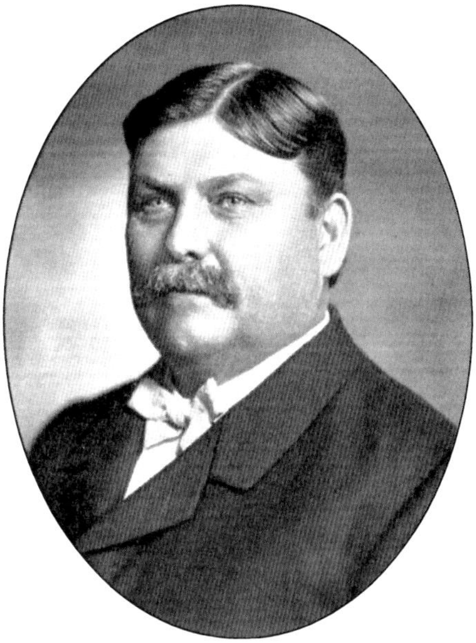

Left: J.F. Haverstick, General Manager of the Central Union Telephone Company, was a member of the Xenia Business Men's Association. He also belonged to the Elks, the Knights of Pythias, the Knights of Honor, and the Independent Order of Oddfellows. (Courtesy of Greene County Room, Greene County Public Library, Robinson's *History of Greene County, Ohio*, 1902.)
Right: H.W. Owens, an architect and owner of a substantial contracting firm in Xenia, was a member of the Xenia Business Men's Association. (Courtesy of Greene County Room, Greene County Public Library, Robinson's *History of Greene County, Ohio*, 1902.)

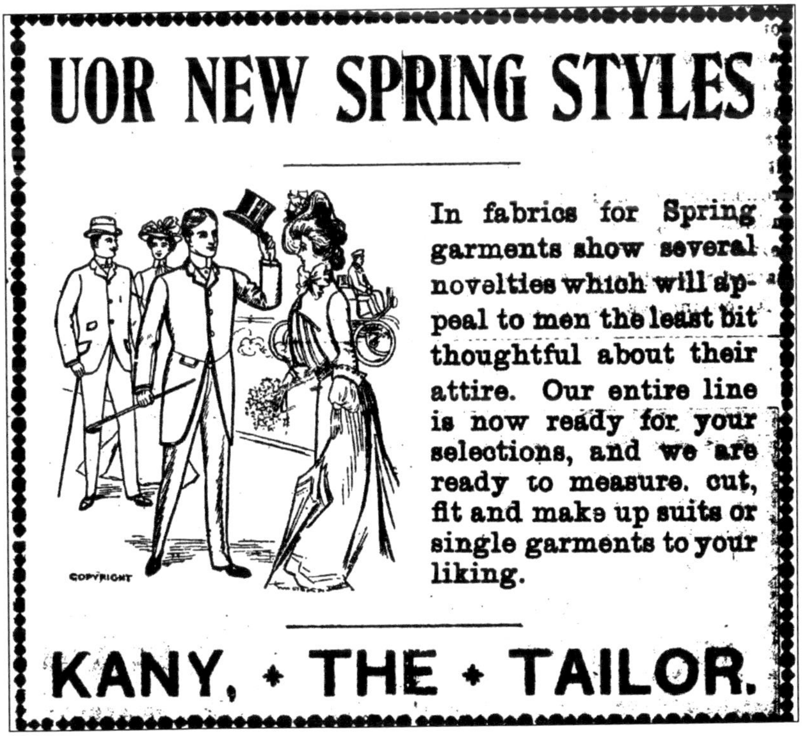

Jacob Kany, merchant tailor, was a member of the Xenia Business Men's Association. This advertisement for the Kany store, typo included, was published in the *Xenia Semi-Weekly Gazette* of March 15, 1901. (Courtesy of Greene County Archives—Time Capsule Document.)

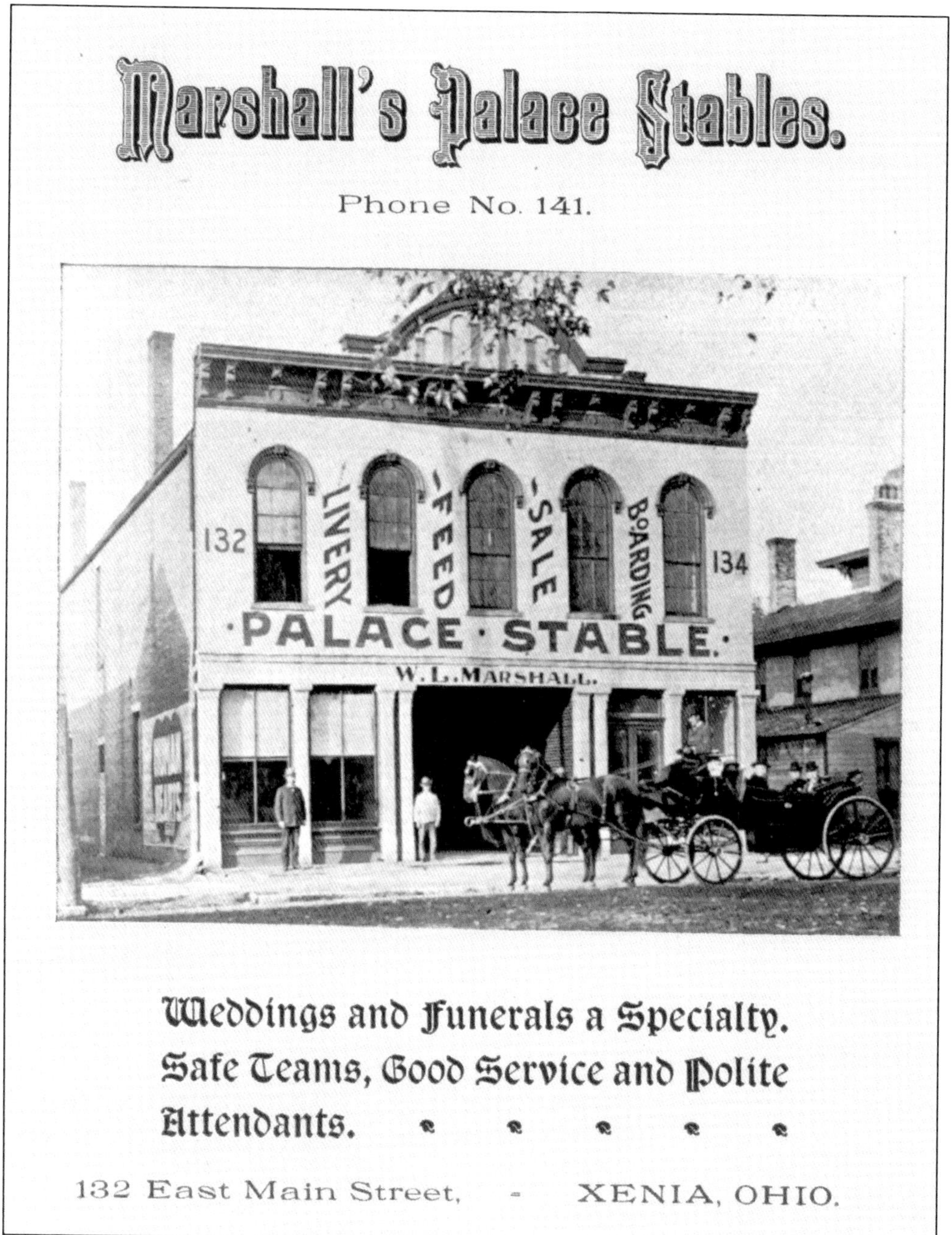

An advertisement from the St. Brigid's Church souvenir booklet is shown here. The building housing Marshall's Palace Stables is now the home of the Greene County Records Center and Archives, where many of the county's historic documents are preserved. (Courtesy of Greene County Archives—Time Capsule Document.)

L.O. Broekhoven of Columbus, Ohio, published this Xenia and Greene County Directory that was placed in the time capsule. (Courtesy of Greene County Archives—Time Capsule Document.)

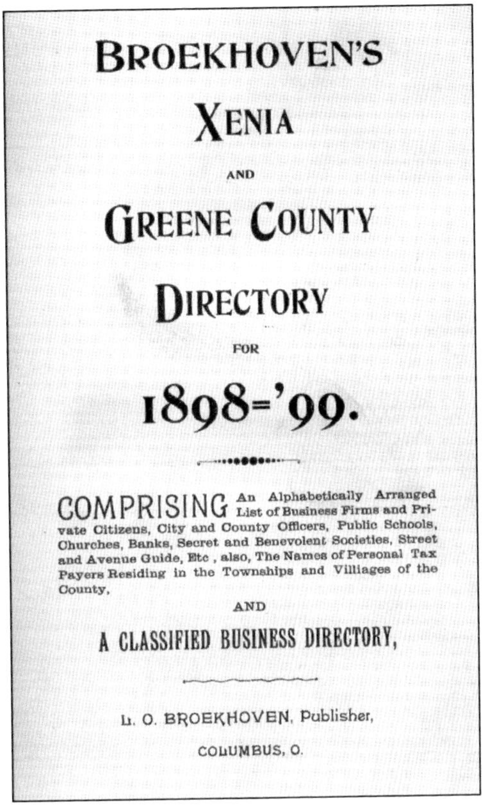
BROEKHOVEN'S
XENIA
AND
GREENE COUNTY
DIRECTORY
FOR
1898-'99.

COMPRISING An Alphabetically Arranged List of Business Firms and Private Citizens, City and County Officers, Public Schools, Churches, Banks, Secret and Benevolent Societies, Street and Avenue Guide, Etc , also, The Names of Personal Tax Payers Residing in the Townships and Villiages of the County,

AND

A CLASSIFIED BUSINESS DIRECTORY,

L. O. BROEKHOVEN, Publisher,
COLUMBUS, O.

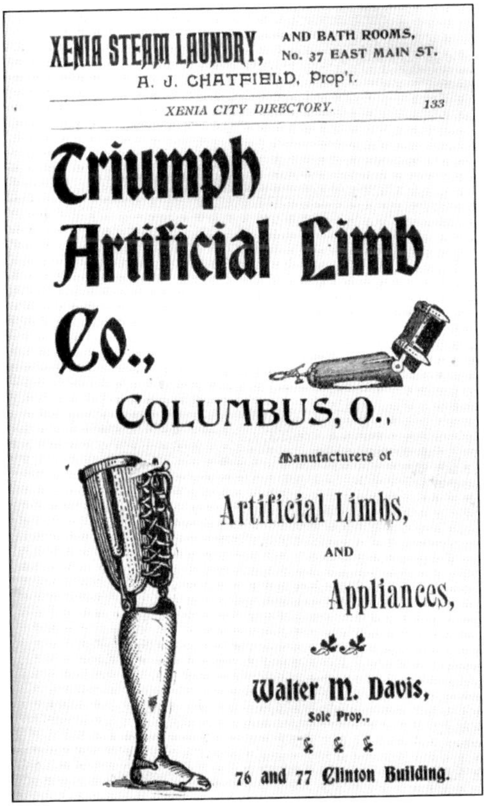
XENIA STEAM LAUNDRY, AND BATH ROOMS, No. 37 EAST MAIN ST.
A. J. CHATFIELD, Prop'r.

XENIA CITY DIRECTORY. 133

Triumph
Artificial Limb
Co.,
COLUMBUS, O.,
Manufacturers of
Artificial Limbs,
AND
Appliances,

Walter M. Davis,
Sole Prop.,

76 and 77 Clinton Building.

This page of the directory advertised not only the Xenia Steam Laundry, but also this interesting business from Columbus. (Courtesy of Greene County Archives—Time Capsule Document.)

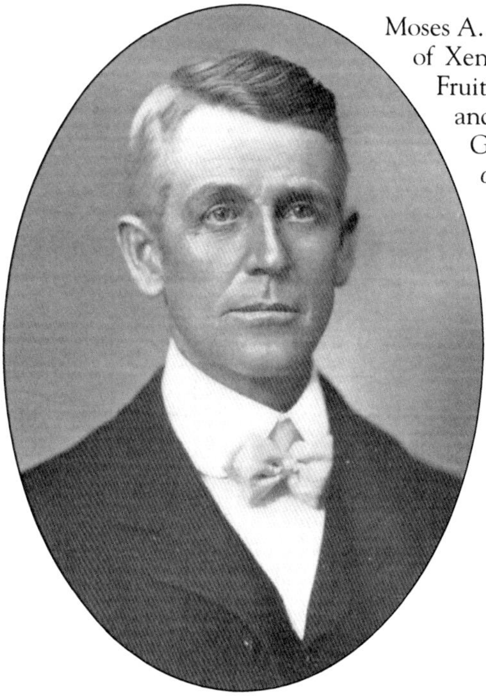

Moses A. Hagler is listed in the city directory as a resident of Xenia Township. His farm, known as Ridge View Fruit Farm, had an orchard that included peach, plum, and apple trees. (Courtesy of Greene County Room, Greene County Public Library, Robinson's *History of Greene County, Ohio*, 1902.)

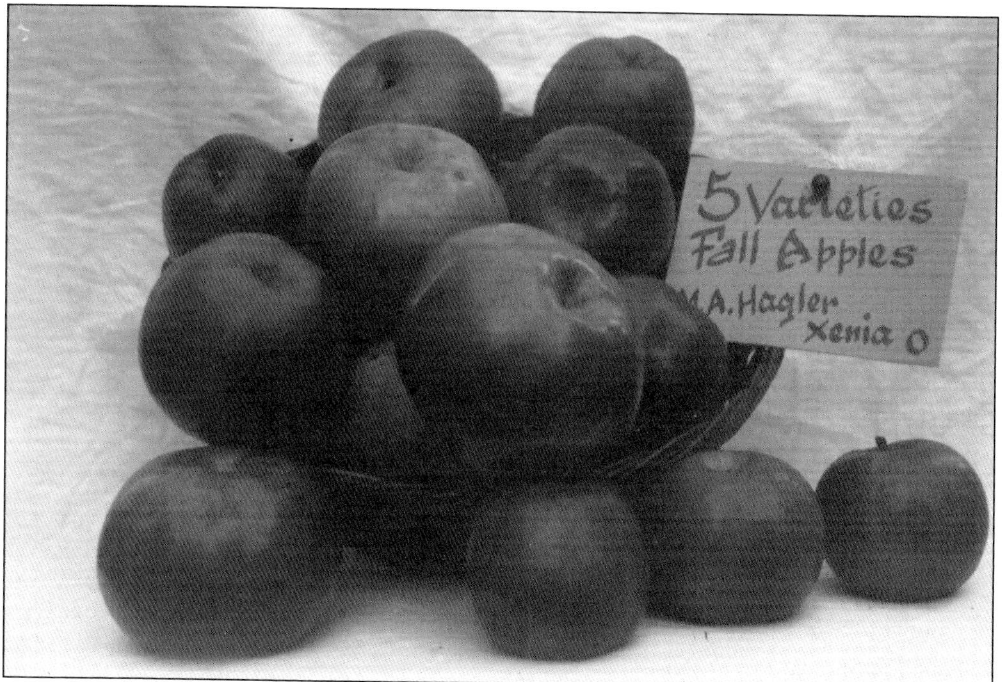

Some of Moses Hagler's prize apples are shown here. (Courtesy of Greene County Room, Greene County Public Library.)

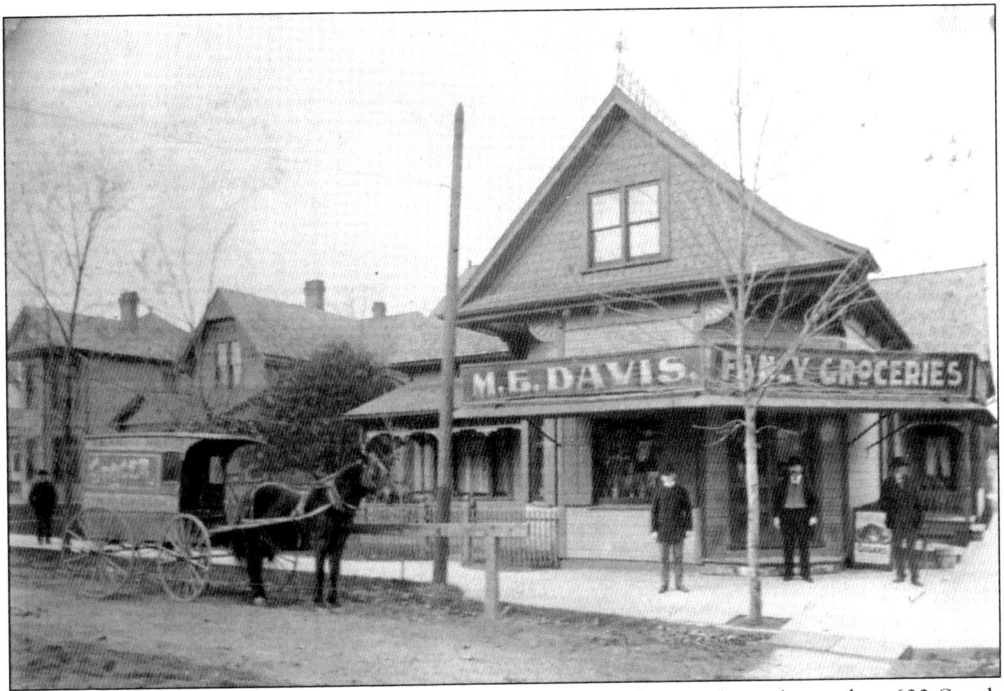

Miles E. Davis, Groceries, is listed in the city directory as having been located at 600 South Detroit Street. (Courtesy of Greene County Historical Society.)

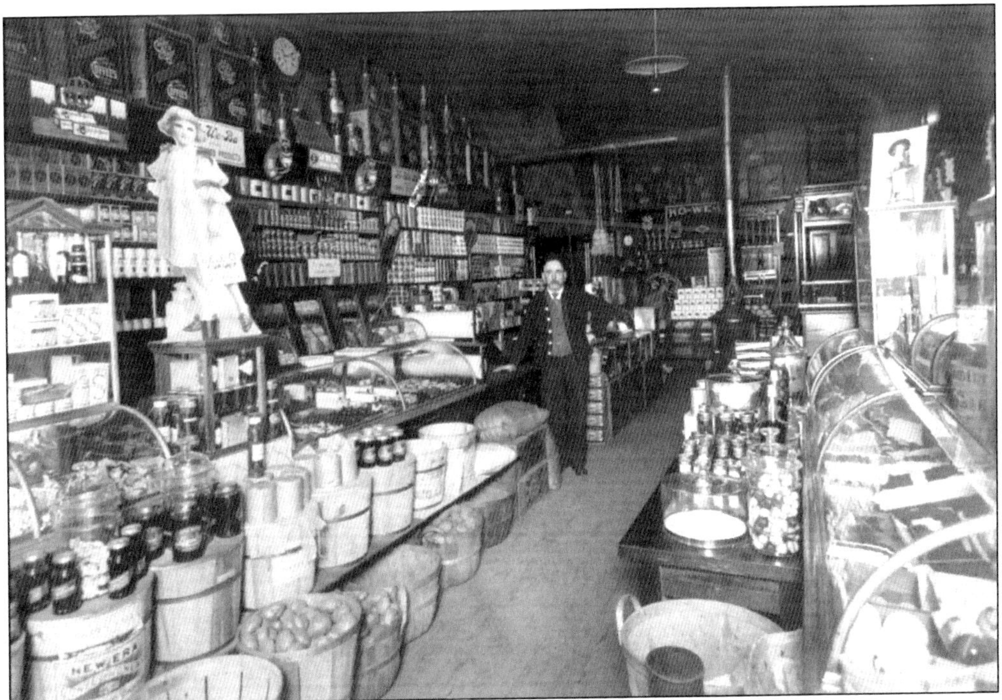

This is an interior shot of the Davis grocery shop. (Courtesy of Greene County Historical Society.)

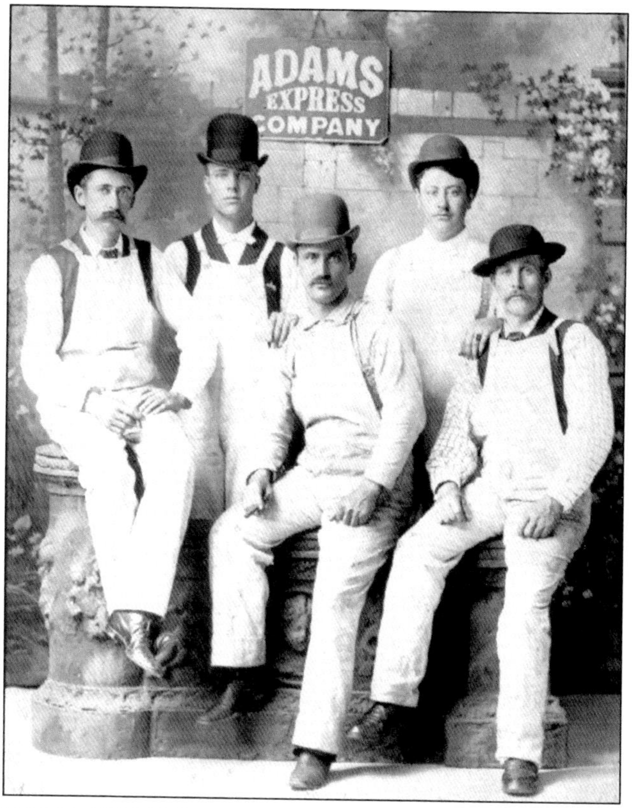

According to the city directory, the Adams Express Company was located at 25 Green Street. John C. Folger was the agent. (Courtesy of Greene County Room, Greene County Public Library.)

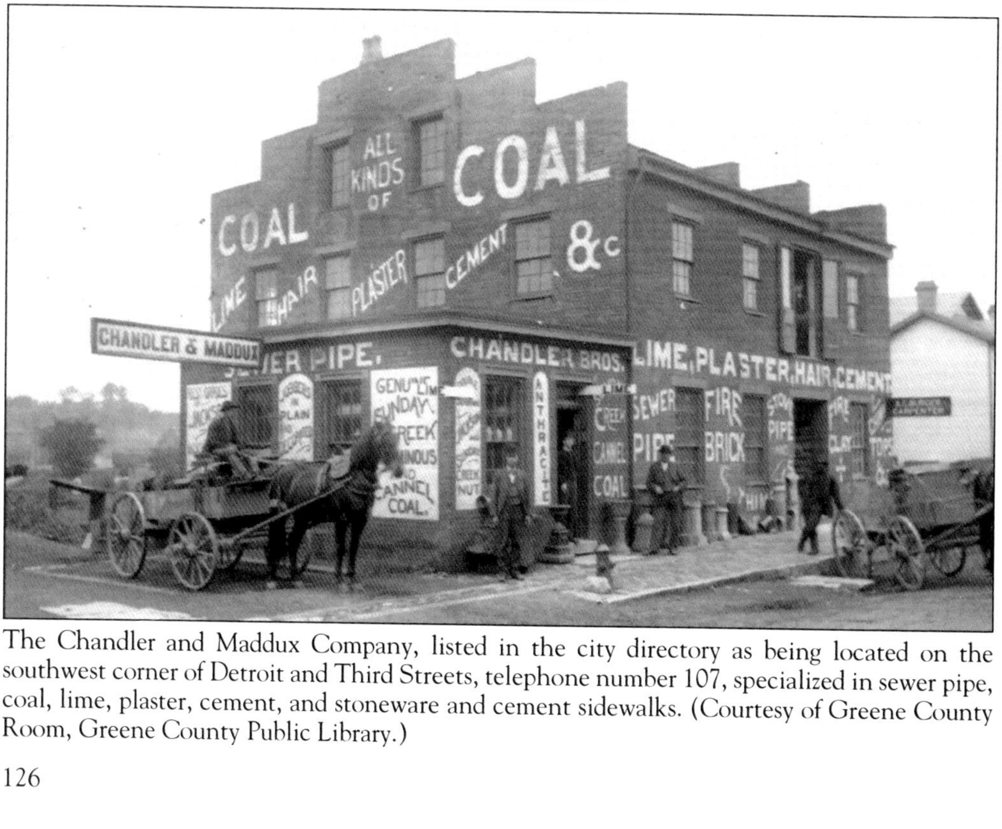

The Chandler and Maddux Company, listed in the city directory as being located on the southwest corner of Detroit and Third Streets, telephone number 107, specialized in sewer pipe, coal, lime, plaster, cement, and stoneware and cement sidewalks. (Courtesy of Greene County Room, Greene County Public Library.)

Index of Time Capsule Contents

1. Advertisement, Boots, Bales and Conklin, quarrymen (business card)
2. Advertisement, Eavey and Casad, Coal Dealer
3. Advertisement, J.P. Bocklett, Machinist
4. Advertisement, McArthur's Syrup
5. Antioch College, Catalogue, 1899–1900
6. The Benevolent and Protective Order of Elks, Xenia, list of charter members, invitation to installation ceremonies, 1901
7. Book, *After Thirty Years* (Roster of Greene County Soldiers in the Civil War), by George Robinson, 1895
8. Book, Bible, signed by Eber Reynolds, High Priest, Royal Arch Masons #36, Xenia
9. Bricklayers and Masons International Union, photos (2)
10. Bricklayers International Union, #16, Ohio, list of members, 1901
11. Chautauqua Literary Club, history
12. Citizens' National Bank, original officers 1881, current work force 1901, annual report 1901
13. Courthouse Building Commission, summary report
14. D. Bradfute and Sons, list of angus cattle at Meadowbrook Stock Farm, Cedarville, 1901
15. Daughters of the American Revolution, Catherine Greene Chapter, charter members, program 1900–1901
16. First Presbyterian Church, Xenia, brief history, church manual, 1901
17. First Reformed Church, history
18. Free and Accepted Masons #352, Jamestown, by-laws, 1872
19. F. & A.M. #352, Jamestown, membership list, 1901
20. F. & A.M. #574, New Burlington, history, list of officers and charter members
21. F. & A.M. #49, Xenia, by-laws, 1901
22. F. & A.M. #49, Xenia, account of internment of Jacob Smith, founding member
23. F. & A.M. #49, Xenia, 1806 recognizance deed, signed by John Smith, founding member
24. Grand Army of the Republic, button, donated by S.T. Baker, Jamestown
25. G.A.R., Lewis Post #347, by laws, list of members and officers, 1901
26. Greene County Bar Association, photo, list of members, 1901
27. Greene County Medical Society, by-laws, membership roster, 1888
28. H.K. Laird, Mayor, Jamestown, mayor's letterhead, signed and dated, 1901
29. Hennesy Brothers & Evans Co., list of contractors for 1901 courthouse
30. Home Building and Savings Co., constitution and by-laws, c. 1900
31. Improved Order of Red Men, Xenia, history
32. Independent Order of Odd Fellows, Shawnee Encampment #20, Xenia, officers
33. J.R. Crain, postmaster, Jamestown, collection of stamps
34. Journeymen Stonecutters of North America, Xenia branch, list of cutters of the 1901 courthouse cornerstone

35. Junior Woman's Club of Xenia, history, members list, 1901
36. Masonic Directories, Xenia,Yellow Springs,New Burlington, 1901
37. Knights of Pythias #56, Ivanhoe Lodge, Xenia, history, list of officers
38. Knights of Pythias #668, Silver Star Lodge, Alpha, history, charter members
39. Newspaper, *Cedarville Herald*, 3/9/1901
40. Newspaper, *Cincinnati Enquirer*, 3/15/1886 (account of Xenia Flood)
41. Newspaper, *Cincinnati Enquirer*, 2/23/1901
42. Newspaper, *Greene County Press* (Jamestown), 3/8/1901
43. Newspaper, *The Home Weekly* (OS&SO Home), 3/8/1901
44. Newspaper, *The Jamestown Journal*, 3/8/1901
45. Newspaper, *The News* (Yellow Springs), 2/22/1901
46. Newspaper, *The Observer* (African-American), 12/18/1897
47. Newspaper, *Osborn Local*, 11/9/1900
48. Newspaper, *Xenia Daily Gazette & Torchlight*, 3/14/1901
49. Newspaper, *Xenia Herald*, 2/28/1901
50. Newspaper, *Xenia Herald*, 3/14/1901
51. Newspaper, *Xenia Republican*, 2/7/1899 (account of Greene County Bar Association banquet)
52. Newspaper, *Xenia Republican*, 2/20/1901
53. Newspaper, *Xenia Republican*, 3/13/1901
54. Newspaper, *Xenia Semi-Weekly Gazette and Torchlight*, 3/15/1901
55. Ohio Masonic Home, Springfield, reports of officers, 1900
56. Ohio Soldiers' and Sailors' Orphans' Home, annual report, 1900
57. Peoples Building and Savings Co., by-laws, 1893, annual report, 1900
58. Poem, "Au Revoir: Imposing and Fitting Ceremonial on Forsaking the Old GC Courthouse," W.A. Paxson
59. Poem, "Joe Dean's Indignation Meeting", Waldo D. Edenburn
60. Poem, Untitled, W.A. Paxson
61. Publication, Dr. D. Jayne's Medical Almanac, 1901
62. Publication, Stone Cutters' Journal, March 1901
63. Royal Arcanum, Shawnee Council #415, Xenia, assessment, officers, 1901
64. Royal Arch Masons #36, Xenia, stone from "Solomon's Quarries, Jerusalem"
65. Sons of the American Revolution, Nathaniel Greene Chapter, roster, photos, members' lineages, historical data
66. Sons of American Veterans, badge, donated by G.A. McLaughlin, Jamestown
67. St. Brigid's Church, illustrated history
68. Sugarcreek Christian Church, Alpha, history
69. Trinity Methodist Evangelical Church, church history, 1864–1901
70. U.S. Post Office, Xenia, list of employees, 1901
71. Union Veteran Legion, Encampment #133, Xenia, 1/15/1894
72. Union Veteran Legion, Ladies Auxiliary, Xenia, officers, members list, 1901
73. Wilberforce University, annual report of trustees, Combined Normal and Industrial Dept., 1900
74. Wilberforce University, catalogue, 1899–1900
75. Woman's Club of Xenia, history, list of members, 1901
76. Xenia Business Men's Association, souvenir from 1901 courthouse celebration
77. Xenia City Directory, 1898–1899
78. Xenia (City of), city officers, report on condition, 1901
79. Xenia (City of), copper plate engraved with names of Xenia officers, dated 3/15/1901
80. Xenia High School, Class of 1901 roll, comments
81. Xenia High School, Class of 1902 roll
82. Xenia High School, Class of 1903 roll, comments
83. Xenia High School, Class of 1904, first section, roll
84. Xenia High School, Class of 1904, second section, roll
85. Xenia Library Association, brief history, list of board members, 1901
86. Xenia Public Schools, report on organization for 1900–1901
87. Xenia Water Company, brief history, 1901